DEC 2 0 2018

W9-BRG-013

THE BANKER
— AND —
THE BLACKFOOT

Also by J. Edward Chamberlin

The Harrowing of Eden: White Attitudes Toward Native Americans

Ripe Was the Drowsy Hour: The Age of Oscar Wilde

Come Back to Me My Language: Poetry and the West Indies

If This Is Your Land, Where Are Your Stories? Finding Common Ground

Horse: How the Horse Has Shaped Civilizations

Island: How Islands Transform the World

THE BANKER

— AND —

THE BLACKFOOT

AN UNTOLD STORY OF FRIENDSHIP, TRUST,
AND BROKEN PROMISES IN THE OLD WEST

J. EDWARD CHAMBERLIN

BlueBridge

Published in the United States of America in 2018 by BlueBridge, an imprint of United Tribes Media Inc. Published by arrangement with Alfred A. Knopf Canada, a division of Penguin Random House Canada Limited. First published in Canada in 2016 by Alfred A. Knopf Canada.

B l u e B r i d g e
An imprint of
United Tribes Media Inc.
Katonah, New York

www.bluebridgebooks.com

ISBN: 9781629190174

Library of Congress Control Number: 2018954756

Jacket design by Cynthia Dunne
Cover images: Chief Mountain: abishome / Getty Images; John Cowdry: Courtesy of the Cowdry Family Collection; Crop Eared Wolf: Courtesy of the Glenbow Archives
Text design by Cynthia Dunne
Map designed by Erin Cooper

Printed in the United States of America

10 9 8 7 6 5 4 3 2 1

for the Cowdry family
and friends

and in memory of
George Laforme
(1942–2016)

THE FOOTHILLS, 1885–1905

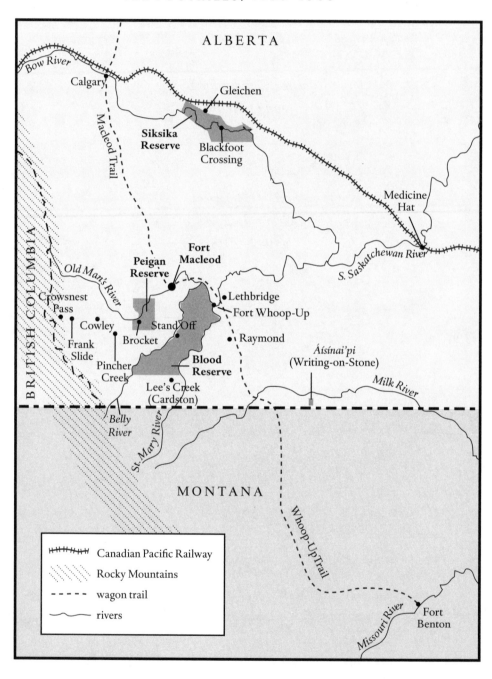

CONTENTS

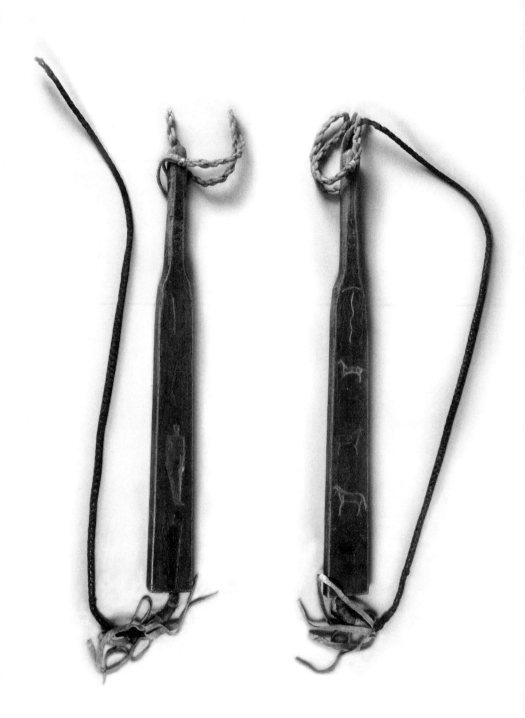

JACK COWDRY AND CROP EARED WOLF

It must have been just after Easter, and I was sitting on my grandfather's knee in the backyard of our house in Vancouver. He was smoking a meerschaum pipe carved into the shape of a prancing horse, and I said I was going to be a cowboy and ride a horse just like that. He said he knew some cowboys and some Indians too; and they both believed in Jawbone. I asked, "What's that?" and he said it meant being as good as your word. Then he said, "I believe it's time to tell you a story . . ."

IT WAS A LOVELY SPRING DAY in the foothills of southern Alberta. The snow-covered peaks of Chief Mountain in Montana and the Rockies further north—the Blackfoot "backbone of the world"—were shimmering on the western horizon, the colors of the grasses heightened by shadows when clouds crossed over, and the abiding wind whispering its promises of permanence and change. Riding down the main street of Fort Macleod in the spring of 1885, my grandfather saw a Blackfoot man riding toward him leading a string of horses ambling along at a lazy pacing trot, looking like country dancers on the way to a performance. He noticed from a distance that the Indian rider sat his saddle at an unusual slant, so the shoulder of his coat blanket was what my grandfather first saw of him; but when they came closer he turned to greet my grandfather in a sign-language gesture of welcome, and they exchanged names.

Makoyi-Opistoki, said the Blackfoot horseman. *Crop Eared Wolf. John Cowdry*, said my grandfather. *Jack.*

Crop Eared Wolf signaled his interest in my grandfather's horse, so Jack took the cue and made a wavy motion as he put his hand on the high withers in front of his saddle to indicate how comfortable his horse was on a long ride, and clenched his fist on the long, flat croup from his horse's hindquarters to the dock of his tail to signal lots of strength there. Crop Eared Wolf nodded courteously as though he was learning something for the first time; but my grandfather recognized from the easy way he sat his horse, even with the slight awkwardness he had noticed, that he was an experienced horseman and would have known all that at a glance. Then Crop Eared Wolf asked, in English, about its color. "Chestnut sorrel," said my grandfather, knowing that the Blackfoot had over a hundred words for the colors of horses, none of which he had yet learned. Crop Eared Wolf chuckled, and pointed to my grandfather's hair—which was the same color as his horse, burnt chestnut—and dubbed him *Sorreltop Jack*. My grandfather knew that the Blackfoot often named their horses for their color, and that Crop Eared Wolf might be making fun of him, but he took to the name anyway because he admired his horse and was proud of his hair. Before he had time to reply, Crop Eared Wolf said he was sometimes called Many Horses—and that he did in fact have many horses—but he preferred the name Crop Eared Wolf because wolves had taught the Blackfoot how to hunt in groups, and how to work together. You can still see them in the night sky, he said. *Makoyi-yohsokoyi* was the Wolf Trail. The Milky Way.

He pointed to my grandfather's knees, which were bent as he sat in the saddle, signaling surprise that he rode with short stirrups—like the Blackfoot, in fact, but unlike most newcomers to Blackfoot territory, such as the North-West Mounted Police officers who had come some ten years earlier and almost all the ranchers and cowboys who had followed them. My grandfather said he liked being able to shift his weight from side to side or forward when he needed to, showing how he did so—then stood in his stirrups smiling, and said it was also because he was short. He had noticed Crop Eared Wolf seemed to be too. He didn't say so, of course, but he did ask him why he rode with long stirrups, and Crop Eared Wolf indicated that he had been shot in the leg during a fight with the Cree twenty years earlier. Jack could tell he was proud of his time as a warrior.

They talked away for a long while, not always understanding each other but coming comfortably back to horses in a conversation that seemed to work just fine across the languages. Until Crop Eared Wolf asked my grandfather, in English phrasing that was fairly blunt, why he had come to Fort Macleod and Blackfoot territory.

And now my grandfather did feel uneasy and paused. The fact is, he wasn't sure, and had been wondering the same thing a few weeks earlier as he rode from his homestead in a place called Pile of Bones in Saskatchewan across the prairies some four hundred miles west to the Alberta foothills. To break the silence, the newly crowned Sorreltop Jack said it was for the adventure of it, just like it was for Crop Eared Wolf, he suggested, when he went on raids—a comparison he immediately realized was silly enough to probably be insulting. Quickly, he said it was because he was bored. Which sounded pretentious. So he added that people had been going to new places, and meeting new people, forever. Isn't that how the Blackfoot got here? he asked. Crop Eared Wolf looked a little surprised at the idea, and said he himself was here because he was adopted when his parents got sick and died, and Red Crow, the chief of the Blood tribe—the *Káínai* in the Blackfoot language, he added, for my grandfather's improvement—chose him to come into his tipi and be his son.

That got Jack talking about his own family, and how his father, Thomas Cowdry, had traveled thousands of miles from England, where he was born, because times were hard there, sailing for days across a large and treacherous body of water to give his family a chance for a better life. As he said this he thought about the challenges now facing the Blackfoot with the buffalo gone. And because he didn't want to suggest that moving somewhere else when times got tough was what the Blackfoot should do, he said, quickly again, that traveling to other places was simply what his people had done for hundreds of years. Rambling around the world was like following the roaming buffalo and the ripening berries over the prairies and into the foothills from season to season. Sometimes his people had made friends, and sometimes not, he said, but he hoped he would make friends here. As he spoke he could tell from the way Crop Eared Wolf looked at his sorrel's big ears that he was asking the horse, "Did *you* hear *that*?" . . . and he knew he was really talking nonsense now. After all, the Blackfoot were the real settlers in a territory they had occupied for as long as anyone could remember— deliberately moving from place to place in their own homeland, rather than "wandering" about. The wanderers were folk like himself, looking for a home.

Crop Eared Wolf listened politely as my grandfather bumbled on, trying to dig himself out of the hole and recover some credit. He was a dozen years older than my grandfather, who had just turned twenty-eight, and he appeared to be enjoying their conversation; and, except for the fact that he knew he was sometimes talking foolishness, my grandfather was too. But since he didn't want to bore Crop Eared Wolf, and had no satisfactory answer to the question about why he had come to his country, and they had said enough about horses for now, he pretended he had somewhere to go. Which wasn't true, because he didn't even have anywhere to stay except at the Macleod Hotel. So with courtesy, and a comfortable confusion of English and sign language, he said he hoped they would meet again one day, and they rode off in different directions, my grandfather northwest toward the Porcupine Hills and Crop Eared Wolf to his home on the Blood reserve at Stand Off, southeast of Fort Macleod.

My grandfather had come to Blackfoot territory for a lot of reasons, but one of them was curiosity. He and his brother Nat had gone to homestead on the Saskatchewan prairies three years earlier from their family home in Ontario, and had made a success of it. They even managed several hard winters living in a little sod house, with temperatures regularly dropping to forty below, and occasionally down below minus fifty. But they had heard about a warm winter wind called a Chinook which could come to the foothills in the midst of a cold spell and raise the temperature by as much as fifty degrees overnight, melting an inch of ice in an hour. They liked the sound of that after the last winter.

Signaled by a wonderful arch of cloud and a belt of blue sky, a Chinook is always a surprise; but, like many surprises, it can be hazardous, melting the rivers just when people have decided the ice is thick enough to take their horses and cattle across, or freezing melted groundwater so hard afterward that the cattle can't get at the grass beneath. Jack had heard a Blackfoot story in which the Chinook was imagined as the breath of a beautiful maiden who had wandered from home and got lost in the mountains to the west; and he knew that beautiful maidens, in legend at least, are often dangerous. And then there was the local tale about a traveler who tied his team of horses to a post sticking up in the snow one night. A Chinook came, and in the morning his horses were dangling from the church steeple. Warm winds like the Chinook, blowing down the slopes of high mountains when the conditions are right, are known in other places around the world; but perhaps nowhere do they have the magical character they enjoy in the lee of the Rocky Mountains and the foothills of Alberta. And yet for all the legendary surprise of a Chinook, which so far my grandfather had only heard about, meeting Crop Eared Wolf was as wonderful a surprise as he could have imagined. Even more wonderful, though he didn't know it at that first meeting, would be the friendship that developed between them over the next twenty years. That friendship is at the heart of this story.

And at the heart of their friendship was a gift that Crop Eared Wolf gave my grandfather some years later. It was a quirt—a riding crop or whip—carved and painted by Crop Eared Wolf in traditional Blackfoot iconography. It told the story of his tribal heritage and heroic exploits in war parties against old enemies such as the Sioux, the Shoshone, the Cree, and the Crow, and of his courage on raids to "bring home" their best horses, which he did with such flair and finesse that his exploits were admired by the same officers of the North-West Mounted Police who were trying to wipe out that venerable Plains Indian tradition. My grandfather had arrived in Fort Macleod at a time when war parties and horse stealing were still taking place, though their days were numbered. By 1885, when they first met, Crop Eared Wolf's time as a warrior in that tradition was almost over, but he was a dangerous man to insult and you didn't want him as an enemy, as several belligerent Indian agents (as these government officials were called back then) later discovered. Along with his wartime exploits, his reputation was tied to horses, which he had "brought home" from the camps of his enemies—the best horses, belonging to famous chiefs. He was very, very good at this, one of the best on the northern Plains, and very, very good at boasting about it, his accounts among the most notable records of that time and place. Boasting and toasting and truthtelling, my grandfather said affectionately, knowing that these are at the root of such storytelling. That was the warp and woof of the fabric of Blackfoot horse culture—securing the horses and telling the story. Words and images, like dances and drumming, were not just *about* events—they were events themselves. Crop Eared Wolf's quirt was more than a witnessing to the things he had done in his life. It was a ceremony of belief in storytelling as well as a chronicle of events in Blackfoot history. He carried it in the ceremonial parades in the years before he took over as chief of the Blood tribe from his father, Red Crow; and then one day he gave it to my grandfather as a gift.

My grandfather kept the gift to himself for most of his life, its significance deeply personal but with puzzling responsibilities. He knew it was a kind of public trust, as well as a witness to Blackfoot history and to their way of telling and "writing" it. Writing without words is a narrative, lyric, and dramatic tradition that goes back tens of thousands of years; it includes woven and beaded belts and blankets, masks and hats and chests, knotted and colored strings, carved and painted trays, poles, doors, verandah posts, stone runes and rock paintings—and quirts. He knew he had to keep the quirt safe. It wasn't Jack Cowdry's trophy; it was Crop Eared Wolf's testament.

He never displayed the quirt in the house where we lived, or even talked much about it. But after Crop Eared Wolf died in 1913, he kept it close; and he took it with him to the nursing home where he lived for the last months of his life, and where he died in 1947 at the age of ninety. The obligation that came with that gift and flowed from that friendship didn't die with him, and this book is my way of keeping it in circulation.

In one sense the quirt is a signature of *all* storytelling. Images, writing without words, carved and painted on an object—in this case, a riding crop—that has both functional and formal value, make it strange and familiar to us all at the same time; and those contradictions of strangeness and familiarity that it represents are, like those of belief and doubt, absolutely central to storytelling. We teach children about this when we say "once upon a time" and mean "right now"; and they soon learn to be surprised, each time as if for the first time, by the twists and turns in a story they have heard a hundred times before. This delight in the surprises of storytelling seems to be deeply human; and it is certainly common across cultures. If we lose the custom or the habit of belief that sustains this contradiction between the familiar and the strange, we lose the stories. And if we lose some of these stories, we lose our sense of who we are and where we belong. And dreadful things happen.

Which is why this book is partly about certain kinds of stories and storytelling that give meaning and purpose to lives that are losing both or finding both, stories that do not take us away from reality but bring us back to it. And it is about stories that give us pleasure, a much misunderstood test of beauty and truth and goodness from time immemorial. Blackfoot storytelling, like many peoples', is not simple, with past and future not so much separated by words and deeds and genealogies as they are connected by them through dreams and dances and declarations and memories and myths and medicine bundles that bring the real and the imagined into conversation. Science and art are interwoven with spiritual chronicle and cultural ceremony. This seems to have been recognized by many of those who came to settle in the foothills of the Rockies in the late nineteenth century, bringing their own strange storytelling with them and using it, as the Blackfoot did, to sustain their belief in themselves. They knew how precious that was; so there could be no excuse for the attempts that were made at the time to interfere with the Blackfoot spiritual ceremony that was the annual Sun Dance. When that was tried by several Canadian agents of Indian affairs, by some of the missionaries, and by a few—fortunately only a few—of the police, many people in the settler community rallied to put things right.

For a brief time—largely in the two decades between 1885 and 1905—many people, native and non-native, tried to fashion a commonwealth in Chinook country that would accommodate both Blackfoot sovereignty and new settlement and would give life to the spirit of the treaty made a few years earlier between the Blackfoot and the "Great Mother," Queen Victoria, on behalf of Canada. It was a time of uncertainty at every turn, with unfamiliar living conditions and livelihoods and unsettled sovereignties, as well as unpredictable weather. But it was also a time when many people in the foothills, awkwardly but ambitiously, looked for ways of getting along and getting on with the things that mattered to them all. Not everyone, of course, and not always; but often enough that their story offers hope for all of us today.

Uncertainties were a fact of life for people on the Alberta prairies, shared by the Blackfoot with their fellow frontier settlers and Plains Indians south of the border in the United States. In fact, during the first ten years following Canadian Confederation in 1867 that border was effectively ignored by almost everyone, with traders and cowboys with their cattle coming north, and Blackfoot regularly traveling to Montana territory to join the buffalo hunts and to visit with their kinfolk there among the Blackfeet. Visits to Montana and Idaho (which became states in 1889 and 1890, respectively) were a frequent necessity for Alberta settlers and Canadian government agents during this time in order to establish—or maintain—commercial and official communication in the region. There were conflicts, many of them of ancient origin, between some of the Plains tribes on both sides of the border, though a treaty in 1855 between the Blackfoot and the American government and some of the other Plains tribes kept the peace for a while. And whatever their differences, the tribal peoples of the Plains had much in common in their secular and sacred practices. Still, raids continued to take place, and enemy horses—prized by all the Plains peoples—continued to be taken, while buffalo hunts and sacred ceremonies such as the annual Sun Dance brought some of the tribes together across the national boundary.

For the Indians (who in Canada now favor the term First Nations, or more generally indigenous peoples) the border was an inconvenient colonial invention, though on the northern Plains it eventually marked some significant differences between Canada and the United States—differences shaped by social, economic, and political factors and written into storylines that continue to influence national ideologies in both countries. That said, the settlers were often anything but settled, and many Americans displayed a restless spirit that took them north across this western border. (Alberta back then was part of the Canadian territory called North-West, stretching from the Great Lakes west to the Rocky Mountains and north to the Arctic ocean. Manitoba had joined the 1867 Confederation of Ontario, Quebec, New Brunswick, and Nova Scotia as a province in 1870; British Columbia joined in 1871. Alberta and Saskatchewan did not become provinces until 1905; and the land to the north of the 60th parallel is now divided into the territories [rather than provinces] of Yukon, Northwest Territories, and Nunavut.)

The story of this western border was distorted by the illegal whisky trade—the term "whisky" covering a wide and wooly range of brews and liquors—from the United States into Canada. After the Civil War, Fort Benton, on the upper Missouri River in Montana, flourished as a center of commerce and communication. It was the main staging point for travel to and from the western frontier, and celebrated as the "Chicago of the Plains." From there, bull trains carried supplies north to the grasslands and foothills of the Canadian West on a trail to Fort Whoop-Up, one of the most important trading forts in southern Alberta. For several decades, it lived up to its name as a place where whisky and wild times were the order of the day, though the trade itself dealt also in guns, blankets, cooking utensils, as well as a wide range of other commodities to exchange for buffalo hides. That well-traveled route from Fort Benton north was called the Whoop-Up Trail; and it also became a supply route for goods to the small settlements and ranch communities that were springing up in the foothills of the Rocky Mountains.

By the 1870s, whisky had become the scourge of many of the Plains Indian tribes, including the Blackfoot, and the new Dominion of Canada was worried that its ambition to settle the West in a peaceful manner (and thereby to connect the country "from sea to sea," as it promised in its national motto: *a mari usque ad mare*) was being threatened by the disruption and disorder that the illegal whisky trade was promoting. Even though the Blackfoot certainly did not share Canada's ambition to advance settlement, they did share its concern over this trade, because many of their communities were being devastated by the binge drinking that it encouraged. The government in Ottawa decided to establish a police (rather than a military) force to deal with the illegal international trade and assert Canadian "law and order" in the West; and in 1874 a contingent of the newly formed North-West Mounted Police (the forerunner of the present Royal Canadian Mounted Police, which is now both the national police force and the contracted provincial police in eight of ten provinces) established their headquarters at what became known as Fort Macleod. The policemen stopped on the way at Whoop-Up, where they were at first troubled by the sight of a homemade American flag flying from the fort, but then discovered only a single trader there who offered them dinner.

But their message got through, and with remarkable speed, considerable skill, and the cooperation of the Blackfoot leaders they stopped the whisky trade and developed good relations with many of the tribes on the northern Plains, sternly applying the criminal laws of the new nation to both the Indians and the settlers, who were still fairly scarce on the ground. This application was a surprise to some of the newcomers, especially those who expected a much less disciplined frontier spirit, and it was a curiosity to the Blackfoot; but friendships and good faith and an inevitably erratic commitment to keeping your word bound everyone—native and newcomer—into an uneasy alliance, sustained in large measure by a tradition of what is called "common law" (derived from local customs rather than statutes), which English-speaking Canada had inherited from the British. It depended upon a cultural acceptance of certain restraints on individual action, and an aversion to vigilante justice; and that was precisely what the North-West Mounted Police were there to enforce as impartially as they could, making it clear to the ranchers that if any of them shot an Indian, even one who was stealing their cattle, they would hang. All of this was made easier by the fact that local judges were not elected but appointed, many from within the ranks of the police.

Of course, it was nowhere near a perfect regime, and its enforcement had all the inconsistencies of any human enterprise. But it nourished social habits that were significantly different from those which developed south of the border, where the celebration of individualism free of restraint was coupled with resistance to the hierarchical "Old World" controls that many had left behind in Europe, shaping a culture much more inclined to the uninhibited exercise of unruly action—the Wild West of memory and myth. Of course, the United States was as much a nation of laws and an advocate of order as Canada was. But as in any arena of public policy, much depended upon the extent to which communities believed in these laws, and who was enforcing them; and in the northwestern American border states enforcement was in the hands of elected sheriffs and judges, acutely conscious of local attitudes they were there to serve—and when they didn't meet the expectations of the communities, citizens often took matters into their own hands.

And then there were the guns. Cowboys on the Plains often carried guns, both long and short, for protection against wolves and snakes; but in the Canadian West this was tempered by strict handgun laws imposed by the police and liquor licensing regulations that effectively kept guns away from the saloons. Many cowboys in the Canadian foothills did not even own a gun, and there was very little sense that anyone needed a gun for protection from somebody else. South of the border, some of the gun violence was a legacy of the Civil War, its hostilities still fresh. But mostly it was an expression of the rugged individualism and the sometimes deadly codes of honor that were part of the diverse character of life on the western frontier, and popularized the defiance of authority. And it fostered a form of independence that was both proudly self-sufficient and frequently self-centered, as reflected in the words from the popular cowboy song "Whoopee ti yi yo, git along little dogies," with its memorable line, "It's your misfortune and none of my own."

Illuminating life across the border, Owen Wister's landmark 1902 book, *The Virginian*, is widely acknowledged as the first western novel, celebrating the virtues of cowboy freedom and self-reliance. The inspiration for Wister's title character is generally credited to Everett (Ebb) Johnson, a cowboy from Wyoming who came to Alberta on a cattle drive in 1888 and stayed to become foreman of one of the great ranches in the foothills, the Bar U. One of his best friends back in Wyoming was Harry Longabaugh, who had ended up in jail in the town of Sundance. When he got out, Johnson invited Longabaugh to come and work on the ranch in Canada, and he was the best man at Johnson's wedding. Longabaugh was popular with the ranchers and cowboys and he mostly stayed clear of the law, except when he was arrested for cruelty to a horse, a grievous sin in the horse country of the foothills. The charge was dropped, but Longabaugh got restless. He soon returned to his old ways—and to another old friend, Butch Cassidy—as the Sundance Kid.

Diversity was evident in communities on both sides of the border, as well as out on the cattle range. It is now recognized that perhaps a quarter of the cowboys there were African American, many of them experienced in handling horses and livestock on plantations during slavery and free at last to take up the hard and homeless life of a cowboy. Some became ranchers and settled into a home on the range, others excelled at the rodeos that sprang up in the West—even though many of their lives were infected by racial prejudices that did not end with emancipation. And so were the lives of some of the Mexican *vaqueros* who came north with experience that helped shape the great ranching heritage of the West, and with Spanish words that became part of the language of its storytelling. But in cowboy culture throughout the West, skill and dependability almost always trumped race—eventually. The names of towns and rivers and mountain ranges in the region confirm the variety of ethnic and cultural communities that came to find a new life, struggling like everyone else to make a home in the midst of social, economic, and political conflicts that intensified as the territories turned toward statehood and provincehood, and the nations turned toward "managing" the Indians.

Which they did in different ways, though with sadly similar motives. In 1871, the United States formally ceased entering into Indian treaties, citing its inability (or unwillingness) to fulfill its financial and other treaty obligations, and deciding that instead of breaking more of its promises it would stop making any. The same year, Canada *began* its treaty-making, which had been the principal method of securing alliances in the British policy toward Indians before American independence, and one that had been formally assumed by Canada in 1867 under the terms of the British North America Act that created the new nation. During the 1870s, Canada entered into seven treaties with Indians on the prairies, each of them involving a commitment by the Indian tribes to keep the peace and obey the laws promoted by the North-West Mounted Police, and to allow settlement (as well as railway and telegraph lines) across their territory. In exchange, the government promised to help them in the transition from buffalo hunting (which had sustained the Plains tribes, both materially and spiritually) and to supply them with food and medicine to deal with the deadly invasion of new diseases that had taken a terrible toll, and to provide radically diminished but protected "reserve" land on which the Indians might establish permanent homes (rather than summer and winter hunting and gathering camps) and take up agriculture.

The results were both starkly different and distressingly similar on each side of the border. In the United States, a war against the Indians that had begun in 1830, with Andrew Jackson's "removal" of tribes from the southeastern states to what became known as Indian Territory west of the Mississippi, spread throughout the western territories. Sometimes this was in response to Indian aggression against settlers who appeared on their land without request or permission—the same aggressive response they would have given to any stranger, including any unfriendly Indian tribe—and sometimes to remove an inconvenient "problem." And so the Indians were rounded up and confined to "reservations," even as the sovereignty of the states was being recovered after the Civil War and new states were being formed out of old Indian territories.

In Canada a measure of peace was preserved, though it was broken in 1885 when Louis Riel, the leader of the Métis (who had returned from his exile in Montana), declared a provisional government for the territory, prompting an uprising of Métis and Aboriginal people on the prairies that was defeated by Canadian military action. (The Métis were buffalo-hunting people of Indian and Euro-American ancestry who were heavily involved in the earlier fur trade, and had developed a distinct culture on the Plains.) Only a few of the Indian tribes on the Canadian prairies joined the uprising, which was itself remarkable given that by this time Canada had broken many of its treaty promises, and had instituted a grim cluster of regulations and administrative regimes under what was called the Indian Act that were unapologetically assimilationist, and severely compromised the ability of the Indians to continue as a separate people.

One factor that helped the Blackfoot in the Alberta foothills was that, unlike the United States, Canada did not try to take away Indian horses. The Blackfoot were one of the great horse cultures of the northern Plains, and even after the buffalo were gone their horses remained a source of pride, celebrated in their storytelling and in local parades and horse races and rodeos—the winner of the premier event at the first Calgary Stampede in 1912 was a Blackfoot Indian.

One of the complicated cross-border situations that Canada had to manage was the arrival of Sitting Bull in 1877, a year after the Battle of the Little Bighorn, with about a thousand fellow Sioux, joining several thousand others who had fled to Canada during the previous winter. Sitting Bull insisted that his traditional hunting grounds included territory now claimed by Canada, and that his people deserved the protection of Canadian law, and he proudly displayed medals given to his grandfather and other Sioux leaders for their support of the British during the American War of Independence and the War of 1812. Sitting Bull was received cautiously, and when he refused to return to the United States, he was in turn refused reserve land or food or other support in Canada, but was—somewhat nervously, given his well-publicized antipathy to settlers—allowed to stay. By 1881, his followers close to starvation, he returned of his own accord to Fort Buford in Montana and surrendered.

On both sides of the border, the Euro-American societies that overwhelmed the Indians in their territory were remarkably similar in habits and heritage, and in ambitions; and the grasslands and semi-arid climate on the northern Plains were virtually identical. Many Americans came to Canada with the cattle that formed the basis of the great ranches in the foothills of the Rockies, bringing with them many of the social and cultural practices of the American West, and their fear of Indians. But they encountered not only the North-West Mounted Police, who were the law of the land, but also the Blackfoot, still proud and at peace as well as relatively independent. The Blackfoot were quite capable of resisting many of the totalitarian edicts of the Canadian Indian agents—often with help from the police, who felt that *they* were in charge; and with help from many of the ranchers, who had relatively good relations with the Blackfoot. Even some of the missionaries took the side of the Indians in their determination to maintain their ceremonial traditions.

The civil laws and their enforcement certainly differed across the border line. But so did the land law that governed ranch and farm country, and this profoundly affected the relationships between farmers and ranchers. Both Canada and the United States had inherited an old storyline, one that celebrated a progress of Western civilization from hunting and gathering to herding and farming. In this view, Indian territory was "primitive" and agricultural development was "progressive," by turning the land into useful production rather than letting it sit "idle."

Dislocation of Indians and dispossession of their lands in the interests of "progress" was undertaken on both sides of the border.

But then the two frontier stories diverge. In the United States, farming was accorded a superior status and received greater support, while in the Canadian West—especially in the near-desert climate of the foothills, where farming was at best a marginal enterprise—ranching was encouraged and supported with an "open range" policy underwritten by government leases to large ranching operations. By contrast, the antipathy toward monopolistic control in the nineteenth-century American West, and the ideology of the crop-rooted farmer as the pioneer and the grass-grazing rancher as the problem, persuaded the American government to resist the granting of large leaseholds to individual ranchers. The result was not only the fragmentation of the grassland "commons" and the breakup of fragile waterways into thirsty farm units, but an unregulated competition for land—between farmer and rancher, as well as between Indians and settlers—that generated dangerous range wars and (since there was no security of tenure for the ranchers) deadly overgrazing. Almost as much as the contrasting regimes of law and order, this was at the heart of the differences between the Canadian and the American West.

But as we shall see, contradictions were the order of the day in the border country of Alberta and Montana during this time, and the border itself remained porous even as it became more permanent. Perhaps nothing commemorates the connections across the border better—and continues to inspire a sense of community there—than Chief Mountain, sacred to the Blackfoot as well as to their border country cousins, the Blackfeet. From Fort Macleod, in the Alberta foothills, you can see it clearly on the southwestern horizon; but the mountain itself is in Montana.

1

FORT MACLEOD

THE COWDRY BROTHERS—John and his older brother Nathaniel, or Jack and Nat—had gone from Ontario in 1882 to homestead in the district of Saskatchewan in what was then the Canadian North-West Territories. Nat was tall and trim, Jack was short and sturdy, and both were just plain curious about all sorts of things. Together they were a good match for the work that lay ahead of them. They built a sod house with thick-rooted prairie grass cut into bricks the size of doormats that they piled on each other to make the walls, framed a roof out of pieces of wood from a dilapidated wagon, and then laid more sod on top. They were among the first dozen or so settlers, securing land at ten dollars for a quarter section (160 acres) and plowing it with a neighbor's steel moldboard plow pulled by a Percheron mare. They'd bought the horse along with a cart from a Red River trader, to start a small farm near a little settlement called Pile of Bones by the banks of Wascana Creek. The name Wascana was translated from the Cree word for bones, *oskana*, and referred to the buffalo bones piled by the banks—some say because of a belief by the Cree that the buffalo would not leave an area littered with their bones. But the buffalo were gone from the Plains by the time the brothers got there, and in due course settlers cleared the bones and sent them east to be ground into fertilizer, for which there was a ready market. And in late 1882 Pile of Bones was renamed Regina, in honor of Queen Victoria.

Jack and Nat settled fairly easily into their first season on the prairies, looking up an uncle who had gone there as a surveyor a few years earlier, and making friends with the other folks in the neighborhood, among them the Hudson's Bay Company manager at nearby Fort Qu'Appelle, Archie McDonald—he was called a "factor" in the jargon of the fur trade—and his Métis wife, Nellie Inkster. From them they learned how to live in the North-West Territories, established in 1870 and including some seven million acres—most of the Canadian land west of the Great Lakes to the Rocky Mountains and further north. They spent many evenings talking with the couple and their other new friends—Métis and Cree, traders and settlers—about treaties and "Indian territory," and squabbling over whether the seat of government of the North-West Territories should henceforth be Fort Qu'Appelle or Regina. The latter won out over Fort Qu'Appelle, becoming the new capital of the territory.

The brothers stayed on the dryland prairies around Regina for the next three years, their farm surrounded by grassland stretching out to bluffs and sloughs around Qu'Appelle. By 1885 they had gathered together enough money from farming, and from the sale of some land they had bought when they first arrived, to give them a start in a new adventure. They had heard of opportunities further west in the cattle country that lay in the foothills of the Rocky Mountains, now flush with the prospect of shipping by rail to eastern markets and on to Great Britain. And of course they had heard the stories about those warm winter breaks brought by the Chinook winds. The success of the dozen-year-old North-West Mounted Police in bringing a certain sort of orderliness to the western prairies of Canada was encouraging, given the tales of Indian wars and vigilante violence that trickled up from the American West. And in Jack's mind, the reputation of the Blackfoot was a big draw. They were by all accounts one of the greatest horse cultures and Indian nations of the northern Plains, and word was that they had turned from fearless warriors who rattled the other Plains tribes into stern peacemakers who had signed a treaty with Canada a few years earlier—and were already resisting its bureaucratic brutalities and calling the country to account for breaking its promises.

In the 1880s, much of the huge expanse of the Canadian North-West Territories had until recently been referred to as Rupert's Land, named in 1670 by King Charles II after his cousin Prince Rupert of the Rhine when the king authorized a royal charter granting the "Company of Adventurers of England" a monopoly on the fur trade and control of all lands whose rivers and streams flowed into Hudson Bay; the Hudson's Bay Company was thereby accorded rights to a million and a half square miles of western and northern Canada stretching from Labrador to the Rocky Mountains and further. Charles believed that the land was his to give because no other Christian monarch had claimed it; and it was an old joke that "HBC" stood for "Here Before Christ."

In 1869 the Hudson's Bay Company turned the charter over to the newly formed Canadian government, for a price of course, giving Canada control over a domain in the West several times the size of the 1867 Dominion. But the rights of the First Nations and the Métis had not been addressed by Canada in the course of that transfer, though they had certainly been asserted from time to time in the preceding two centuries. And Canada's responsibility to do so was clear, for it had inherited the British policy of making formal treaties with the indigenous peoples it encountered in its imperial undertakings, a policy that had been articulated some hundred and thirty years earlier by William Johnson—a wealthy entrepreneur, militia leader, and Indian agent for the British government living in the 1740s and later decades in what was then the colony of New York.

Fluent in Mohawk, Johnson came to respect the Iroquois; and he saw alliances with the Indian tribes as a matter mostly of expedience, though sometimes of necessity. His policy reflected that view. "I know that many mistakes arise here from erroneous accounts formerly made of Indians," he wrote. "They have been represented as calling themselves subjects, although the very word would have startled them, had it been ever pronounced by any interpreter. They desire to be considered as allies and friends." If you call them "subjects," he continued, you had better have an army behind you.

So in the early spring of 1885, with some fairly incoherent ambitions and no careful planning, Jack and Nat Cowdry loaded a wagon, hitched up four horses, trailed several more behind in what the cowboys called a "cavvy" (a bunch of horses that are not being ridden or harnessed), and lit out on the trail to Calgary and then south to Fort Macleod.

The trip across the prairies wasn't especially hard for Jack and Nat, considering those winters in Pile of Bones, and the weather held cool and clear; but it was challenging, with wolves following the wagon on one stretch, and a group of young Blackfoot men making themselves evident as outriders when they got near Calgary. They weren't worried, though they were watchful—just like the Blackfoot. Sign language often made the difference and kept the peace, so they made signs as they had learned to do from the Cree. For hundreds of years, signing had been the lingua franca of Plains Indians speaking very different languages (the Blackfoot spoke an Algonquian language, unlike speakers of Athapaskan languages nearby), and the signing reminded everyone of what they had in common, while they decided what they didn't. It was also a nice reminder that language itself may have begun with gestures rather than words. For Jack, the gesture that mattered was a handshake; but since he also loved to smoke a pipe, and knew about the long pipes of the Blackfoot and the significance of sharing one together, he had an idea how they might get halfway there with their new traveling companions. So he and Nat stopped their wagon, lit a pipe, and passed it back and forth between them. The Blackfoot men waved a welcome, and rode off in another direction.

On their journey to the foothills, the Cowdry brothers passed through miles and miles of native grasslands where the cattle had wandered over the winter. The buffalo were almost all gone, and ranching was about to take over the prairies. This was near-desert country, described in the middle of the nineteenth century by the geographer John Palliser as semi-arid grassland unsuitable for large-scale farming. The temptation to turn foothills country over to crops was a wet-season dream in a region whose most permanent feature was not that it was flat but that it was dry (though some early visitors had a misleading welcome when they arrived during years of relatively heavy rainfall).

But almost everywhere it was ideal for cattle, ranging across the open plains like domestic buffalo in spring and summer, and herded in fall and winter into the foothills—where shelter and water were plentiful in the wooded coulees (small ravines) and native fescue grass provided feed except during the most drastic winters. The open range was the commons of sentimental song and story, a place where interests coincided and stewardship was shared. Keeping the short-grass prairies and the foothills in good condition benefited everyone, for otherwise they would have to feed the cattle over the summer and winter on the home ranch, and many of them could little afford to do that; and even if they could, it wasn't always possible to secure hay in those early years. So keeping the range open and relatively unfenced became a high priority for the ranchers there.

The river that ran by Fort Macleod, where the Cowdry brothers were headed, was called Old Man's after *Napi*, the Blackfoot god who made the world. The reason the world is so full of wonders, the story goes, is that *Napi* was a trickster and a mischief-maker, just like the river. For the first decade that the newly created North-West Mounted Police had been in the region, Old Man's River was responsible for intermittent spring floodings that plagued the original fort they'd built on an island in the middle of the river; just the year before Jack and Nat arrived they'd finally replaced it with a new barracks on the banks above Old Man's, and this spot would become the town of Fort Macleod. Willow Creek, close by to the north, had been the townsite preferred by the few dozen settlers in the district who were not in the police force; but agricultural priorities came before urban development—Willow Creek offered good farmland—and the new fort's location with its lovely prospect overlooking the Old Man's River was chosen. Though it was (as one resident ruefully described it) on "a piece of ground guiltless of ever having produced ought but a plentiful crop of stones," a contemporary newspaper's description of the view from the town was without irony:

> *Situated on the south bank of the Old Man's River, [it] commands a view which, for variety, beauty and grandeur, is hard to be excelled. Away to the north, at a distance of about a mile, may be seen a small remnant of the old town in the shape of a few log shacks yet resting upon the bosom of the waters. . . . To the northwest, almost in a line with the main street of the town, rise wooded summits of the Porcupines, while away to the west, and circling southward, the magnificent peaks of the rocky range [Rockies] . . . Chief Mountain standing out by itself a conspicuous landmark, which can be seen at a distance of 200 miles. While to the north, and immediately in front of us, the Old Man's River, winding through its changing scenes of mountains, hill and dale, pursues its way. . . . It is the finest section of the North-West.*

The new fort was sturdy, but some of the buildings that sprang up around it looked as though they might fall down in the winds that blew constantly in the foothills and across the plains. A lady who arrived from the East and settled on a ranch nearby described the townsite dismissively as "one of the last places to live in all the world . . . covered with small stones which the never-ceasing wind drives hither and thither with little clouds of dust. . . . How the people live here happily I do not know and I don't think they are very happy." (She had attended a ball at the North-West Mounted Police barracks which she also did not enjoy, having been asked to dance by a man who "with his half-breed wife had been cheering himself with more than one drink.") And a grumpy twenty-year-old newcomer, who had arrived in 1884 to open a drugstore, said the town "consisted of a crooked lane, it could not be dignified by the name of street, lined with log stores and shacks, the former having square-faced frame fronts, and their whole appearance decidedly ramshackle and distressing." Within eighteen months, he was off to nearby Lethbridge. But most of the newcomers happily stayed, and helped to give the young town a more organized character, with the fort barracks where the police lived to the north of a wide main street with a hotel and a trading post, blacksmith shop, shoemaker and several other stores, and stables and houses and a couple of churches in behind. Within a very few years, there were two blacksmiths, two butcher shops, fifteen stores, four churches, nine saloons, over fifty residences and nearly three hundred people.

Mail to that part of Alberta had been slow until quite recently, with contract delivery by cart and wagon and coach in summer, and sled in winter. Post destined for the East went from the North-West Mounted Police barracks in Fort Macleod, where it was stamped with U.S. postage, to Fort Benton and then onto the Missouri River on its way to Toronto or Ottawa or Montreal. In winter, when the Missouri froze up, mail to eastern Canada had gone from Fort Benton by stage to Helena and south to the railway town of Corrine, Utah.

But in 1883, when the railway reached Calgary, mail service improved dramatically. Weekly mail from Calgary to Fort Macleod began in January 1884 under contract to wagons from one of the local ranches and continued until 1893, when a railway spur line came down from Calgary. To carry dispatches, the North-West Mounted Police used riders and special mail wagons and sometimes Blackfoot runners like Deer Foot, who could make it from Calgary to Fort Macleod and back in two days, and from Calgary to Edmonton and back in four.

One of the tributaries of the Old Man's River is called the Belly River, a direct translation of the Blackfoot word, for it feeds and waters the land where Red Crow's Blood tribe had traditionally made its winter home. It begins as a little stream up by the sacred Chief Mountain, which stands sentinel among the great mountains to the west that you can see from Fort Macleod, towering above the plains and foothills where the buffalo once roamed and where cattle now grazed. A legend tells of a great chief who grazed his horses, the finest and fastest in the West, on the flat land on top of the mountain where special grasses grow.

Nearby, to the west of town, were the coulees where horses liked to gather under cottonwood trees as the wind whooshed and whispered across the prairies in every season. The summers were sometimes so hot that people said the flies walked instead of flew about; but that was when the berries ripened and were gathered—saskatoon berries (*okonoki*) and blueberries and chokecherries and baneberries and gooseberries and bull berries and bearberries, which were sometimes called *kinnikinnick*, a name that really means "a mix-up." The Blackfoot planted tobacco every spring, which they often mixed with *kinnikinnick*, and wild turnips that they dug up at the end of the summer.

Virtually every coulee and cottonwood grove in the territory had a Blackfoot name, of course, and the Blackfoot gave new names to many of the towns; but it is notable that none of them, in the words of the historian Hugh Dempsey, "reflects any antagonism or hostility towards the invading settlers. Some have humorous undertones, but most are logical and to the point." Fort Macleod was named *akápiyoyis*, which means "many houses," while the town of Gleichen, east of Calgary, was called *sokitsi*, or "fat stomach," after the owner of the general store in town. And sometimes the settler and the Blackfoot names were along the same lines. A town west of Fort Macleod, for instance, was named by a rancher with literary leanings after a line from Thomas Gray's popular eighteenth-century poem "Elegy Written in a Country Churchyard"—"the lowing herd wind slowly o'er the lea." Watching the cattle string out just before a winter Chinook and go to water at the big spring near town, and knowing that the bunch grass there provided excellent pasturage and that "lea" means "pasture," he called the town Cowley—keeping company, in nature terms, with the Blackfoot name, which was *akái-sowkaas*. It means "many [wild] prairie turnips."

Coming into Fort Macleod on their wagon in the spring of 1885, Jack and Nat Cowdry needed a stable to put up their horses. They had heard there was one at the Macleod Hotel, which was already legendary in the territory, so they headed straight there. The owner, Kamoose Taylor, was part of the legend. The name Kamoose meant "wife stealer" in Blackfoot, and was apparently accorded him when he married an Indian woman whose family refused to let her go, despite the dowry he offered of a horse, two pairs of blankets, and some tobacco. Or so the story went, with about a dozen variations. Later, after she died, he favored his other first name, Harry.

Like many people in those parts, Kamoose had tried a bunch of things before he settled on one. He had come to the West as a missionary, gone gold mining in the mountains of California, and when he came to the Alberta foothills in 1874 had been the first man arrested by the North-West Mounted Police for bringing whisky into the territory from the United States. Down by the border was no-man's-land, and everybody's backyard; and at a time when the boundary surveyors were still setting out their stakes, nobody paid much attention to the movement of products and people to and from the United States until the Canadian police arrived on the scene with orders to shut down the illegal whisky trade that was wreaking havoc in the Indian communities. But after Kamoose had paid his fine (having had not only his whisky confiscated but also sixty horses and several wagons loaded with buffalo robes and other trade goods), he turned around and built a hotel in Fort Macleod where he welcomed friends and strangers and the police too with good (and this time legal) beverages, good humor . . . and *fairly* good food, everyone said. In response to which, Kamoose posted signs in the lobby warning guests that "Assaults on the cook are strictly prohibited" and "Meals in your own room will not be guaranteed in any way. Our waiters are hungry and not above temptation." However, "The bar will be open day and night. All day drinks 50 cents each; night drinks $1.00 each. No mixed drinks will be served except in the case of death in the family." The Cowdry brothers, tired and dusty after their travels, were met by a sign at the entrance displaying the silhouette of a man's head and the notice "No Jawbone"—meaning "cash only, no credit." Inside, the list of "house rules" included more instructions on how to behave:

All guests are requested to rise at 6:00 a.m. This is imperative as the sheets are needed for tablecloths.

Towels changed weekly. Insect Powder for sale at the bar. [*Kamoose's answer to a patron who complained about the state of the towel hanging above the public washbasin was: "Twenty men have dried themselves on that towel and you are the first to complain."*]

A deposit must be made before towels, soap or candles can be carried to rooms. When boarders are leaving, a rebate will be made on all candles or parts of candles not burned or eaten.

When guests find themselves or their baggage thrown over the fence, they may consider that they have received notice to quit.

Jewelry and other valuable [*sic*] *will not be locked in a safe. This hotel has no such ornament as a safe.*

Saddle horses can be hired at any hour of the day or night, or the next day or night if necessary.

Only regularly registered guests will be allowed the special privilege of sleeping on the Bar Room floor.

Refreshing themselves in the bar, the Cowdry brothers got acquainted with some of the local folks, including the stagecoach driver Frank Pollinger, known to everyone who traveled anywhere in the foothills as Polly. It was said that his horses could only understand him when he swore—like the men who drove the bull trains, called bull-whackers, who were renowned for their inventive curses. Pollinger's oaths were (as the local newspaper, the *Macleod Gazette*, described them) "never microscopic or feeble, but resounding and polysyllabic." It was said he could drive a wagon up a hill so slippery you could slide down the same if you had a toboggan; and Jack Cowdry liked him right away because he reminded him of the drovers who navigated the hills back in Ontario when he was growing up.

They also ran into Inspector Francis Dickens, son of Charles, standing at the bar asking for "something quick at taking hold and slow at letting go," and Jack was delighted to meet this son of England's most famous author, who had died some fifteen years before. After running through his small inheritance, Frank (as Francis was called when he got to Canada) had signed up as an early recruit with the North-West Mounted Police. He had been stationed at Blackfoot Crossing (north of Fort Macleod near Calgary) for several years, but was in town this time on a brief visit from the battlefront with the Métis and the Cree in Saskatchewan, where he had been in nervous command of Fort Pitt when the fort was surrendered in one of the defining moments of the 1885 uprising led by the charismatic Métis leader Louis Riel. So of course the conversation, often agitated, was about the uprising, and the prospects of an Indian war in the territory, and the leadership of Riel (whom Jack Cowdry had met the previous year through his friends at Fort Qu'Appelle), and the bar was lively with opinions. Then Jack recited his favorite passage from *Hard Times* to Inspector Dickens, and started chatting away about the great novelist. But by that time Dickens was well into his cups, a habit he cultivated more reliably than he did policing—or anything much else for that matter, for he was not as good a judge of character and plot as his father, and he had botched several assignments in the foothills before turning his uncertain attention to Saskatchewan. A year later, still in his early forties, Dickens left the force and was all set to follow in his father's footsteps on the lecture circuit in the United States when he died suddenly, in Illinois, of a heart attack.

Dickens was one of an interesting group of individuals around Fort Macleod and in the country nearby: so-called remittance men from Great Britain, sent out by their families to get them as far away from home as possible. As one newspaperman put it, they were often "deported for some small lapse of grace, which in the [Canadian]

North-West would not afford gossip for ten minutes [such as] the unpardonable sin of preferring a pretty barmaid's society to that of a bespectacled aunt, coupled with a tendency to stay out all night." The tales of their escapades, including some courageous (albeit often foolish) adventures, provided entertainment all round.

Many of them put on airs, as they were expected to. "Lord" Lionel Brook—the title was dubious, but genially upheld by the community—was a regular at the Macleod Hotel. He had taken up ranching near Pincher Creek (thirty miles southwest of Fort Macleod) where, in the words of an old-timer in the area, "his picturesque appearance was always to be noted at race-meets and sports . . . He was invariably riding in belted Norfolk jacket, riding breeches and gaiters, wide-felt hat and monocle. The Indians called him 'Window Pane Chief,' and he has been a prince of graciousness to them."

As they settled into town Jack and Nat found that a group of a dozen or so townsfolk, including a number of reformed whisky traders, gathered at mealtime around a long dining-room table in the hotel, affectionately known as Taylor's Table, almost always with Harry Taylor presiding. Lively arguments were routine there too, and invariably the treaty signed with the Blackfoot eight years earlier would come up—praised as a peace pact with one of the most powerful Indian nations on the northern Plains—as would the recent selection by the Blood tribe of a new reserve in their old winter territory close to town, a move that pleased many merchants who looked forward to more trade with the Indians. But the conversation also covered the fences that were going up as settlement increased, protecting livestock and crops on the small farms but closing down the open range on which ranchers depended; the fires along the railway line, which dramatically increased the hazard of grass fires on the dry prairies; and of course the condition of Fort Macleod, which by general agreement was still fairly ramshackle. And Taylor's Table was the seedbed of some visionary speculation on the future of the North-West Territories, and it was there that the Cowdry boys got a quick but thorough education in how the territory looked from the vantage point of the foothills.

2

ON THE BANKS OF THE OLD MAN'S RIVER

DESPITE THE SEEMING SELF-CONFIDENCE of the new nation of Canada, the bureaucrats and their political masters in Ottawa had a lot of anxieties about the First Nations in the West. The simple fact—and (for the government) the worrying figure—was that in 1871 there were over thirty thousand Indians on the Canadian prairies, along with ten thousand Métis, and fewer than two thousand settlers. So the settlers were not only outnumbered, but sometimes outclassed by the great leaders of the tribal nations, individuals of stature and statecraft refined through generations of dealing with other strangers and settlers, including migrating Aboriginal ones. The Europeans were often gifted, occasionally greedy, sometimes wise and generous of spirit; but they were more likely to be amateurs. In the face of these odds, alliances and trust were the order of the day.

The new Dominion of Canada, expanding the British practice of treaty making that had begun well before 1867, did proceed to negotiate a set of treaties with First Nations on the prairies—though Ottawa quickly forgot about the spirit and proceeded to interpret the written text in the narrowest terms, or simply to ignore it. And they left the Métis out of the bargain, their central role in the life of the territory unrecognized, their sovereignty unacknowledged, and their civil status unclear. For that piece of unfinished business, the country would pay dearly.

The treaties were, in principle, peace treaties to secure permission to enter and settle in First Nations' territories, and they included a solemn promise to ensure the continuing welfare of all the Indian tribes, in good times and bad. They were also intended to keep the Americans at bay until "Canadian" settlement was well established along the border. Whatever the treaties look like from the present day, and however many of their solemn promises were soon broken, treaty making on the prairies after the 1867 Confederation did signal a recognition of both Canadian *and* First Nations sovereignty. Canada undertook to "acknowledge the Indian title to his vast and idle domain, and to treat for it with much gravity, as if with a sovereign power"—a strong statement, to be sure, but as so often in the language used to describe Aboriginal lands and livelihoods, there is a catch. In this case, it is in the word "idle," which signals the misrepresentation that warped so much that followed, conjuring up the notion of "idle Indians" and an "empty land" just waiting for European agricultural (and in due course industrial) enterprise to make it "useful." And "civilized."

When treaty making started in 1871, Adams George Archibald, the lieutenant governor of Manitoba and the North-West Territories, wrote, "it is impossible to be too particular in carrying out the terms of the agreements made with these people [the prairie First Nations]. They recollect with astonishing accuracy every stipulation made at the Treaty, and if we expect our relations with them to be of the kind which is desirable to maintain we must fulfill our obligations with scrupulous fidelity." In other words, we must keep our word. Whatever our perspective, the Canadian–First Nations treaties provide a framework, witnessed at the time by spiritual as well as secular leaders on both sides, for revisiting those promises and reconstituting the sense of alliance and friendship, as well as responsibility and respect, with which they were proclaimed in the rhetoric of the time.

The first of the Canadian so-called numbered treaties—they were numerically if not imaginatively labeled One to Eleven—were with some of the prairie tribes east of Alberta; the Blackfoot signed Treaty Seven in 1877. Of course, along with their acknowledgment of First Nations sovereignty, the treaties were designed to clear the way for the railway, for settlement, and for "civil society" in the narrative of the new nation of Canada, and to avoid the Indian wars that had demoralized the United States. And since this treaty-making might not be sufficient to remind the Americans that this land was Canadian, it was expected that the Canadian Pacific Railway would provide a bulwark against American territorial ambitions, binding the new country together with what the historian George Stanley called "bonds of steel as well as sentiment" (and keeping a promise to British Columbia, which had joined Confederation in 1871—a bitter reminder that *some* promises to *some* people were kept). There was early opposition to the railway, as well as to the telegraph line that more or less accompanied it, from the Cree and the Blackfoot across whose territory the lines would run; but the treaties were supposed to address their concerns and establish conditions for both orderly settlement and First Nations self-sufficiency—though exactly what the latter might mean was unclear to everyone. Canada was in a teenage hurry, and the pace of construction of the railway line, for instance, was remarkably fast. One homesteader from Pile of Bones told about leaving in the morning to cut some wood, with no sign of the railway. When he returned that evening, he had to cross the tracks.

The Blackfoot had entered into many pacts with former enemies and future allies, and had signed a treaty with the United States government some twenty years before they accepted a treaty with the Queen of Canada, so their leaders certainly knew about treaties and treaty making. Treaties were a time-honored way of dealing with the crises the Blackfoot faced, including foreigners they disliked and the threat of war. But this was different, and not just because there was a major crisis with the departure of the buffalo and the arrival of the railway and the settlers. The difference had to do with the territorial aspect of the treaty. For the Blackfoot, wars had never been about acquiring territory but about revenge or prestige, and this treaty with Canada was above all a treaty to prevent war and keep the peace. Using such a treaty to deal with territorial matters was completely unfamiliar to the Blackfoot, and more or less inconceivable. They said repeatedly that the Great Spirit, not the Great Mother, had given them the land and only that same Spirit could take it away.

But there wasn't much room for negotiation in the brief that the Canadian government negotiators had been given, and none at all when it came to that kind of territorial covenant. That said, there is plenty of evidence from the treaties entered into across the prairies that leaders on each side, however grudgingly, believed that what they were doing was for the best, and that the treaties bound both sides with promises to keep.

There is no question that the Blackfoot didn't understand some of the implications of the treaty. But they did understand keeping your word. So did the government negotiators David Laird, the lieutenant governor of the North-West Territories at the time, and James Macleod, recently appointed commissioner of the North-West Mounted Police, who in 1874 had led the force when it first arrived in the territory and built the fort named after him. In their view, the treaties were like a watching brief taken up by the Crown, ensuring that Canada would remain "seized of the issue," as lawyers say, in perpetuity, for nobody was sure what the future would bring—except change. However mysterious the text of the treaties might have been to the First Nations and however uncertain their future, the spirit of the treaties to this end was clear both in the written account provided by the treaty commissioners and in the oral record of the First Nations. *Both* sides became treaty people.

Jack Cowdry used to repeat Henry David Thoreau, saying, "If I knew for a certainty that a man was coming to my house with the conscious design of doing me good, I should run for my life." Crop Eared Wolf and his father, Red Crow, certainly didn't need to be warned against "improvements" that would diminish being Blackfoot or encroach on the identity and integrity of their tribe. They refused to be browbeaten or belittled by the bureaucratic agents and missionary believers who came with designs to do them good; and instead of running, they fought for their lives with all their might and all their imagination. They were warriors, after all.

They were also peacemakers, making common cause and friendships with newcomers who respected their beliefs, and with whom they imagined a new kind of commonwealth in the foothills. That was what Treaty Seven was all about, and Red Crow had in an important sense accepted it because of his friendship with his neighbor, Commissioner James Macleod. "I entirely trust *Stamixotokon* [Bull Head, the Blackfoot name for Macleod]," he said. "He made me many promises—not one of them was ever broken"; and this was echoed by Crowfoot, who was another Blackfoot leader. They didn't use the word "commonwealth." But the word isn't a bad place to start understanding what was happening in a territory where many in the community believed that the contradictions of settlement and sovereignty could somehow be accommodated—a community comfortable with a confusion of medicine bundles and bibles, Blackfoot drums and piano recitals, Sun Dances and social dances, horse racing (at which the Blackfoot excelled) and polo (the first in North America, some say), and rodeos and roundups to celebrate both the horse culture of the Blackfoot and the skills of the cattle range.

A community, in other words, in which conflicts would be settled by consensus in the territory, not by the politicians or bureaucrats in Ottawa who knew nothing of the world in the West they lived in or the people they lived with. The "wealth" in commonwealth meant first of all "well-being"; its contrary was what the nineteenth-century cultural critic John Ruskin called "illth"—a grim coinage for the condition that threatened many First Nations peoples during this period, and came to pass afterward.

Although they were holding on to their heritage and history, the Blackfoot weren't living in the past. They never had; their way of life had always required stern attention to the present and to the future. They would have disappeared centuries earlier if that had not been so, if they had not been a thoughtfully adaptable people, or if they had not been ready for change. They had taken up with horses some hundred and fifty years before this, and stories about that radical transformation continued to be told by elders. Horses were a good surprise. The loss of the buffalo was not. But their stories told of both sorts of surprises.

The newcomers too lived by their own stories and songs and ceremonies and looked to the future rather than the past, though like the Blackfoot they held on to their traditions—both spiritual (in church services and the texts upon which they depended) and material (such as clothing and food), as well as in the arts and crafts that brought them together—because doing so centered them. But they knew they had to be ready for the next surprise in those uncertain times; and in this, the Blackfoot were an inspiration, and their acceptance of uncertainty a comfort.

In 1885, the year the Cowdry brothers arrived in Fort Macleod, many things were uncertain for many people. For the Blackfoot, the world was changing in unfamiliar ways and at a bewildering pace, with the buffalo having disappeared, and danger everywhere. Some dangers they were dealing with, as newcomers came from every direction; but new diseases, brought by traders and settlers and whisky, continued to devastate their communities. And the Métis uprising that spring against the Canadian government introduced a new level of anxiety and violence on the prairies, unsettling relations not only between newcomers and natives but also among the First Nations themselves, with many people uncertain about their own loyalties, much less everyone else's.

Renewed unease among the Métis was hardly surprising to anyone who was paying attention. Back in 1869, after the Hudson's Bay Company charter transfer, the Métis in Red River (under the leadership of Louis Riel) had proposed a provisional government for Rupert's Land and the North-West; but instead the province of Manitoba was created. Increasingly frustrated and fearful over the next decade, Riel's Métis supporters—urged on by white settlers angry that their appeals to Ottawa for a representative government had been ignored—had called him back to Canada in 1884 from exile in Montana to lead them in proclaiming their grievances.

In March of 1885, Riel again declared a provisional government for the territory; and the Cree and Assiniboine, frustrated by the flagrant disregard of promises made to them under the treaties they had signed a few years earlier, rose up and joined the Métis. In the following weeks a series of confrontations took place, with Cree and Métis forces fighting a combination of North-West Mounted Police and Canadian military troops. There were battle victories on both sides, but the war was won by the government; and those Métis and Cree who weren't killed were held for trial. Louis Riel was accused of treason, and his trial began in late July.

The Blackfoot did not take part in the uprising, remaining loyal to their treaty partner, the Dominion of Canada. But Riel's trial and execution kept tensions bristling across the country; and in November 1885, the same month Riel was hanged, the Canadian Pacific Railway was completed from coast to coast, bringing more settlers to Blackfoot territory. New material technologies were also taking hold and new spiritual practices were taking over, and in many ways the next couple of decades presented challenges as great as any culture— indigenous like the Blackfoot's or more or less migrant like Jack Cowdry's—had ever faced.

Anyone at that time who settled in the foothills of the Rockies realized that the Blackfoot—the *Niitsítapi*, or "the real people"—were civilized and sophisticated, and that they were not going anywhere. Most of the settlers, especially those involved in ranching (and one way or another that included almost everyone), knew that their lives and livelihoods depended upon cooperation with the Blackfoot, with whom they often developed close working relationships, albeit occasionally punctuated by indifference on both sides. They cooperated where they could, made friendships where they wanted, all the while transcending some of the boundaries and breaking down some of the barriers that the treaties unfortunately nourished. And although the treaties brought a particularly European energy and enterprise to the business of displacing and dispossessing people, the experience was not new to the Blackfoot, for they had tribal neighbors north and south of the border who from time to time moved against them. But the Blackfoot survived; and now, with a new order upon them, they were determined to prevail. They were experienced both at making war and at making peace—Treaty Seven had their signature on that. But surrender had never been part of their statecraft.

There were many friendships in this time and place, both among town residents and foothills ranchers and the North-West Mounted Police, and between many of them and the Blackfoot. One ranch historian describes the town during this period with genial affection:

*The varied backgrounds of the inhabitants of this plains outpost
gave Fort Macleod a flavour unique in the [Canadian] north-
west. There were probably more characters per capita in that little
settlement than in any other centre on the Canadian prairies.
Ex-whisky traders . . . went legitimate and rubbed shoulders with
the Mounted Police, many of whom were just as adventurous as
the old traders. Indians from the nearby Blood and Peigan reserves
mingled with local ranchers, cowboys and assorted adventurers.*

Some of these friendships were unequal, as friendships often are,
with one party presuming superiority over the other. But the pride
of the Blackfoot, nourished by leaders such as Red Crow (*Mékaisto*)
and Big Swan (*Akamakal*) and Crowfoot (*Isapo-Muxika*), saw them
through those harrowing times following the decline and disappearance of the great buffalo herds on the northern Plains and the new
treaty with the upstart nation of Canada, and maintained their confidence that they were the equal of anyone.

Back in the Macleod Hotel, around Harry Taylor's table, the conversation turned to the challenges facing everyone in Blackfoot territory.
One of the most energetic regulars was Frederick (Fred) Haultain, a
lawyer the same age as Jack Cowdry, who had come to Fort Macleod
in 1884 and soon was defending a number of dubious clients with
unfashionably stern attention to the presumption of innocence and
the principle of reasonable doubt—not the strong suit of some folks
in town, and sometimes (depending on the accused) bewildering to
the Blackfoot. Fred Haultain and Jack Cowdry became close friends,
and Haultain eventually became one of the most eloquent statesmen
in the North-West Territories, in company with several of the chiefs
of the Blackfoot, for whom he had great respect. He was a champion
of non-partisan politics in the territory, becoming its first (and only)

premier in the days before Alberta and Saskatchewan became provinces; and he was a proponent of forming one single province, not two, which he suggested be called Buffalo (mischievously, some say, but according to Jack perfectly seriously), as a reminder of the natural and First Nations history of the prairies—instead of Alberta and Saskatchewan, named after Queen Victoria's daughter and a prairie river. Haultain did indeed have a mischievous streak, once conspiring with the local Indian agent to glue the Anglican parson's notes together before a service so that he read two sermons on different subjects without realizing what had happened. But Haultain also had a humane sense of right and wrong, going to visit another churchman who had refused to conduct a funeral service for a young girl whose life had been . . . let's just say blemished. When he arrived at the reverend's door carrying a horsewhip, he got a solemn promise that a dignified service would be conducted the next day.

Despite its somewhat intimidating house rules, the Macleod Hotel was in the business of hospitality; and as new competitors came into the local hotel business, they all needed a reliable supply of reasonably clean linen. So laundries opened, many of them run by Chinese men and women who came to town; and one of them, Chow Sam, turned from a spell working at the Macleod Hotel to opening a succession of popular cafés in town, becoming a friend to both Jack Cowdry and Fred Haultain (who later stood as godfather to Chow Sam's daughter Kathleen).

Around town, Jack met others who became his friends. Jerry Potts was one of the first. Born about 1840, Potts was the son of a Scots father and a Blackfoot mother named Crooked Back (*Namo-pisi*); his own Blood name was Bear Child (*Ki-yo-kosi*). He was not yet a year old when he was adopted by a saddler and trader after his father was killed in an altercation at a trading post on the Missouri River; but his new father had notoriously brutal habits, and after a few years he left the upper Missouri region rather quickly for parts unknown, leaving the young lad once again fatherless. Luck was now on Jerry's side: at the age of five he was adopted by another trader, Andrew Dawson of Fort Benton, an amiable man who taught him English as well as the ways of the settler society even as he learned the skills—the arts and the science—of living on the Plains. From his teens, Potts was comfortable with the Indian and the white as well as the mixed-blood trading communities; and by the time he was in his twenties, his reputation as a warrior was well established and widely celebrated. On one occasion, so the story goes, while alone hunting buffalo he met seven Crow Indians, enemies of the Blood tribe. Four had rifles, and the other three had bows and arrows. They invited him to "visit" their camp nearby, and, having no choice (nor any illusions about the invitation), Potts put on a cheerful face and agreed. So they set off, the three Crow with bows and arrows in the lead and the other four with their rifles behind. As they rode along, the Crow—not realizing that Potts had learned their language while traveling with his father—began to talk about him, and he heard them discussing whether to kill him right away or wait until they got to the camp. Easier to do it now, they decided. As soon as he heard the telltale "click" of a rifle, Potts slipped from his saddle, taking his rifle with him. The Crow leader fired at him but missed; and before any of them got off a second shot, Potts was down on his knees firing back, killing all four riding behind him while the three others with bows and arrows fled to their camp. Potts caught his own horse, rode back to gather together a party of Blackfoot warriors, and led them to the main Crow camp, which they destroyed, leaving dozens dead and wounded.

Potts never looked the part of a great Indian scout, being short and stooped and what would have been called "uncomely" in the company of tall and handsome Blackfoot men, but his life was straight out of a novel. It could be dangerous if you tried to join the script and were not as gifted as he was—which few in the territory were. Fifteen years before Jack Cowdry met him, Potts had been involved in an infamous battle on the Belly River near Fort Whoop-Up, when the Blackfoot were attacked by the Cree and the Assiniboine—who had heard of the devastation caused by a small-pox epidemic which killed more than fourteen hundred Blackfoot. Joined by the Peigan, the Blood tribe defeated the Cree and their Assiniboine allies, slaughtering more than three hundred. It was the last major battle between any of the First Nations in Canada, though local hostilities continued for some time over the next twenty years. Potts's role in the battle, tactical as well as militant, became part of his story. At the time the North-West Mounted Police arrived in 1874, Potts was working out of a trading post in Montana for the I. G. Baker company—then one of the most important traders, transporters of goods (mostly by bull train), and cattle drovers on the northern Plains—and he was known as one of the best plainsmen in the territory. The Mounted Police took him on as scout and interpreter, and he suggested the site for their original fort on an island in the Old Man's River. For the next twenty-two years Potts was an indispensable member of the force, guiding and cajoling the officers, winding them up and settling them down all at the same time; interpreting at every turn both the languages and the livelihoods, ancient and modern, of his Blackfoot people; and leading the police and some of the settlers through the territory that was for many of them to become a permanent home.

Jack Cowdry's first rancher friend was Edward (better known as Ned) Maunsell, who had come from Ireland in 1874 to join the newly formed North-West Mounted Police and was part of the first contingent that arrived in the foothills. Late that first summer season he saw the Plains black with buffalo, moving in herds that seemed to go on forever; and over the next five years he watched their numbers dwindle to nothing. When his three-year assignment ended he left the police force, partly because he was bored with the inactivity after the police had effectively shut down the whisky traders—most of the smuggling now was to supply the police as much as the settlers, whose thirst routinely exceeded the regulated supply of liquor in the territory. At the time, consumption of liquor anywhere in the North-West Territories was legal only with a permit, and then only for "medicinal purposes"; and so the local doctor in Fort Macleod, who became Jack's next-door neighbor, was authorized to keep five gallons of whisky and two gallons of brandy in stock. But the regulations were impossible to enforce, and nobody tried very hard. In any case, the main reason Maunsell left the police force was that he had dreamed of starting a ranch from the moment he arrived in the foothills. He saw, as did others, that the country that had supported millions of buffalo could also support large herds of cattle, provided the range was kept open for grazing. From Ireland he brought a knowledge of farming, which helped him supplement his income from ranching by growing potatoes to feed himself and oats to sell to the North-West Mounted Police; and from his time with the police he was at ease with the Indians, many of whom he knew well and trusted more than he did some of the settlers.

Ned Maunsell became Jack Cowdry's close friend; and although they had different temperaments, they both got along well with the Blackfoot, and saw each other through some tough times. The rancher's temper sometimes tested the easy-going Jack, and probably the other way around; but all the same, in 1905 they took to ranching together, buying twelve thousand head of cattle—the entire stock of the famous Cochrane ranch, founded in the 1880s and one of the earliest in southern Alberta—to take their place among the biggest ranchers there. But that's for later in this story.

———

When the Cowdry brothers arrived, Crop Eared Wolf's father, Red Crow, was the head chief of the Blood tribe in the Blackfoot Confederacy. Born about 1830, he had earned the respect of the Blood as a warrior with a storied war record and as a wise leader and statesman, and he had shown one way forward by turning from war to peace and from hunting buffalo to herding cattle, inspiring many in his tribe with his early success in farming and ranching while continuing to breed and build up his herd of fine horses and maintaining the traditions of secular and spiritual knowledge and of ceremony that had sustained his people for generations. He had also earned the respect of the police and the settlers and ranchers and townsfolk, and the sometimes grudging admiration of the Indian agents, to whom he always kept his word—not for their satisfaction, but for the benefit of his people. He was a peacemaker as well as a warrior, and stern in both roles.

The Blackfoot word for the Blood, *Káínai*, means "many chiefs," and Red Crow was also chief of a smaller group—one of a dozen or so bands within the tribe—called Fish Eaters. It seems to an outsider a curious name, for the Blackfoot didn't usually eat fish; but in the old days when food was scarce they would catch fish from the local rivers and in the mountains to the west, building fish traps that worked like the corrals into which they had herded buffalo. That kind of resilience and accommodation was one of their greatest strengths in hard times; and these times were becoming very hard for the *Niitsítapi*, the real people of *Nitawahsin-nanni*, their homeland—Blackfoot territory. They were used to traders, moving with the seasons as they themselves had done for centuries; so while the appearance of more and more settlers might threaten their sovereignty, it was the disappearance of the great buffalo herds that challenged their sense of the world.

Red Crow's stature as a leader of his people in Blackfoot territory was described by his friend the Methodist missionary John Maclean, who had come to the foothills in 1880 and settled with the Blood tribe. Maclean quickly became fluent in the Blackfoot language, and versed in its subtleties. He had many friendships in the Blood community, both with leaders such as Red Crow and Crop Eared Wolf and some of the rebellious younger men of the tribe, as well as with its everyday citizens. He provided food and medicine and loans and companionship and care to anyone who wanted or needed it, along with what he called "soul grub" on Sunday. (And once he was tearing up floorboards of his little house on the reserve to make a coffin for a family who came asking him to bury one of their relatives.) This is what he had to say about Red Crow:

> *His quiet demeanour gives no evidence of his warlike qualities. Yet he was, in the old buffalo days, one of the bravest warriors that lived upon the plains [with a war record of thirty-three raids against the Crow, Shoshone, Cree, and Nez Perce]. I have listened to him at the Sun Dance eloquently relate his military adventures and successes [and] as he walks through the camp, arrayed in his stateliness and adored by his followers, he bears in his attitude the marks of a man of peace who loves his people and is ever studious of their welfare. Sitting in his spacious lodge with the minor chiefs, he discourses about the necessities of his tribe, lays plans for their progress in the arts of civilized life, instructs them how to maintain their law and keep inviolate the morality of the natives. In the old days I have often gazed in astonishment at the record of his brave deeds in the picture writing on his lodge. . . . The scalp-locks were fastened upon it, and the writing in various colours ran around it, which detailed the history of his life. . . . He is essentially a leader of men. Not by force of arms, nor even through the influence of his position, does he rule, although his*

official dignity is a strong factor in maintaining his power over men; but it is his striking personality which enables him to command implicit obedience to the customs and laws of the tribe. . . . His influence is no less among the white people who have learned to trust him, assured that he has always been friendly to their interests while guarding the rights of his own tribe. It is to his friendship, intelligence and good government that they are indebted for the peaceful relations which have existed for many years between the white and red races in the west.

Over a hundred years later, his great-great-granddaughter Annabel Crop Eared Wolf celebrated Red Crow's "wisdom, foresight, courage, accomplishment and strong sense of commitment to the tribe and the ancestral lands [as] the standard of *káínaayo'ssini*," the real *Káínai* way of life.

Back in the mists of time the Blackfoot had first moved onto what became their homeland, following the buffalo up to the North Saskatchewan River and beyond the Great Sand Hills in western Saskatchewan. There are various accounts of their migrations before the buffalo hunt gave a new meaning and purpose to their lives, long before horses came into their hands. But by the 1800s, the Blackfoot had developed extraordinary skills in horsemanship that caught everyone's attention and confirmed their reputation as one of the most powerful people of the northern Plains, a reputation nervously acknowledged by early explorers and traders and by other Plains tribes such as the Cree and the Crow and the Assiniboine and the Sioux. They had formed the Blackfoot Confederacy, a collective of tribes called Siksika (*Siksika* being their word for "black foot," supposedly a reference to the color of their moccasins), and Blood (or *Káínai*), and Peigan (or *Pikuni*, a name celebrating a young man who was scorned for his shabby robe until he became a great warrior). The Blackfoot spoke an Algonquian language, and they had come together with their neighbors the Sarcee (who called themselves *Tsuu T'ina*, or "earth people," and spoke an Athapaskan language) to form a confederation, a formidable defense against enemies on all sides. Not long before, they also had an alliance with the Gros Ventre in Montana, but a dispute over stolen horses had turned them against each other. In Montana too, the Blackfoot had (and still have) many relatives, who call themselves Blackfeet.

Their long and complex history as a great people is still told in stories and songs—often accompanied by dancing and drumming—and in carvings and paintings on skins and robes, and in parades as well as in other performances and protocols that certified their belief in their territory and their traditions. And their history stretches that territory into a world as wide as that which can be viewed from the ridge above the Milk River, southeast of Fort Macleod, where you can see rivers running north to Hudson Bay and south to the Gulf of Mexico—a world as wonderful (and as wonderfully strange) as any that can be imagined. But their history was also—and their world still is—in *Nitawahsin-nanni* itself, and is figured in the carvings and paintings in *Áísínai'pi*, now called Writing-on-Stone Provincial Park (about a hundred miles southeast of Fort Macleod), which tell of material and spiritual happenings going back thousands of years in their homeland.

Crop Eared Wolf's parents died in the 1850s from one of the waves of infectious disease that swept through many of the Plains Indian communities during those years. His sister, who had married Red Crow, persuaded the chief to adopt her little brother. He did so, raising him as his own. And before his death in 1900, Red Crow appointed Crop Eared Wolf his successor as head chief of the Blood tribe, having recognized his bravery and leadership on raids and scouting expeditions during the 1860s and 1870s. He signaled his choice and Crop Eared Wolf's future responsibilities by giving him his favorite tipi design. Tipi designs, with their colors and forms and images and scripts and sometimes scalp-locks, were among the Blackfoot's most public forms of boasting and toasting and truthtelling, as well as of prayer; and this design, called Middle Painted Lodge, dated back to the beginning of Blackfoot spirituality and science and included a wide red band around the middle of the tipi with sacred otters painted on it. It told a story of the devotion to the spirits of his place and his people that was Red Crow's legacy, and would become Crop Eared Wolf's trademark. In return the son promised his father to use all the power he had, and all that the spirits would give him, to defend the land they had chosen for their new home under Treaty Seven.

During the 1880s, as the Blackfoot struggled to come to terms with the devastating disappearance of the buffalo upon which their spiritual as well as material nourishment had depended for generations, they held on to their horses—and their stories about them. Much is made of the enthusiasm of the indigenous peoples of the northern Plains, particularly the Blackfoot, for stealing horses and telling stories about it. It was a way of gaining renown, to be sure, and of demonstrating success in war, like taking possession of an enemy's gun or shield or scalp. But it also had a very important place in the hierarchy of their mythical and historical consciousness. It was an act of mischief outside the law of civil society, and mischief was the signature of the Blackfoot creator hero *Napi*, the Old Man. Mischief can be a way of making enemies, so stealing horses—"bringing them in" or "bringing them home," to use phrases that were customary in Blackfoot accounts—came with considerable risks. Stealth and skill were crucial, along with a subtle and sophisticated knowledge of horses and how they behave, as well as of people and dogs. Much of this tradition of mischief-making is part of European culture too. Hermes, the messenger of the gods in Greek mythology, began his career when he was an infant by stealing cattle from Apollo with rare finesse, thereby making the point that some things are valuable not because they are useful but because they are special. Or—if you are a thief—because they belong to someone else. And in Hermes's case, in order to begin his life with a signature story. Having something to talk about, whether it had happened or was going to happen, was an essential part of being human, and being Blackfoot.

And then there was the pure delight of doing something difficult and dangerous just because it is there to do—in this case bringing in more horses than you need. Thoreau, in another passage that Jack Cowdry admired, talked about the importance of "more than enough" (which Thoreau called "*extra vagance*," adding "it depends on how you are yarded"), of the imagination pushing back against the pressure of reality and redefining it, of doing things that defy utility and sometimes even test morality. That was the argument made about the arts in the late nineteenth century by Oscar Wilde and others—art for art's sake—and it had its counterpart in the tradition of horse stealing that flourished in Blackfoot society into the 1890s. Given the respect accorded to horses in Plains Indian society, fine horses—and more fine horses than enough—were like works of art as well as weapons of war, and in both cases figured as national treasures, their conformation and color and character discussed with scholarly intensity.

The Blackfoot men get most of the attention from historians of the Old West, but newcomers admired many of the Blackfoot women for their authority and judgment as well as their beauty and charm; and nobody who had any intelligence underestimated these women, with their unmistakable pride, their equitable presence of mind, and their considerable influence over sacred as well as secular happenings. One of them, Red Crow's aunt *Natawista*, became especially notable in the 1870s, well beyond the Blackfoot tribe. She had first married Alexander Culbertson, chief trader of the American Fur Company in Fort Benton, after a courtship that followed traditional protocols and an exchange of gifts that included a complete dowry for her from the Blood—buckskin costumes, a new lodge, backrests, and fourteen horses—and from the groom a wardrobe of silk, woolen and cotton clothing, as well as guns, blankets, and tobacco for her father. When Culbertson later took to gambling and the marriage broke up, she became the wife of a whisky trader and rancher named Fred Kanouse, who later ran a rooming house in Fort Macleod; and she remained a force to be reckoned with in tribal affairs. The following is a description of her by Richard Nevitt, a police surgeon in the early days of Fort Macleod, at a dance that followed a day of games and races:

> *The ladies came on horseback; only one, however, had a saddle and that was Madame Kanouse. You should have seen her dress. It was the Dolly Varden style, a large figured chintz just short enough to display the gorgeous stripes of a balmoral petticoat which in its turn was also just short enough to show two very small feet clad in moccasins and the end of a pair of leggings beautifully worked in beads. She also had on a heavy black velvet loose-fitting overcoat and over this a most brilliant striped shawl, the stripes being about three inches broad and alternately red, blue, green and red, with a narrow line of yellow between each colour. Her head gear consisted of a small plaid shawl. The other titled aristocrats were dressed also in gorgeous array, but perforce they yielded the palm to Madame.*

Dressing up wasn't the sole prerogative of pretty women (or remittance men), of course. Dances were very common and widely attended, with weekly dances in Stand Off on the Blood reserve, and regular local dances held throughout the territory in restaurants and private homes. Everyone would dress up in finery, with the cowboys putting on their fanciest trappings and gear for the occasion, and for the ladies. Indeed, with all the demands of their life out on the range, cowboys were often gloriously extravagant in town, routinely spending wages from six months on the trail in as many days, and wearing clothes and gear that displayed a love of show—boots, spurs, chaps, shirts, hats (smaller in the foothills than in the American Southwest, but, just as there, the best were often made by Stetson). There is a story about one roughriding cowboy who arrived in Fort Macleod from Pincher Creek for a ball, his evening clothes rolled up behind his saddle. When he got to town, he borrowed a clean and pressed white shirt, but was unable to get any shoes; so he went to the Hudson's Bay store, where all he could find was a pair of velvet slippers with red roses on the toes. He wore them all evening. This was a complicated and contradictory community—and anyone who thinks flowers are not a favorite of cowboys has not seen decorated cowboy shirts and vests and jackets, then and now.

During the 1880s, it was said that all trails in southern Alberta ended up in Fort Macleod. It was not a frontier town on the margins but a community at the crossroads, a center of challenge and change. The street names, added as the town grew, give a sense of the stature of the characters in the town back then and how they shaped—and still shape—the community. First Avenue on the west side of town is now named after my grandfather; and John Cowdry Avenue meets three boulevards: Chief Red Crow Boulevard, Colonel Macleod Boulevard, and Jerry Potts Boulevard.

Directly to the east of John Cowdry Avenue is an avenue named for Jack's friend Fred Haultain, a man dedicated to a territory that respected the history of its First Nations as well as the hopes of its newcomers. Archie McLean Avenue comes next; he was a horseman and cattleman known to everyone as "Honest Archie," and was one of the four founders of the Calgary Stampede in 1912. Colonel Sam Steele, like Colonel Macleod an original with the North-West Mounted Police, has the next avenue named after him; he served in various parts of the West before taking command of the detachment in Fort Macleod between 1888 and 1897. Then there is an avenue named for Annora Brown; born in 1899, she taught school for several years and then turned to painting and became famous for her representations of the weather and the wildflowers and the Blackfoot and settler citizens of the foothills. Lillie Grier, who arrived in Fort Macleod the same year as Jack Cowdry, to take up teaching in its first organized school, claims the next avenue; she later traveled to the Yukon during the Klondike Gold Rush with her husband, D. W. Davis (of whom more later), before returning to Macleod as a widow in 1906 and living in the foothills for the next thirty years. And finally there is an avenue on the east side of town named after my grandfather's friend Edward Maunsell, one of the earliest ranchers in the territory.

So Fort Macleod is "framed" on the north of town by a great Blackfoot chief, a famous North-West Mounted policeman, and a renowned plainsman; and on the east and west by a rancher and a banker.

3

AN UNUSUAL BANKER

THE YOUNG COWDRY BROTHERS had first thought about opening a livery stable when they got to Fort Macleod, because Jack knew about horses and Nat knew about grain and hay. Early on in their homesteading days in Pile of Bones, Jack had set off for Winnipeg to buy a couple of draft horses and found himself there in the company of horse traders from what seemed like all parts of the world— in a town that was fast becoming a center of commodities trading. Winnipeg was just starting its extraordinary late-nineteenth-century expansion, with thousands of people pouring into town.

But there was already a good stable in Fort Macleod. Then a hotel came to mind, since the town welcomed lots of travelers. But they decided there was no sense in starting out in competition with Kamoose, even though they figured a new hotel would gather good business and competition would no doubt keep both on their toes.

But it was their new friend Ned Maunsell who got them going in a different direction. Some years earlier, Ned's older brother George had worked for the Boundary Commission, surveying the new border with the United States, and when that was finished he joined the North-West Mounted Police (as Ned had done), leaving when his tour of duty was done in 1878 and joining Ned to gather stock and start a ranch. All they needed was money to buy some cattle; but they had decided to wait until spring so they would not have to over-winter the herd, which gave them some time to raise the cash. Their family in Ireland had promised to help them, and they wrote asking them for funds; sure enough, in late March, the funds arrived . . . sort of. What actually arrived was a letter of credit promising that "so-and-so" would pay them "such-and-such" on demand—a check of sorts, but not one easily cashed in those times and in that place, because "so-and-so" lived hundreds of miles away in Deadwood, South Dakota, and the only way to get the money without going that far was to find someone nearby who would believe both in them and in the good word of "so-and-so."

Unfortunately for the Maunsells, the nearest bank to Fort Macleod at the time was three hundred miles away in Helena, Montana. The few outfits that extended credit in or around Fort Macleod, like the I. G. Baker store, had never seen a letter of credit and wouldn't give the Maunsells the money. Still, three hundred miles to Montana was better than eight hundred to South Dakota, so Ned Maunsell headed off in late winter to try to get the money. His guide was Tony La Chappelle, who ran a tobacco and candy emporium—with billiard tables and locally renowned cider in the saloon at back, where poker players gathered around a couple of tables day and night. If you asked the limit, you would be told "floor to ceiling." La Chappelle might seem to have been a curious choice, but he was one of the best guides in the territory, an ex–whisky trader who knew every trail between Fort Macleod and Fort Benton, and had often traveled on further to Helena. On their way south, not far from Fort Macleod, a storm came up and they made camp; but their horses got away. So Maunsell went searching for them, and after a few hours he thought he saw them on a ridge in the distance and headed in that direction through the storm—but they turned out to be a few stray buffalo. By that time, Maunsell was far from camp, and snow was blowing hard. He thought he knew the direction but couldn't see his way and stepped right through the ice into a river. He stumbled on, and by some miracle made it back to their camp; but by that time his feet were frozen. La Chappelle wrapped them in rags soaked in coal oil, and got him back to the medical ward in Fort Macleod; but it took a couple of months before he got his feet back in circulation. All in order to cash a check.

Maunsell and his brother eventually got the money, bought the cattle, and started a small ranch. When he first told the story to Jack Cowdry, Maunsell grumbled not just about the difficulty of cashing a check but also about the lack of a local line of credit for someone like him, still struggling with the ups and downs of the cattle business. There were traveling bankers, working for the big banks based in the East, but they were more interested in operations with thousands of head of cattle; and they usually didn't know the local customers well enough to want to extend credit, especially without much (or often any) security.

James Macleod, too, grumbled about the lack of a bank in town. When Jack Cowdry met him in 1885, Macleod had left the North-West Mounted Police and was working as a magistrate. He told about riding all the way to Helena in the early days of Fort Macleod just to pick up the policemen's pay. He also admitted that he had never been very good at bookkeeping, and when he was commissioner of the North-West Mounted Police from 1876 to 1880, the force had come under attack for mismanagement. A good banker would have been a good friend to have back then, he said. And now too, he added, for he was trying to juggle his duties as a magistrate with a small horse-breeding operation to supply the police force.

Jack knew that he and his brother could work together, and Nat was up for almost anything. If Harry Taylor could build a hotel and Ned Maunsell could start a ranch and Tony La Chappelle could run a store-cum-saloon and Jerry Potts could—well, Jerry Potts was incomparable—surely they could open a bank. It would serve the community in the same spirit as Taylor served his hotel customers, with a genial welcome and a good-natured warning about the rules. But Jawbone would be the rule, unlike at the hotel. If you were going to do business with their bank, you had to be as good as your word. Jack used to say that "credit"—as in a line of credit or a letter of credit—means "he or she believes." To be a banker, he would insist, you have to believe—and dream a bit too, right alongside your customers. And both Jack and Nat had worked as clerks in a bank before heading west, so they actually knew something about the business.

It was clear that Fort Macleod was at the center of a lot of activity for which a bank could be helpful. In the bar at Kamoose's hotel, Nat and Jack heard a slew of complaints from cowboys who hadn't been paid on time (because the ranchers didn't have a bank to see them through with cash until they had sold their cattle), and from Kamoose and others in business who lost out because the cowboys didn't have money to spend. Even the missionaries, despite their well-advertised dedication to God rather than mammon, were calling for a bank—and for advice about managing the donations they received, their paltry stipends from headquarters, and purchases from local merchants and tradesmen. And the officers of the North-West Mounted Police and the Indian agents responsible for fulfilling treaty obligations to the Blackfoot complained that they didn't have a place to deposit their wages and safeguard the funds they received from Ottawa to do their work. Small businesses needed all the banking help they could get, for it was the small businesses that supported the town with more than supplies. As one pretentious ranching patron from England noted, after describing Fort Macleod as nothing more than "a wide muddy lane, with a row of dirty, half-finished wooden shanties flanking each side," the town did business which "would gladden the heart of many a shopkeeper in a country town in England, aye, if he could put his net profit at even one-fourteenth of that which rolled into the pockets of the possessor of one of those shanties." These were shopkeepers who needed to be able to extend credit to the ranchers to buy the cattle and pay the cowboys as they struggled through hard times or expanded in good times. And the citizens of the town needed a hand, especially in those years, to build something more than a half-finished wooden shanty.

A few local merchants in Fort Macleod, including I. G. Baker, did offer loans to the folks they knew, but generally only for the purchase of items from the store. As Ned Maunsell would tell you— he was not a shy man—even then they didn't always come through when you needed them. (And some of the missionaries made loans to the Blackfoot for wagons and harnesses and horses, using money that came to them from church headquarters back east.) So all the settlers, the businesses in the region, the ranching community, the North-West Mounted Police, the Indian agencies, and those Blood and Peigan who came to town regularly hoped for a bank that wasn't owned by someone from somewhere else (like Halifax, Montreal, Toronto, or Winnipeg). This wasn't just western distrust of easterners; there was some suspicion that a few of the regional and national banks based in those distant towns were vulnerable in the uncertain economic circumstances and high-flying business expectations that arrived with the railway. And they were right.

Almost without exception, Jack and Nat's new friends and acquaintances were encouraging. And after all, the brothers thought, they did have a little experience. So in the fall of 1886 they started a bank, called Cowdry Brothers, with modest funds of their own. It seems they had a good instinct for whom to believe and what to believe in, for Cowdry Brothers Bank prospered for the next two decades. Jack also liked finding out how to do things—things that people needed money to do, like building houses and growing crops and raising cattle and milling wood and digging mines and starting or running businesses, which was good because almost all his early loans were to folks who had no security, and he spent a lot of time in these years visiting his customers in their homes and workplaces. His loans were usually for short periods of three or six months, which was typical for the time; but he almost always extended the loans when asked, often with suggestions about how to make things work better—or with sympathy when a hard winter had frozen the livestock, or a summer fire had burned the crop. Both happened regularly in the foothills, where uncertainty was a way of life and surprises came as regularly as the seasons. "You need to wait for a better year," he'd say, a fellow traveler both with his needy customers and with the depositors who were trusting him to safeguard their money (and thereby underwriting his loans); and then he would make the loan interest-free for the next stretch. By all accounts from economic historians, the little bank played a big part in the success of ranching in the foothills, and in the economic development and cultural character of southern Alberta.

Going back millennia, when commodities like cattle and horses were the currency, their agreed-upon value was the basis of commerce. In this, banking currencies have a lot of similarity to language. The visionary Marshall McLuhan once proposed that "by the meaningless sign linked to the meaningless sound we have built the shape and meaning" of the world. He was describing how we believe in words, which are made up of arbitrary signs and sounds that are given meaning by conventions. The association of commerce with language is very old; and with coin and paper currency, just as with language, we depend on a collective belief in its value. One community's currency can often be another's curiosity, a counterpart to the "strangeness" of someone else's language, or customs. But custom itself, and especially the custom of belief in arbitrary signs and sounds, is shared across cultures. Understanding this is fundamental to understanding other people.

Many Blackfoot took to the new money economy as confidently as some of them took to the new language of English; but just as most of them kept their Blackfoot language, they also kept their traditions of bartering, trading horses or cattle as well as exchanging them for tipi designs and medicine bundles. Medicine bundles contained elements of sacred ceremony—such as sweetgrass, tobacco, and paint—as well as individual objects including pipes, tipi flags, otter skins, war shirts, and knives. They were opened and "read" after the first thunderstorm in spring, or on special occasions to transfer ownership or fulfill a vow. Almost all the Blackfoot balanced both traditional and new technologies quite comfortably in these early years, maintaining trade relations as support systems as well as commercial opportunities.

Back then, banking attracted a familiar measure of scorn for its supposedly predatory instincts and its well-developed habit of scavenging pennies from the poor. But there was a moral philosophy in the Western world that countered this during the nineteenth century, arguing that the poor who did not have any security to pledge needed access to money to get a start in life, or to pay for goods and services in a bad season. They needed someone to believe in them, and lend them money. In the preface to his play *Major Barbara*, published in 1907, George Bernard Shaw wrote, "money is the counter that enables life to be distributed socially: it *is* life as truly as sovereigns [gold coins] and bank notes are money. The first duty of every citizen is to insist on having money on reasonable terms." This rang true in Fort Macleod. Nobody had security in the foothills—unless they had very rich backers (and then they certainly didn't need a loan from Cowdry Brothers). Most had only their good word, and with it a promise to keep.

Although it may seem sentimental today, "keeping your word" was a fundamental value for newcomers as well as Indians in the foothills at that time, highlighting the connection between language and currency. One of the earliest chroniclers of the foothills, the *Calgary Herald* journalist L. V. Kelly, opens his 1913 book, *The Range Men: The Story of the Ranchers and Indians of Alberta*, with a praise song:

> *John Cowdry, who conducted a private banking business in the town of Macleod from 1886 until 1905, through the hey-day of the best years of the ranching business, never had a word of trouble from any of his customers. Often he advanced money on a man's mere word and never was his confidence abused. A man's word was his bond in those primitive days. The cowboys and ranchers were honest, clean and straight in all their money dealings even though they might pick up a calf [that is, mark a maverick calf with their own brand]. When Cowdry sold his private banking business (Cowdry Brothers) to the Canadian Bank of Commerce in 1905, the bank took over from the Cowdrys some four hundred and eighty-seven thousand dollars of loans, of which amount the Cowdrys had to guarantee fifty-two thousand dollars for [six] months. After the expiration of this time Cowdry was released from this guarantee, and out of that fifty-two thousand dollars he had to pay something under two hundred dollars, an astonishingly pleasing average to any banker.*

One story (told in the Cowdry family and in books about those early years) catches the character of this unusual banker. Jack was standing behind the counter in his bank, a little wooden shanty said by one contemporary to be known to every man and woman in southern Alberta. It was springtime, with warm weather blowing on a breeze that was making soughing sounds across the marsh marigolds by the river, while the snow-covered mountains to the west looked in the clear air like they were just next door. He was watching a group of Peigan riding across the edge of town on their way home from south of the border. A few cowboys were about, getting supplies before heading north to their ranches and roundup.

And then a stranger came into the bank and looked around. There was nobody else there. He pointed a gun at Jack. "Hand over the cash," he demanded, "or I'll shoot."

Bank robbers were the stuff of frontier legend, but not yet of Fort Macleod. This one was young—who wasn't in those days?—and what we might call stressed out. Jack, who was only a few years older, was cool and casual. Or so the story goes. He turned around, kicked the safe door shut, spun the handles to set the lock, and swung back to face the stranger. "Shoot me, and be damned," he said. Then, before the young fellow could do just that, Jack scolded him for his stupidity, suggested that he should get on his horse and ride out of town before the Mounted Police came by, and then gave him twenty-five dollars out of the counter till to speed him on his way. He never said whether it was a cowboy, or an Indian. To Jack Cowdry, it didn't matter; and saying who it was would imply that it did. The first bank robbery in southern Alberta was an unusual robbery. And the first private bank in southern Alberta was an unusual bank.

4

WHEN THE POLICE CAME

"WE WOKE TO FIND THE COUNTRYSIDE covered in buffalo,"
wrote nineteen-year-old Ned Maunsell in the late summer of 1874,
camped not far from what would become Fort Macleod on the Milk
River ridge with his utterly exhausted fellow North-West Mounted
Police officers, brightly attired in their red uniforms, toward the end
of their long ride westward across the prairies from Fort Dufferin in
Manitoba. Their arrival was noted by the Blackfoot elder Father of
Many Children in his "winter count" (kept on a tanned skin) as
"Ennakex/otsitotorpi/akápioyis"—"Police/when they came/Fort Mac-
leod." A couple of years later, Father of Many Children recorded,
"Itakainiskoy"—"When there were plenty of buffalo." Three years
after that, in 1879, he wrote, *"Itsistsitsis/awenimiopi"*—"When first/
no more buffalo." Then, in 1883, *"Istsienakas/otsitotorpi"*—"Fire
wagon, when it arrived." The buffalo had gone; and the Canadian
Pacific Railway and settlers had come.

The North-West Mounted Police force, established in 1873 by the
Canadian prime minister, John A. Macdonald (and partially inspired
by the Irish Constabulary), was to bring "law and order" to the fledg-
ling Dominion. Its commission had been hastened by the massacre of
nearly two dozen Assiniboine in the Cypress Hills in Saskatchewan
by liquored-up wolf hunters and a few Métis following the theft of
their horses (perhaps by Cree raiders). And then there was the dan-

gerous kind of disorder being caused by the whisky traders, illegally bringing rotgut spirits from the United States to trade in Canada. The border was just being surveyed at that time, and it certainly wasn't yet observed as a sovereign marker by the traders, whose scruffy style masked a shrewd and sometimes ruthless business instinct. Many of them became prominent figures in late-nineteenth-century society, as some of the Prohibition magnates did a few decades later. (And when have traders ever been stopped by national boundaries anyway? As Thomas Jefferson wrote, "merchants have no country.") The Canadian government was also anxious to show its colors to the American neighbors but not to go into battle or provoke a war.

The police force would parade the new Dominion's sovereignty to the First Nations and newcomers alike and maintain the regime of law and order that they were sent to establish, appointing its officers as either stipendiary magistrates or justices of the peace. Although this overrode the long-standing British principle of an independent judiciary, it encouraged efficient and (at least in the early years) often equitable enforcement of the law on behalf of First Nations, which nourished good relations—and disagreements that were straightforward rather than surreptitious—between the Blackfoot and the Crown.

Ned Maunsell and the North-West Mounted Police contingent had ridden hundreds of miles that summer season, heading west from the Red River with around three hundred men to patrol more than 300,000 square miles of territory. They saw buffalo herds that covered the land as far as the eye could see, and a prairie landscape that was as dry as the desert but blessed with creeks and rivers and hills and valleys along the way. For the men—many of them boys, like the cowboys they met—the unknown was the most fearsome menace on the ride westward; even though the region had been a part of the Dominion for several years, it was foreign territory.

A plaintive song, "The Red River Valley," was going the rounds at that time. It was about a young woman mourning the departure of her man, and people north of the border assumed (and most folklorists now agree) it was about the Red River settlement in Manitoba—though cattlemen might have thought it could be about another Red River, bordering Texas and Oklahoma. That southern river was a major crossing for the cattle coming up to northern railheads, and they would have heard stories and perhaps sung songs about those great cattle drives

Although the North-West Mounted Police men had some training, and a few of them considerable expertise in military routines, their knowledge of horses was limited—and their lives depended on their horses, since they certainly had none of the skills on foot over the open prairie that the Blackfoot or the Cree had inherited from their ancestors. Not knowing any better, they routinely camped down by the prairie sloughs and picketed their horses there to graze on the pond grass, because most of the grass up on the ridges seemed to have been eaten up or tramped down by the buffalo. But still their horses were in bad shape, and they couldn't understand why. As William Pearce, an experienced contemporary surveyor and articulate champion of ranching in the foothills (as well as an opponent of land speculation, called by his enemies the "Czar of the West"), noted,

> *It was only necessary to give the horses enough time to fill themselves with the grasses on the ridges to enable them to stand the trip in first class condition. Throughout southern Alberta it was invariably reported that the North-West Mounted Police when they first came into the country could not understand why their horses were so foolish as voluntarily to seek the ridges for grazing where there was apparently little pasturage in preference to the slough grass. . . . For some years after their arrival the police seem to have had little*

knowledge of the relative food value of the grasses. . . . . *If they had*
not been able to procure a considerable quantity of oats from the
Boundary Commission . . . they would have been paralyzed in their
movements on account of the condition of their horses. As it was they
were very greatly hampered. Looking back it seems incredible that
they were not wholly paralyzed.

They should have listened to their horses; but they were lucky,
and—helped along the way by the first peoples as well as some of the
newcomers on the Plains, they made it to the foothills. Their horses
weren't so fortunate; many died on the trek, and few of those that
made it to Fort Macleod lived for more than a few months.

During the years up to the early 1870s, antagonisms between the
tribes in the region north and south of the border—at the time roughly
marked by sod or rock pyramids about six feet high—were complicated by the scourge of whisky. It was brought into the territory by
traders from the United States, and mixed with anything available—
opium, turpentine, vanilla extract, various patent medicines and pain-
killers, red ink, tobacco, and slough water—to create liquor that
wreaked havoc among the Indians as well as the settlers. The response
from many of the Blackfoot to the North-West Mounted Police mandate to abolish the trade was supportive, even though some of them
had taken to drink. Or maybe *because* they had. Jerry Potts, for instance,
liked to drink, and whisky was his frequent companion all his life; but
he was sympathetic to the police mission because he hated the whisky
trade, which had caused the death of his mother and half-brother in a
drunken camp brawl in 1872. (He got revenge a few months later,
killing the murderer, ironically named Good Young Man.)

Even stone-cold sober, which he was most of the time on duty
with the police, Potts was a character. His notoriously laconic style
of speech became his trademark, and sometimes contrasted sharply

with the earnest intent of others. Leading a party that included the governor general of Canada (the Marquess of Lorne) on a scouting visit to the West in 1881, Potts was asked by the impatient marquess—who had been riding all day and was getting exasperated that they hadn't reached their destination—"What's over the next hill?" No reply. So he asked again, "What's over the next hill?" Still no reply from the taciturn Potts. Finally the marquess repeated his question with all the imperial authority he could muster. "Now say there, my man, what's over the next hill?" "Another hill," replied Potts and returned to his musings. The marquess must have been listening to some other things that Potts said, however, for later he spoke out in support of the Blackfoot when their rations promised under treaty were being cut back by a government in Ottawa that was having trouble balancing its books, and by Indian agents in the field who were happy to have an excuse to show who was in charge.

After leaving their camp on the Milk River ridge, one of the first stops in the foothills for the North-West Mounted Police contingent was to be the infamous Fort Whoop-Up (near to what is now Lethbridge). It had been a trading post for whisky and buffalo robes for fifteen years and it had a Wild West reputation worthy of its name, burnished by stories like the following—taken from a letter written by a resident of the fort named Snookum Jim (his name at least is true) to a friend in Fort Benton the year before the North-West Mounted Police rode by.

> *Dear Friend,*
> *My partner, Will Geary, got to putting on airs and I shot him and*
> *he is dead. Your potatoes are looking well.*
> *Yours truly,*
> *Snookum Jim*

Fort Whoop-Up was near where the Belly River and the St. Mary River join the Old Man's. Even though whisky traders had their own "personal trails," forts like Whoop-Up certainly weren't hidden—after all, they were trading posts, dealing in robes and other commodities even if some of their trade was illegal. (And anyway nothing was hard to find if you had Jerry Potts along, as the police did at that point.) The post had been established by two Montana traders, John Healy and Alfred Hamilton, in 1869; Healy was married to the daughter of one of the Blood chiefs, Many Spotted Horses, who gave him permission to build in his territory. He adopted a Blood child who became known as Joe Healy (Flying Chief), whose parents had been killed in a raid in Montana. Joe Healy later became a notable figure in the community, regularly called upon as an interpreter. When Crop Eared Wolf died in 1913, he was even a serious, though unsuccessful, candidate for head chief of the Blood tribe.

As they rode up anxiously to Fort Whoop-Up, the North-West Mounted Police saw the Stars and Stripes flying from its flagpole, which didn't help calm their nerves. But after a comically dramatic flourish of setting up their field guns and preparing for battle, Potts led Colonel Macleod toward the fort, his nonchalance prompting some members of the force to put his intelligence into question. But that was always a mistake; and in this case he almost certainly knew more than he let on, for they found only one white man there, along with several Indian women; and instead of a fight they got a good dinner for the entire troop. D. W. Davis, the American trader in charge of Fort Whoop-Up on behalf of I. G. Baker and the Fort Benton traders, was temporarily absent; but some weeks later, when the North-West Mounted Police returned for a mop-up, D.W. (as he was known) served them another hearty dinner that many wrote home about, complete with vegetables from his garden. No matter who you were, hospitality was a trademark in the foothills—unless you came to kill your enemies or steal their horses. Living in a world of courtesies was crucial. D.W., like others in the whisky trade (such as Kamoose Taylor), quickly turned legitimate. He became manager of the large I. G. Baker store in Fort Macleod, which is where Jack Cowdry first met him in 1885; and encouraged by his friend Kamoose, D.W. stood for election in 1887 to the Parliament in Ottawa, where he would very effectively practice his skills as a dealer for the next decade.

Although the Blackfoot may have been uneasy at the arrival of the North-West Mounted Police, they could see that they overwhelmingly outnumbered the newcomers; and without any notion of how many white people there were in the world, they were not too worried. In fact, given what they quickly understood to be the mandate of the force—to eliminate the whisky trade—they were quite happy to help. The whisky trade had ravaged the Blackfoot community—one trader reported that at least seventy Blood had been killed in drunken quarrels in the winter of 1871/72 alone—and few of the families of Blackfoot chiefs had been free of drunken tragedies, so there was hope that the police would be able to stop the trade. Which they did, and remarkably quickly.

Riding northwest from Fort Whoop-Up, the North-West Mounted Police followed the Old Man's River. They made camp on an island in the river where Potts recommended that a fort be built, right in the heart of his homeland, between Blood and Peigan territory. The fort would be easy to defend, if that ever became necessary; wood for building and fuel was close by, and hay could be grown in the river bottom in summer; and the river had plenty of fish, with deer and elk and small game in the brushlands and antelope and buffalo still roaming the grasslands. They called it Camp Macleod after their commanding officer, set up a corral for the horses, and then built a stable before beginning construction of the fort (supervised by the resourceful D. W. Davis) on October 13, 1874. Having split up the troops along their way across the prairies to set up other forts, they now had only a hundred and fifty men. Three years later, with scheduled departures (such as Ned Maunsell's) and defections, they were down to 113, with as many horses. A small medical unit was attached to the fort and became the first hospital in southern Alberta; they built a larger one ten years later when the new fort was constructed on the townsite. And within the next few years, a hospital (run by the Grey Nuns of Montreal) was opened on the Blood reserve, celebrated in the local newspaper as "the first Indian hospital in North America." A year later it received the gift of a pipe organ from one Eusèbe Brodeur, an organ builder from St. Hyacinthe, Quebec, who was a brother of the sister superior.

Jerry Potts, despite his early reputation as a warrior, and his habit of standing a good distance from a friend of his while they took pistol shots at each other to shave their whiskers, was a mostly genial presence in and around town, and became a very good friend of Jack Cowdry's in the late 1880s and 1890s. His taciturn manner was the subject of many anecdotes, but he was not nearly as hot-tempered as some stories suggest, and he usually tried to take the easiest way. If that meant a measure of violence, so be it. But one of his favorite stories showed a different side. In May 1875, over thirty of his horses were stolen by Assiniboine raiders, who took them to Montana. A year earlier he would have mounted up and gone on a raid to recover the horses. But, alert to the new order of things, he secured a letter of introduction to the U.S. Cavalry from Colonel Macleod and went south, where he was escorted into the Assiniboine camp by a cavalry officer and gathered up his horses, mercilessly mocking the infuriated horse thieves, who were as unaccustomed to such a bloodless coup as he was.

Potts's abbreviated style of speech in English made it easy to underestimate him when it came to the subtleties of civilization, and he sometimes seemed at a loss when institutional or legal jargon came into play. But Jack Cowdry said that for all his seeming disengagement from whatever was going on around him, he was always on the watch and was a very good listener, one who could make you make sense by the quality of his attention—provided he felt you had something interesting to say.

After the police had built the fort and settled in for the winter, Potts insisted that since they were camped in Blackfoot territory, they should meet with the most widely respected statesman-chief of the Blackfoot as soon as possible. So on the first of December that year Colonel Macleod rode north to Blackfoot Crossing on the banks of the Bow River to meet Crowfoot, a head chief of the Siksika tribe at the time. One of Jack's favorite stories (also widely told in the histories of the western Plains) had to do with that meeting. Surrounded by nearly two thousand Indians, their tipis spread out for miles across the prairies, Macleod spoke first, paying tribute to Crowfoot and his people, asking permission to come into their country, praising the chief's statesmanship, promising to safeguard the Blackfoot tribes from the scourge of whisky and their lands from settlement before a formal treaty was made between the Great Mother and the chiefs, and to maintain the peace for all people. And he said that his word would be his covenant with them, and that he would always keep his word. He spoke for about three minutes, conscious of ceremonial protocol as the guest. "We are glad to be here," he concluded. Jerry Potts translated, and Crowfoot listened carefully.

Then Chief Crowfoot began a long speech, in the Blackfoot language, during which he picked up a handful of earth and held it to his chest while he pulled out the grass and flung it in the direction of Colonel Macleod, motioned to the river flowing east and to the mountains in the west, pointed at the Mounted Police horses with unmistakable scorn, and described a herd of buffalo going over a buffalo jump and then a buffalo hunt on horseback, eyes flashing and feet stomping and arms waving and voice rising. Macleod, who had not yet learned Blackfoot and couldn't understand a word, got nervous. Worried by the chief's energetic—and maybe belligerent?—gestures, Macleod turned to Potts and asked, "What's he saying, Jerry?" "Damn glad, too," replied Potts.

That meeting between Colonel Macleod and Chief Crowfoot, for all its rhetorical differences, marked the beginning of a remarkably good relationship between the Blackfoot and the North-West Mounted Police, which meant between the Blackfoot and Canada. And this extended to Red Crow, chief of the Blood tribe, whom Macleod recognized in the community around Fort Macleod as a leader to be reckoned with, and to be trusted. And he himself was respected by Red Crow. Friendships helped, as they almost always do; and the friendships that developed between Macleod and Crowfoot and between Macleod and Red Crow owed much to Jerry Potts, and played an important part in the successes of that period. So did keeping your promises.

Did those two ways of welcoming, from two conventions in which courtesies and candor counted but were bound into different languages and different ceremonial traditions, mean that Colonel Macleod and Chief Crowfoot lived in two worlds? The answer might be yes and no. Customs shape the way we live in the world, and govern everything from codes of conduct to political actions. They also influence our scientific and religious stories, our histories and myths. We instruct our children in the complicated customs that govern these—which is to say, that govern and guarantee belief—

and they sometimes seem very strange to those from another community. But that strangeness described earlier paradoxically gives us all something in common—the arbitrariness of words and signs. Translations like Jerry Potts's underscore this by their apparent inadequacy, highlighting the artifice of every ceremony, including the most familiar of all, the ceremony of language. Aside from his exceptional skills as a scout, one of the reasons Potts became such an important figure in the foothills during this time was not his quirky character or his laconic style but the way in which, perhaps by instinct and perhaps by design, he both drew attention to the strangeness of different customs and found a way of accommodating them by offering his own strange mediation. He was an avant-garde artist as well as an idiosyncratic (and at times somewhat confusing) interpreter, alerting everyone to the artifice of all communication. Certainly Jack Cowdry thought that much of Potts's apparent bumbling was deliberate. Defamiliarization, the modernist literary critics call it. Making the familiar strange and the strange familiar—that's what the arts do all the time. Perhaps Potts was just before his time. Or maybe right on time. And he helped the newcomers recognize how every chronicle of events, as a record of what happened, must also be a ceremony of belief if it is to be taken as true.

5

ARISTOCRATS OF THE PLAINS

"IT WOULD HAVE BEEN AS EASY to count or to estimate the number of leaves in a forest as to calculate the number of buffaloes living at any given time during the history of the species previous to 1870," wrote the zoologist William Hornaday two decades later. Long bull trains freighting supplies across the Plains, consisting of a number of wagons each drawn by a dozen or more oxen, often had to stop and remain quiet for several hours to permit the buffalo to pass; and wherever they were encountered in herds the buffalo would blacken the Plains, moving as though one unbroken robe sometimes twenty miles in width and sixty miles in length—the sight overwhelming observers and defying accurate description. And counting was made more difficult by the fact that at certain times of year, such as after the summer rut, the smaller autonomous herds would come together in mega-herds. (The proper scientific name for buffalo is "bison"; but since we are going with some nicknames in this story, we'll stick with buffalo.)

Iinii was the Blackfoot name for buffalo. Originally giant, then by evolutionary steps smaller, buffalo had lived in North America—in one form or another—for half a million years. For some ten thousand years buffalo had flourished on the Plains, in numbers estimated to have been as high as thirty or forty million.

Sometimes as tall as six feet at the shoulder and up to twelve feet in length, and weighing upward of a ton, one buffalo alone commanded respect, and thousands running in a herd were an awesome sight. And an absolute necessity, for buffalo gave the Plains Indians almost everything they needed by way of food and clothes and footwear, along with hides for tipis and shields and all sorts of tools and glues. Their sinews were used for thread and bowstrings, their stomach liners for water and food containers, ribs for sled runners, and skins to write on. The spirit of the buffalo informed the lives of the Plains Indians in many ways; and their seasonal migration dictated the movement of the tribes when the buffalo moved around the hills and across the plains in vast herds that blackened the whole country and blocked out the grass. Buffalo hunts became major events, and often nourished rare cooperation among the Indians of the Plains.

Aboriginal people, more or less ancestral to the Blackfoot, had been in southern Alberta for thousands of years. Blackfoot culture, like all human culture, originally moved on foot, and this influenced the small size of their social and economic units, and the ways in which such bands could come together in tribal communities to improve hunting capacity. That turned out to be an effective arrangement even after they took to horses in the early 1700s, but there were certainly inconveniences when they only had dogs. Tipis had to be small, so that they could be hauled on a travois by the dogs; and limited movement meant that they were much more vulnerable to the weather, and much less able to modify their lives or their livelihood than they proved to be when horses came along. Before horses, the Blackfoot followed the buffalo on foot, creeping up on them downwind or surprising them from behind a bluff, spearing them or shooting them with bows and arrows. Sometimes they would chase the animals along prairie driveways—marked with stones and shrubs and sticks draped with coyote or wolf hides—into makeshift corrals or "buffalo pounds," or (perhaps as recently as the 1860s) run them through narrowing pens over natural rock outcrops, called buffalo jumps, at the bottom of which they would slaughter them with clubs and spears. Even when the Blackfoot became accustomed to horses, they remembered the stories of older times that they had grown up with, stories of making their way across the Plains on foot, and they told them often to ensure that the lessons of survival were not lost. And scouts still went on foot to assess the movements of enemies or the migrations of buffalo, or when and where the berries were ripening, well into the later 1800s.

In the early years of the nineteenth century, the Blackfoot were frequently camped in the United States at the head of the Missouri and in the rich valleys of Judith Basin, moving back and forth across the not-yet-surveyed border to follow the buffalo, as their ancestors had done for millennia; and they were often described by traders and explorers as "American Indians." But by the 1840s, the Blackfoot were more often at home in the foothills of Alberta, prompted by trade in furs with the British, plentiful berries in the foothills, the availability of wood and water, and shelter from the weather—as well as from the tribal warfare that had left many of their community dead; shelter too from the grass fires that were the occasional scourge of the Plains, bearing down with what the naturalist John Macoun described as "the speed of a fast horse. . . . As [one] came near us the whirling smoke and flames seemed to take the forms of living things that were in terrible agony."

Wolves—and dogs—were said to have taught the Blackfoot how to hunt the buffalo in groups, as Crop Eared Wolf told Jack Cowdry, but wolves also taught them (with transparent self-interest) that animals with hoofs and horns were all right to eat, but those with paws and claws should be left alone. Horses were never keen on this, but when the Blackfoot got horses in the early eighteenth century and called them *ponokaomitai-ksi*, or elk-dogs, horses felt a bit better, because this put them in the company of the dogs that were important to the Blackfoot—they had hauled the belongings of Plains Indians on travois for thousands of years, and were still used that way in some Indian communities on the prairies in the later 1800s. And elk antlers were used in sacred rituals, with women sometimes wearing elk tooth ornaments on their dresses.

Even allowing for the importance of buffalo hunting on horseback, the horse soon meant something much more to the Blackfoot. And the Blackfoot are certainly not alone in their respect for horses, both real and imagined. For millennia, horses have provided a ceremonial center as well as a commercial and military asset for many societies—a still point in a turbulent world. One of the most famous of these equestrian ceremonies, profoundly influencing social, economic, political, and religious life in Europe and beyond, was chivalry. The name brought together the French word for horse, *cheval*, with *chevalerie*, signifying knighthood and expressing archetypal horse culture—which combined gentleness with force and the secular with the sacred—and creating an ideal of wandering within the reality of a settled society: the chivalric knight had one eye on the horizon and the other on his home. Like the nomadic warrior of the Asian steppes or the buffalo hunter and warrior chief of the Plains tribes, the medieval knight lived within a strict set of courtesies that maintained a balance between freedom and discipline, love and war, life and art. One of the great moments of European literature, from the medieval poem *Sir Gawain and the Green Knight*, takes place when King Arthur, hosting a Christmas feast, asks for *"sum mayn mervayle, that he myght trawe"*—some great wonder, that he could believe—and through the door rides a giant of a knight on horseback, beautifully adorned and dangerously powerful.

The Blackfoot believed in such horses, and such horse riders.

They had saddles and bridles and all sorts of other horse tack richly woven and worked for both war and peace, and for the ceremonies of each that had become part of their culture. And they were certainly aware of the other great Plains Indian horse breeders of the time, being avid and envied breeders themselves. The great mid-nineteenth-century Blood chief Many Spotted Horses had a herd of over five hundred paints and pintos, many of which would have been Appaloosas, bred along the banks of the Palouse River by another famous horse culture, the Nez Perce. Other horses would have been raided from the Crow or the Cree or Assiniboine, or the Shoshone or the Sioux. Blackfoot breeding both for performance and for conformation was renowned; and they loved particular colors. Like sorrel.

Horses came to the Americas by Christopher Columbus on his second voyage in 1493—he arrived with twenty-four stallions and ten mares and a significant number of cattle. Some say he simply brought horses *back*, for there were stories (scientific, it turns out) about ancient "dawn horses" (*Eohippus*) that roamed the rain forests and swamps of the Americas many millions of years ago. Later, some of their descendants traveled across the land bridge to Asia and onward to Europe and Africa, while those that stayed behind in the Americas disappeared around ten thousand years ago, victims of climate changes and predators, including humans. (But some insist that a few horses remained, hiding in the box canyons and highland gorges of the West.) In any event, on the island of Hispaniola where Columbus landed, the horses he brought over thrived, creating in remarkably short order substantial herds along with skilled horsemen who adapted Spanish equestrian techniques and equipment to the new environment. When the Spaniards moved on to the other parts of the Caribbean, Central America, Venezuela, and Brazil, they found the horses were slow to adapt to the tropical regions; but when they got to the pampas of Argentina and the plains of the American

Southwest, the horses knew they were home again. In times when feed was scarce, the Spanish set the horses free to roam; and within a few years the pampas were, in the words of one observer at the beginning of the seventeenth century, "covered with escaped horses in such numbers that when they go anywhere they look like woods from a distance." They were spreading out too across the Great Plains, and a traveler reported in 1777 that in the Rio Grande area of Texas there were so many horses that "their trails make the country, utterly uninhabited by people, look as if it were the most populated in the world."

The indigenous people took to horses in different ways. Initially, the Spanish were careful not to let horses into enemy hands. But the uprising of the Pueblo Indians against the Spanish conquerors in 1680, which drove two thousand of them from the Santa Fe area and killed hundreds, resulted in large numbers of horses escaping. Even so, the Pueblo Indians responded cautiously. By contrast, within a generation of acquiring their first horses (some by happenstance, others by theft), the great warrior tribes of the Apache and Comanche were doing things on horseback that astonished even the skilled Spaniards, and horses were soon in the hands of other Plains tribes. There is a story that the Shoshone and the Nez Perce rode horses before they ever met a white man; and an Indian named Shaved Head was said to have been the first to "discover" horses among the mountain Indians and bring them to the Blackfoot in the 1720s. When the horse arrived the Blackfoot changed their hunting techniques (even though some of them continued to hunt on foot), surrounding the buffalo with a large number of horsemen and shooting the animals as they milled about in a circle, or chasing them, with each rider singling out a buffalo to kill. By the 1830s the Blackfoot were almost exclusively hunting by the chase, still using lances or clubs or shooting with bows and arrows until breech-loading rifles became available in the 1850s and repeating rifles in the 1870s. (Muzzle-loading muskets were very difficult to reload while on a running horse.) Racing along beside a herd at high speed, the rider would bring his horse close to the buffalo he had picked out, slot an arrow (from the couple of dozen in his quiver) to his bowstring, and aim at a spot described by William Hornaday as "from 12 to 18 inches in circumference . . . immediately back of the foreleg, with its lowest point on a line with the elbow." As the arrow was shot, a well-trained horse would swerve away from the buffalo to avoid disaster if she collapsed in front of them, and swing back if a second shot was required. The rider would have coiled the long end of his bridle rope under his belt, so that if he was thrown and not seriously hurt he could retrieve his horse and continue the chase.

Hunting on horseback required great skill, as well as a knowledge of the anatomy and physiology of the buffalo and their different instincts and movements when running in a herd or running alone. It also required fast horses, selected and bred for speed and agility; and young Joe Healy, who had followed the last of the buffalo herds into Judith Basin in Montana in the late 1870s, told Jack Cowdry over dinner in the Macleod Hotel one night about how a couple of first-class buffalo-hunting horses would be kept in each band. In another account by a contemporary, the buffalo horses "seemed to know better than the men what to do amid the dangers of a hunt, for when suddenly a buffalo turned upon them they sprang aside to escape the danger and pursued afresh." The Blood were proud of the fact that they were often in charge of the hunt because they had the fastest horses.

The sophisticated arrangements that sustained buffalo hunting both before and after the arrival of horses, with other tribes joining in depending on where the buffalo were and how they were congregated, generated economic and social conditions that often surprise those who hold on to stereotypes of hunting and gathering societies, especially nomadic ones like the traditional Blackfoot. "Subsistence" was never a minimal condition for the people of the Plains, nor was it for any of the Aboriginal peoples of the Americas; and subsistence and surplus were certainly not competing conditions in Blackfoot society. Subsistence meant having everything you needed, spiritually as well as materially; it was a condition of sovereignty within nature rather than dominion over it. And surpluses were relatively common, with buffalo meat and berries dried and stored for distribution during the winter season.

There had long been a regular accumulation of wealth in the form of medicine bundles as well as sacred and secular songs in Blackfoot society, but after the early eighteenth century, horses as emblems of prestige and power became another kind of surplus quite consistent with a subsistence economy. Of course there were periods of hardship and scarcity, as there are in all times and places; but capitalism and socialism are European "isms" and schisms, not those of the Plains Indians; and surpluses, while not exactly routine, were a familiar part of life, nourishing the kind of balance between work and play, and between the demands of the day and the display of beauty in visual and verbal arts as well as dance and music, which we all cherish.

The disappearance of the buffalo must have seemed inconceivable to those who had grown up watching tens of thousands of animals pass by in a season (though we should all have a sense of what that feels like from watching once-familiar species become nearly extinct in our contemporary world). The buffalo collapse was foreshadowed by some of the Indian seers, and by those who had followed the seasonal movements of the buffalo, with runners and scouts bringing back information more sophisticated than contemporary GPS technology, information that included detailed reports on the flora and fauna upon which the buffalo depended, and the size and health of the calf crop. And they knew that the intermittent cycles of drought often took a terrible toll on the herds.

In the territory, by the 1870s many Blackfoot saw the end coming, though not nearly as quickly as it did; and there is little doubt that the Blackfoot agreement to Treaty Seven was brought about in part because some signs of trouble were clear. The government negotiators painted a gloomy picture, noting that the current presence of buffalo on the Canadian Plains contrasted starkly with the situation south of the border, where the buffalo had almost disappeared from many of their traditional grazing lands. The Blackfoot knew this, moving back and forth across the border, but as one elder said, "We thought we had more time." They didn't. Nor did the buffalo, who were gone from the northern Plains within a decade.

Some warning signs had been noted, but just as in another environmental disaster—the collapse of the Atlantic cod fisheries toward the end of the twentieth century—they were often dismissed, or misconstrued. In the case of the cod, many of those who spent their lives harvesting them, and even the scientists with nothing at stake (except their reputations), got it wrong. But beginning in the nineteenth century fishermen had noticed that the oil content of cod livers—a lucrative product—depended on where the fish were caught. This worried them, and they wanted more attention paid to local habitat and spawning cycles, to counter the widespread belief that cod roamed throughout the northern Atlantic relatively unaffected by regional catches. Even as notable a scientist as Charles Darwin's friend Thomas Huxley, alert to the concern but oblivious to its urgency, proclaimed (in an address to the Great International Fisheries Exhibition in 1883 in London) that, while it might be possible to exhaust some inland fish species such as river salmon, the number of ocean fishes such as cod was "so inconceivably great that the number we catch is relatively insignificant, and . . . the multitude of the destructive forces at work upon them [in their natural environment] is so prodigious that the destruction effected by the fishermen cannot sensibly increase the death rate." Barely a hundred years later, the great cod fishery had been virtually eliminated.

Just so, the buffalo dominated the Canadian Plains until the 1870s, their numbers also inconceivably great and seemingly inexhaustible, even though it was clear that their range was being encroached upon and their habitat imperiled by human settlement and by fences, a menace for almost any wild animal. But other troubles were mounting in the territory as a lucrative trade in buffalo hides and robes attracted both skilled Plains Indian and Métis hunters and an assortment of enterprising non-native buffalo hunters. Their collective enterprise devastated the herds and destroyed a way of life that had defined Plains Indian culture for millennia (just as the trades in sealskins and whale oil came close to wiping out entire species along with many island and coastal cultures around the world). In all these cases, the slaughter was aided and abetted by new technologies. In the case of the buffalo, horses certainly played their part, but it was the trade in robes—fostered by the demand for buffalo skins for machinery drive belts, improved tanning methods (with strong lime), and contemporary clothing fashions—that did them in, with railways providing easy transportation to markets and the repeating rifles bringing an industrial-scale enterprise to the hunt. Well-equipped and brutally wasteful Euro-American hunters played a major role in the carnage, as they set out to gather up a valuable commodity as fast as they could, in any way they could, and with nothing like their own way of life at stake. One of them alone, Josiah Wright Mooar, was said to have killed some twenty thousand buffalo between 1870 and 1879, in his case mostly along the Texas

Panhandle. And perhaps the most famous buffalo hunter of the five thousand or so Euro-Americans who were engaged in the enterprise, William Cody (a.k.a. Buffalo Bill), had an extraordinary record in 1867 of killing an average of eighteen buffalo a day in an eight-month period to supply a company contracted to feed railroad workers. Cody was a showman, and his accounts are not always to be taken at face value; but this one seems to be fairly accurate.

The arrival of the North-West Mounted Police, followed within a couple of years by the treaty commissioners and the opening of the territory for settlement, signaled a momentous change in the life and livelihood of the Blackfoot in the foothills of Alberta; but the breathtakingly fast demise of the buffalo changed their world more than strangers ever could. And to make it more traumatic, they went hand in hand.

The government in Canada took note but did next to nothing, intermittently passing legislation that was unenforceable, and encouraging slaughter that was unsustainable and settlement that was throttling the life out of the buffalo's range. Instead, Ottawa spent time and energy exaggerating Indian hostility south of the border in order to implement treaties designed to pacify First Nations on the Canadian prairies, and to justify the expenditure involved to a mostly eastern public that was grumbling about their taxes.

Whom and what to blame? As the scale of the devastation became apparent, the Blackfoot occasionally blamed the Cree, with whom they had historically belligerent relations, and the Métis, who did not have the same sense of the territorial protocols of the buffalo hunt. Many said that the Sun Spirit was angry because they had let the white man wreak such havoc. But the Blackfoot recognized that they were parties to the trade, and thereby to the slaughter. However they interpreted this particular crisis, the Blackfoot were acutely aware that both natural and supernatural powers were infinitely greater than human ones, for better or for worse, and that the will of the Creator, unfathomable as it might be, governed both ordinary and extraordinary events. Indeed, in ways acknowledged by some of the early missionaries, the Blackfoot had the kind of faith—though not the specific forms of belief—that Christianity espoused: the same power that could say "every beast of the forest is mine, and the cattle upon a thousand hills," in the words of Psalm 50, could strike off those multitudes of animals.

Since the scale of the loss wasn't apparent until two years after Treaty Seven, some of the Blackfoot thought they were being punished for signing the treaty, pointing to the fact that three of the Blood chiefs who signed it died before the year was out. But overall, the Blackfoot response to the disappearance of the buffalo during the following decades demonstrated their ability to change while remaining the same. Hugh Dempsey, who has listened to many stories told by those who were around back then, reports that "their tales of the last days of freedom and the destruction of their old ways of life were not filled with bitterness or anger. They were told plainly and simply as facts that could not be changed through the passage of time."

The Blackfoot had come into this time as one of the most powerful peoples of the northern Plains—"aristocrats of the plains"—and a great horse culture, rivaling those of the Asian steppes and the Arabian desert centuries earlier, and the chivalric culture of medieval Europe. With their powerful status among the great Indian tribes of the West came a wealth of experience in the ways of the world, which for them included centuries of wars and diseases and climate changes that had intermittently altered their tribal and territorial alliances. To be sure, this seemed like no other time in their history. But their storytellers told of other drastic events that they had survived, and after which their sovereignty had sometimes even been enhanced—as was the case when the horse transformed their lives a mere hundred and fifty years earlier.

And although the collapse of the buffalo was devastating, and happened brutally quickly, the Blackfoot knew from such stories passed down to them of climate changes that had transformed not only the plant and animal populations but the geography of their whole world, the waters rising and falling and land thrusting up and wearing down all over the plains—some of it happening long before human habitation on the planet and linked to their stories of the creation of the world as we know it. And there were much more recent memories, told by men and women who were alive back then, of the so-called Little Ice Age that began in the Northern Hemisphere in the 1300s and lasted well into the 1800s. As Dempsey writes, "elders related stories that encouraged conformity to band mores and a common understanding of the band's place in a charged super-natural world." Which isn't that different from what many of us are taught. We learn early that there are some things we cannot control, and must surrender to. The weather. Disease. Death. For some, reli-gion teaches us to accept such things. Science shows us we don't always have to. Balancing the stories of religion and science, and admitting that sometimes both get it wrong, is something we have not yet learned to do very well.

Every tribe in the Blackfoot Confederacy was divided into bands, each with its own chief. This was a practical organization, as well as a matter of traditional principle, for the small number of men and women and children in a band—perhaps twenty or thirty families—was an efficient group for traveling and camping, and the bands got together when the buffalo were moving in large herds, as well as in the winter camps and during wartime.

Each tribe, in turn, had both a war chief and a peace chief, though the distinction seems to have been easily misconstrued by outsiders, for both would have war records, and either could claim authority by the force of his argument on a particular subject. That said, one of them would be acknowledged as the head chief, and his decisions held on most everyday matters. But in times of serious trouble, the war chief would come to the fore. The lines of authority were relatively clear, and disagreements would normally be talked through until a decision was taken—and then the authority of one or the other was (usually) strictly observed. Recognizing this, and admiring its effectiveness, the Canadian police fostered close and constructive relations with the chiefs, relying on them to maintain order and good governance in their community at a time when these traditional lines of authority were well respected. Over and over again, conflicts and controversies that had the potential to be divisive and possibly dangerous to the wider community were dealt with by the chiefs, sometimes sternly. The key was the continuing presence and the power of customary tribal sanctions and incentives. When these were subverted or destroyed, as they were by the relentless social engineering of the 1876 Indian Act in Canada, designed to control the Indians and (as the years went by) to assimilate them, and administered by its all-too-often autocratic field agents, things changed in many communities.

Traditionally, life in camp was centered around the tipis, made with long poles tied together in a cone, covered with buffalo hide and decorated with designs telling of events and powers both material and spiritual. The tipis could be taken down and put up easily when the families moved between their summer home out on the plains and their winter residence closer to the mountains; a fire kept the tipi warm in winter, while a flap at the top let out the smoke and kept the inside cool in summer. The plain style of the tipi masks a sophisticated sectioning of space that caught the elements of curve and cone which defined the dwelling itself, with private and public areas clearly defined and decorated accordingly, comfort being paramount. Indeed, in the 1800s the interior was as comfortable as a Victorian parlor, with cushions and carpets and blankets and backrests, and when family and friends came the hosts would offer food and share a pipe to make them welcome and give thanks. The floor plan was elliptical rather than circular, with the buffalo hide cover held down by large stones that would be left in "tipi rings" from year to year when the tribe moved between winter and summer camps. The entrance to a tipi normally faced east to the rising sun, and that side of the tipi was the public space, while the west side was private and used for sacred ceremonies. The hearth was always in the center.

And from early days right through the late 1800s, fun in camp was a feature of Blackfoot life. There were games for children and adults; singing and storytelling; drumming and dancing: the tea dance, for instance, where men and women would compete to see who could drink the most tea and still keep on dancing; and the laughing contest dance, when two groups would choose a man from one side and a woman from the other to see who could get the other to laugh first by singing and telling stories and making funny gestures, the loser providing the meat and bannock and other food for the dance the next week. And there was the most important dance—indeed the most important ceremony—in the Blackfoot community, the sacred annual Sun Dance, sponsored by a woman and held after the Berry Moon in summer when the saskatoon berries were ripening.

The significance of the Sun Dance was first of all religious; but the line between the secular and the sacred was not neatly drawn in Blackfoot society—indeed in some respects there wasn't any line at all. Spiritual powers as much as material sustenance nourished both individual and collective well-being, as they often have in the history of humankind; and the Sun Dance was as important for its celebration of the tribal communities as it was as a consolidation of individual welfare. So when some of the missionaries and police opposed the Sun Dance on grounds that it encouraged the telling of stories of enemy raids and horse captures, always undertaken at risk and sometimes (as with Crop Eared Wolf's experience) occasioning injury or even death, they caught the importance of the Sun Dance while missing its significance.

6

TREATY SEVEN

COURTESY COUNTS FOR MUCH, especially when customs differ. It creates responsibility, and respect. When the leaders of the Blackfoot Confederacy gathered at Blackfoot Crossing on the Bow River in mid-September of 1877 to consider the offer of a treaty from the government of Canada—or more precisely from the Great Mother, Queen Victoria—courtesies were the currency of the formal exchanges between them and their counterparts, the government negotiators James Macleod, commissioner of the North-West Mounted Police, and David Laird, lieutenant governor of the North-West Territories and special Indian commissioner. Courtesies masked both anxieties and ambitions, and they characterized the rhetoric on both sides.

The timing was set to coincide with the seasonal routines of the confederacy. (In fact some of the Blackfoot such as Joe Healy, and a few leaders including the Peigan chief Big Swan, were away hunting what buffalo they could find when the negotiations began.) The gathering was originally to be in Fort Macleod, at the center of Blood and Peigan country; but Fort Macleod was where the North-West Mounted Police were located, and Crowfoot refused to meet in a white man's fort, insisting instead on his Blackfoot tribe's traditional gathering place, Blackfoot Crossing.

The tribes in the Blackfoot Confederacy acted together in agreeing to what was presented to them by the new Dominion of Canada on behalf of Queen Victoria, while they struggled with conditions that were variously incomprehensible, inconceivable, or misunderstood.

The first misunderstanding, however, was the government's assumption that Crowfoot was chief of the Blackfoot nation; but there was no such thing as a single Blackfoot nation. It does not seem to have been deliberate (though it almost certainly made success more likely) but it indicated something about the boilerplate character of treaty making. The treaties, by British and European tradition, were nation-to-nation agreements. Yet the Blackfoot was a confederacy of tribal sovereignties, each with its own political and constitutional dynamics. The misunderstanding was particularly ironic, given that Canada itself had followed the United States in departing from the eighteenth-century European idea of absolute and indivisible sovereign power residing in nation-states, opting instead for divided sovereignties flowing from the people and vested in provincial or state and federal governance. The Blackfoot Confederacy had its own political formalities and functions which the North-West Mounted Police appreciated even if they did not always comprehend, and upon which they based their practice of dealing with the chiefs of band and tribal jurisdiction.

So when Crowfoot was singled out by the government as *the* chief, a status that emerged because of his considerable diplomatic skills in dealing with the newcomers and his undeniable leadership abilities, some of the other chiefs—several of them with greater influence among the Blackfoot tribes than Crowfoot—were understandably irritated. Red Crow of the Blood, for example, had a larger following and often exercised greater authority in decisions of the confederacy; and the Blood and the Peigan were both unhappy with the change of venue from their territory to Blackfoot Crossing, and were strategically late in arriving for the negotiations. Indeed, Red Crow initially thought that the presence of the Blood tribe's war chief (and one of its great orators), Medicine Calf, would be enough, and there would be no need for him to attend. And many from throughout the confederacy were not at all sure about the treaty. Some (such as Medicine Calf) were strongly opposed; many were confused by its commitments; and some just didn't think it was all that significant. The "winter count" for that year kept by Blackfoot elder Father of Many Children recorded *"Itsiparkap-otomiop"*—"When we had a bad spring." No mention was made of a treaty; and even the next year was described simply as a "mild winter."

David Laird opened the gathering with a tribute to both the Great Spirit, who in his words "has made all things—the sun, the moon, and the stars, the earth, the forests, and the swift running rivers," and the Great Mother, the Queen, "who by the Great Spirit rules over this great country and other great countries."

> *And now the Queen has sent Colonel Macleod and myself to ask you to make a treaty. But in a very few years the buffalo will probably be all destroyed, and for this reason the Queen wishes to help you live in the future in some other way. She wishes you to allow her white children to come and live on your land and raise cattle, and should you agree to this, she will assist you to raise cattle and grain, and thus give you the means of living when the buffalo are no more. She will also pay you and your children money every year, which you can spend as you please. By being paid in money you cannot be cheated, as with it you can buy what you think proper.*

Discussion took place over several days, and the chiefs of the Blackfoot tribes conferred among themselves, often seeking the advice of elders. Crowfoot turned to one named Pemmican, whose wisdom, spiritual as well as material, he respected. Twice he went to his lodge, and twice Pemmican would say nothing. Then, on a third visit from Crowfoot, he spoke:

> *I want to hold you back because I am at the edge of a bank. My life is at its end. I hold you back because your life henceforth will be very different from what it has been. Buffalo makes your body strong. What you will eat from this money will have your people buried all over these hills. You will be tied down, you will not wander the plains; the whites will take over your land and fill it. You won't have your own free will; the whites will lead you by a halter. That is why I say don't sign. But my life is old, so sign if you want to. Go ahead and make the treaty.*

Crowfoot was disturbed; but shortly afterward, Red Crow came to him with the decision of the Blood, who were by no means unanimously in favor. As for Red Crow, he was cautious, but he trusted his friend Colonel Macleod; and having gained the support of his tribal council—not an easy task with some powerful chiefs opposed—his message to Crowfoot was that the Blood would sign if he and his followers would. That afternoon, Crowfoot gave his famous acceptance speech to the commissioners.

> *While I speak, be kind and patient. I speak for my people, who are numerous, and who rely upon me to follow that course which in the future will tend to their good. The plains are large and wide. We are the children of the plains, it is our home, and the buffalo has been our food always. I hope you look upon the Blackfeet, Bloods and Sarcees as your children now, and that you will be indulgent and charitable to them. They all expect me to speak now for them, and I trust the Great Spirit will put into their breasts to be a good people—into the minds of the men, women and children, and their future generations.*

> *The advice given me and my people has proved to be very good: if the Police had not come to the country, where would we all be now? Bad men and whiskey were killing us so fast that very few, indeed, of us would have been left today. The Police have protected us as the feathers of the bird protect it from the frosts of winter. I wish them all good, and trust that all our hearts will increase in goodness from this time forward. I am satisfied. I will sign the treaty.*

He was followed by Red Crow, who expressed confidence in his friend James Macleod, rather than in the paper document. For him, being as good as your word was the test, and Macleod had passed it.

> *Three years ago, when the police first came to the country, I met and shook hands with Stamixotokon (Colonel Macleod) at Belly River. Since that time he made me many promises. He kept them all—not one of them was ever broken. Everything that the police have done has been good. I entirely trust Stamixotokon, and will leave everything to him. I will sign with Crowfoot.*

And for his part, Macleod was well aware not only of his personal responsibility but also of that which the Blackfoot had conferred upon the government.

> *You say that I have always kept my promises. As surely as my past promises have been kept, so surely shall those made by the Commissioners be carried out in the future. If they were broken I would be ashamed to meet you or look you in the face; but every promise will be solemnly fulfilled as certainly as the sun now shines down upon us from the heavens.*

It is easy, given the past century and a half, to doubt the good faith of the two commissioners; but they meant what they said, just as the Blackfoot leaders did.

The occasion of Treaty Seven was remarkable in many ways. It was an occasion that seemed, even more than the numbered treaties that preceded it, to signal something special and to symbolize not only all the promises of the other treaties but the participation and collective promise of the non-Indian people of the Plains, in this case the rancher and settler community that had come to live in Blackfoot territory. As one later commentator noted, "probably never in the history of the North-West Territories had so many people assembled in one place at the same time." The Blackfoot and Sarcee, along with several bands of Stoney to the north toward the mountains, were signatories, and made up the majority of people present; but almost all of the residents of Fort Macleod attended, along with many from Fort Calgary (as it was called then) along with missionaries, traders, police, and Plains Indians and Métis from across the territory.

A description by Frank Oliver, from Fort Edmonton, gives a good sense of the gathering.

> There was a numerous and miscellaneous assortment of unattached Indians, half-breeds and whites from the more Northerly plains and the Edmonton settlements on the North Saskatchewan and other Northern points, who were without any special reason for their presence except a desire to see what was to be seen and to tread hitherto forbidden ground. Of these I was one. Eastward from the camp, the valley for miles was full of horses which seemed to be unguarded. But if the herd were approached, a Blackfoot head promptly popped up from among them. This was accepted as notice to move in another direction. Horses were wealth, power, prestige,

quick transport that made Indian life on the buffalo plains most pleasant and desirable. They were the most valued possession of both Indian and whites, and were guarded accordingly.

Another witness, North-West Mounted Police inspector Cecil Denny, brought a more informed eye to bear on the scene, though one that also overflowed with newcomer sentimentality. Something was happening to—and with—the new country called Canada as it entered into a covenant not just with "some people," but with an ancient civilization. It was a moment of decision . . . and of what an observer schooled in the tradition of British romantic poetry would have called dread.

There must have been at least a thousand lodges in camps on both sides of the river. . . . Their horses, herded day and night, covered the uplands to the north and south of the camp in thousands. It was a stirring and picturesque scene; great bands of grazing horses, the mounted warriors threading their way among them, and, as far as the eye could reach, the white Indian lodges glimmering among the trees along the river bottom. By night the valley echoed to the dismal howling of the camp's curs, and from sun to sun drums boomed from the tents. Dancing, feasting, conjuring, incantations over the sick, prayers for success in the hunt or in war, all went to form a panorama of wild life vastly novel and entertaining, and seen but once. Never before had such a concourse of Indians assembled on Canada's western plains; never had the tribes appeared so contented and prosperous.

And never before had they been so worried, he might have added. Laird and Macleod—Macleod especially, because he lived there— recognized the challenges of life in that time and place where the settlers were the wayfaring nomads and the Indians were the home-land custodians dealing with unpredictable turns of fortune.

Treaty Seven was the last of the numbered treaties to be signed during the 1870s, fulfilling (from the government's point of view) the commitment Canada had made when it acquired control of Rupert's Land, as well as the promise to British Columbia when it entered Confederation in 1871 that a transcontinental railway would be built across the great sweep of land held by the Indian tribes. To do that, the government knew it would need to make large land concessions to the company building the railway and later allow for immigration and settlement all along the line; but that could not happen until the land was ceded by the Indians. Which is what the prairie treaties were all about.

There is no question, when all the rhetoric is set aside, that the government commissioners were agents of settlement in the West. But they were also dedicated to the well-defined principles of inter-national treaties between nations, and well aware they had inherited those principles from the tradition of British–Indian treaty policy enunciated in the 1700s by William Johnson, principles assumed by Canada on Confederation. This was reiterated by Colonel Macleod at the gathering for Treaty Seven, and had been signaled earlier by Adams Archibald when the first numbered treaty was being negoti-ated in 1871. This was a peace *and* partnership treaty.

The Blackfoot tribes were experienced in international negotia-tions and treaty making with both allies and enemies; in 1855 its chiefs had made a treaty with the United States government, a treaty that included several other tribes. So they knew what treaties were about. They were about peace—for now, at least. But they had good reason to be anxious as they gathered at Blackfoot Crossing. They had been devastated by the smallpox epidemics that had swept the

Plains after the coming of the new settlers; the state of the buffalo was deeply troubling; the encroachment by the Cree and the Métis on their hunting grounds was a constant bother; and the scourge of new diseases had become a frighteningly unpredictable threat, having reduced their population by almost half over the past several decades.

With hindsight, they were right to be anxious, and the reasons go profoundly deeper than some of the actions—or inactions—that would be sanctioned by Ottawa, which included its sometimes deadly failure to provide the rations mandated by the treaty. *Canada did not keep its word.* That is at the heart of the matter, a breach of faith which has had profound, and poisonous, consequences for Canada.

There were many problems in the structure and style of the nego-tiations. But there were also moments of surprising promise. At its best, the treaty promised a new kind of covenant between that prai-rie world and the people who lived in it, as well as with the spirits of the past and the future that inhabit and inform it. And it clearly represented a formal acknowledgment of the sovereignty of the tribes. It is often said, usually to underline the duplicitous nature of the negotiations, that this sovereignty was not acknowledged; but it *was*, both by the spirit of treaty making and in the letter of the treaty. The anthropologist and historian Michael Asch, in his book *On Being Here to Stay*, catches one important indication of this (beyond the eighteenth-century principles of treaty making) when he notes that the language of the prairie treaties accords the chiefs and head-men the same status to sign a treaty on behalf of their people as the commissioners had on behalf of the Crown. And there was *no* indi-cation that Treaty Seven would change this; indeed, there are plenty of indications in the earlier numbered treaties, which Treaty Seven echoes, that the sovereign relationship between the Crown and the signatories would be a continuing one.

And yet there is something more. For all the nation-to-nation dynamics (or some would say deceptions) of the treaty, it was also a *sacred* agreement, entered into by both sides with a very real sense that it was made under the authority of a higher power, with the Great Spirit presiding beyond the politics of either the Blackfoot or Canada; and the promises made on both sides were guaranteed not only by a specific treaty liturgy but also by sanctions equivalent to swearing on the Bible or smoking a sacred pipe. In that sense, the spirit of the treaty *is* the treaty, for it was the spirit that underwrote its commitments. Orality plays its part in this, and this is just beginning to be acknowledged as fundamentally important. In the case of the treaties, the presumption that they are mutually binding contracts rests on the knowledge that there has been prior mutual consent; and since the agreement was reached orally before the treaty was signed, the full extent of the oral agreement needs to be taken into account . . . and can even claim precedence.

Finally, the "letter" of the treaty, its language, included terms that were either poorly translated to the Blackfoot or untranslatable, and the implications for territorial authority—which up until then had been challenged only in tangible ways by those ready and willing to risk war—were never given the attention they required. While Crowfoot may have been the most aware of all this, he was also the most hopeful that the treaty would benefit his people, facing the loss of the buffalo and the inevitable flow of white settlers onto their lands. The translation of languages, and the naming of lands, has long been recognized as an exercise in power, and by no means only in the Americas.

When Crowfoot agreed to Treaty Seven, he was still accurately describing his people in declaring: "We are the children of the plains, it is our home, and the buffalo has been our food always." And he gave thanks for "the mountains, the hills and the valleys, the prairies, the forests and the waters, and all the animals that inhabit them." His eloquent celebration of the place he called home could be dismissed today as rhetorical or romantic, but it was a linguistic contour that at the time *did* match the landscape of fact. And the rhetoric had muscle.

David Laird spoke in the same covenantal language as Crowfoot when he acknowledged that "the Great Spirit has made all things—the sun, the moon, and the stars, the earth, the forests, and the swift running rivers," reinforcing the sacred bonds of family by continuing: "The Great Spirit has made the white man and the red man brothers, and we should take each other by the hand. The Great Mother loves all her children, white man and red man alike; she wishes to do them all good." Crowfoot too was speaking the words of a new covenant, for that is what the treaties were. A covenant for people who were all bound in good faith by a treaty.

But Canada did not keep its word.

And a crisis was looming. At least one key figure, James Macleod, recognized this; and the crisis he feared arrived early in 1879, when the tribes in the territory faced starvation. The buffalo were gone and promised rations were reduced or withheld. Macleod went to Ottawa that spring to brief and badger the government, returning to the West in July with food supplies and new police recruits. He was accompanied by Edgar Dewdney, the newly appointed superintendent general of Indian affairs for the North-West Territories, and together they visited many of the Indian agencies.

Despite the fact that Macleod's health was beginning to deteriorate under the strain (he had Bright's disease), he traveled more than 2,300 miles by horse that year to conduct his police work, as well as to fulfill his judicial responsibilities as a stipendiary magistrate. But most of all, he traveled to almost every corner of the territory to assess the dreadful circumstances of many of the Plains tribes. (With their signature sense of humor, the Blackfoot name for Dewdney, who kept promising day after day that food would arrive, was *Apinau-kusi*, which means "Tomorrow.") Macleod's understanding of the government's obligations toward the Blackfoot and other treaty nations—he had, after all, been one of two commissioners for Treaty Seven—seems to have been significantly different from that of the administration of Prime Minister John A. Macdonald. Put bluntly, they had promises to keep, and their honor to uphold. When Macleod got to know Jack Cowdry, he told him that he was appalled by the government's failure to keep its promises and furnish foodstuffs for the destitute Indians, adding that the Ottawa authorities seemed to think that the Blackfoot could still gain their livelihood by hunting, "as if everyone didn't know that there is nothing for them to hunt."

The Blackfoot ran out of fresh meat, so dried meat and bacon and pemmican were substituted, along with flour that was often black because it had been made from frozen wheat. The situation was made worse by the measles and scarlet fever that now took many of their children. Among the Blood, disease was devastating for the next couple of decades. In 1881, there were 3,560 Blood collecting the annual treaty money; by 1890 that number was halved, and by 1896 it was down to 1,300, with annual deaths double that of births. The arrival of relatives from the United States, many in wretched shape, to join their Blood families complicated the situation; and the Canadian economy was struggling too, though treaty provisions should have been a protected budget. The result on the Canadian prairies was desperate hunger, starvation for some of the First Nations, and unrest among them all.

Jack Cowdry's rancher friend Ned Maunsell was at the Treaty Seven negotiations, and his experience in those years gives a sense of how this played out for everyone on the ground. The Indians were eating dogs and snaring gophers; and Maunsell and his brother, living in a log cabin they had built to start their ranch, had much sympathy for them but little food for themselves. One day a local Blood man came by, and they did what anyone would do in the foothills at that time, they gave him tobacco and a meal. The next day he came back with his wife and child. Again they fed them. For weeks after, every time they lit a fire Indians would see the smoke, take it as a signal, and arrive at their door. Soon the Maunsells were nearly out of food, and couldn't keep up the hospitality; but neither would they eat in front of the starving Blackfoot. So they took to eating cold bacon and bread in the bush.

They eventually got some food from a neighbor—there were only about a dozen settlers between Fort Macleod and Lee's Creek (now called Cardston) at that time—and finally had a proper meal. And the next day, in one of those wonderful coincidences, the cattle they had bought when they finally got that letter of credit cashed arrived on the trail from Montana. During the few weeks following, their herd was raided several times—fresh meat!—and they lost a good number of cattle which they could ill afford to part with. In exasperation, the Maunsells—both being former North-West Mounted Police officers—went with several other ranchers to meet Colonel Macleod and see what could be done. "If you can identify the Indians who killed your cattle, they will be punished," Macleod said, knowing full well that was impossible (and adding that in his experience some of the settlers were stealing more cattle than the Indians, because everyone was hungry and because some of the newcomers were scumbags). "If we corral our cattle together at night, can we defend our property?" the ranchers asked. "If any of you fellows kills an

Indian, he will be hanged," replied Macleod. "Then will we receive compensation for the cattle killed by the Indians?" "No," answered Macleod. "This country is not yet open for settlement [the ranchland leasing regulations were not in place until 1880] and you brought the cattle in entirely at your own risk."

Maunsell wasn't happy; but he said that this whole experience made him conscious of how they were all in it together, especially when it came to getting enough to eat. Under the same circumstances, he admitted to Jack Cowdry, he and his brother "would have stolen themselves, if they found a place to steal from, and something to steal."

The Blackfoot Confederacy was as complex, as fluid, and as full of tensions as the Canadian federation, but the Blackfoot responded to the departure of the buffalo and the arrival of the new immigrants to their ancestral territory by bringing centuries of craft and culture and statesmanship into conversation with new realities and new imaginings. They signed that peace treaty instead of going to war, even as they took stock of the changes that were upon them, changes brought about by forces they did not fully understand. At the same time, and as a kind of assurance that everything was not lost, they held with fierce determination to their religious ceremonies and to their authority as the custodians of sacred as well as secular knowledge and practice.

Disoriented by the treaty and dislocated by its reserve provisions and the restrictions on customary practices that were imposed by capricious Indian agents, the Blood tribe turned its attention to the changing location of their reserve.

The Dominion Lands Act of 1872 that staged the settlement of the Canadian West was designed to distribute the public domain to settlers in homestead parcels; but on the semi-arid Plains, where agriculture was at best marginal, allotments (of 160 acres) were seldom large enough to make farming feasible. This is where the ranching arrangements in the foothills, with leases (not allotments) on the open range and substantial landholdings under treaty, maintained the imaginative illusion—if not the reality—of a domain that was territorial rather than proprietary; and the Blackfoot were very much part of this imaginative domain. The rancher "users" were privileged, to be sure, for they had special consideration in the government's granting of leases; but in the main they were good stewards, keeping the grasslands in remarkably good condition—and keeping settlement away from the open range, for a while at least. Both forms of land tenure—individual proprietorship and communal custody—had their awkwardnesses; but the second was much more congenial to Blackfoot understandings of a homeland, and it was also in line with the ranching culture of the foothills. In turn, the settlers' antipathy toward "idle" land protected for grazing instead of promoted for plowing made for common cause between the ranchers and the Blackfoot, for whom the open range without fences was fundamentally important.

The Blackfoot's strong survival instinct made them determined to find ways of securing self-sufficiency by sustaining their cultural heritage even as they adapted their lives and livelihoods to deal with the new circumstances. For some, this meant compromising their traditional territorial connections. Led by Chief Crowfoot, the Siksika tribe took a reserve bordering the railway—while the Peigan took land close to their traditional hunting grounds near Pincher Creek and the Porcupine Hills. At first the Blood had gone along with the Siksika, and accepted land adjoining the Siksika reserve. But they didn't fancy the barren plains along the Bow River, and the memories of their hunting and gathering lives and the movement of summer and winter camps were still fresh in their minds.

So they requested a change, and in a move that should have been replicated across the country as First Nations took stock of the reality of their treaty and reserve life, the Blood tribe chose a new reserve in 1883 near to their traditional winter camping ground by the Belly River. This land turned out (not surprisingly, given its location on the buffalo plains) to be at the heart of ranching country; and at over 545 square miles, the Blood reserve remains the largest in Canada, with the second-largest Aboriginal population (next to the Six Nations reserve near Brantford, Ontario).

The government attempted to secure what it called, in transparently aggressive language, the "surrender" of some of their reserve land; but in the Blood territory of Chief Red Crow, his son and successor Crop Eared Wolf, and Crop Eared Wolf's son Shot Both Sides (who in turn became chief), all resisted this—Crop Eared Wolf with a fierceness and effectiveness that has been inspiring to the Blood tribe for a century now. The Peigan maintained the size of their reserve as well, though coerced into a couple of surrenders, later reversed. And between 1912 and 1918, the Siksika took a decision to surrender land that reduced the size of their reserve but for a time made them the wealthiest Indian community in Canada (and wealthier than many of their settler neighbors in and around Calgary). The Blackfoot Confederacy held together by allowing partners to go their own way—something they had learned long ago.

7

THE ROUNDUP

BEEF WOULD DO EVERYTHING, it was said. It would feed the Indians. It would provide a relatively safe return on investment (except during the occasional bad winter). It would fill the freight cars of the new railway and foster both national commerce with eastern Canada and international trade with the United States and Great Britain. It would nourish a good local market and contribute to the economic success, the popular ideology, and the political sovereignty of the territory. And it would save the native grasslands in a region where drought was the long-term norm; if you put too many cattle on the grass for too long, you destroyed your ability to winter your stock. And that would wipe out you and your ranch. It was that simple.

The 1880s marked the beginning of the "beef bonanza." In 1881, there were nine thousand cattle in the whole of the North-West Territories. Just five years later, by 1886, there were a hundred thousand in the grasslands of the foothills alone; by the turn of the twentieth century, a half million. And Fort Macleod was at the center of this new cattle-ranching community.

Cattle ranching in the foothills brought together the indigenous Plains cultures with the heritage of horse and cattle ranching from Spanish America, and the customs of the cattle trail and the cowboy became a kind of chorus to Blackfoot horse culture. Range-savvy cattle were at a premium, and the best of them were brought in from south of the border, with both cattle and cowboys from Texas and Colorado, Wyoming and Montana coming to the grasslands and ranches of the foothills. Eastern stockers—cattle bought to finish for market rather than to build up a herd—often turned out to be poor at wintering on the western range, a euphemistic way of saying that they died in large numbers. Newfangled ways of "spoiling cattle" by feeding them through the winter with hay and grain were regarded with suspicion, if not contempt; one rancher boasted that if he could get through a winter on whisky then his stock could survive on snow. The ability to rustle for food, cows that were good mothers to the calves, and calves that were weaned early so the cows were strong enough for the next season were the most important attributes of a good herd.

Jack Cowdry's love of horses made him comfortable with both the Blackfoot and the cowboys (some of them Indians, of course) around Fort Macleod. The best of them were very good horsemen—whether herding cattle (often purchased south of the border) back to the home ranch, or checking the cattle on the winter range, or gathering them in the spring roundup. They had to be. They spent most of their waking hours in the saddle, day after day, month after month, year after year. They worked and played with riding and roping skills that were necessary on the ranch and in the rodeo, just as they worked and played with language, creating a lexicon of technical terms—many of them from Spanish—twisted and translated into cowboy lingo: *la reata* migrated to "lariat," *vaquero* to "buckaroo," and *dar la vuelta* (wrapping the end of a rope around the saddle horn) to "dally." A "willow" was a range mare, a "waddie" a cowboy riding one, and a "slow elk" a cattle beast poached by a waddie out of work.

The singing of a cowboy also fell between work and play, and Jack Cowdry certainly knew more cowboy songs than there were stars in the sky. He said that singing a song, or just the sound of a human voice, helped settle cattle—a notion still current in dairy barns around the world; and at night especially the cowboys would sing to the herd. When they ran out of tunes, they would launch into a litany of profanities, often comically contradicted by some religious humming; or they might recite the words on a coffee label or a can of condensed milk. And during the day, they would whoop and yell and hoot and holler to move the herd along. The importance of cowboys' songs as part of a specifically literary as well as a broad cultural heritage throughout the Americas was illustrated when the folklorist John Lomax was invited to speak—and to sing cowboy songs—at the annual meeting of the Modern Language Association of America in New York in 1909. (He had just completed his graduate work at Harvard under George Kittredge, a distinguished literary scholar who was successor to the university's first Professor of English, Francis James Child. Child, in turn, was the editor of the famous collection *The English and Scottish Popular Ballads*—the Child Ballads, as they were often called. Both Child and Kittredge insisted that what is sometimes marginalized as folklore and folk song belonged with the Norse and Icelandic and Celtic and Germanic folk traditions, and with the stories and songs of Old and Middle English and eighteenth- and nineteenth-century America.) Lomax published the ballads he collected in his *Cowboy Songs and Other Frontier Ballads* in 1910 (with an introductory letter from former president Theodore Roosevelt, to whom the book is dedicated). Like so many literary texts, these songs were about lives and livelihoods, longing and lamentation. Their casual tone defied the circumstances they often portrayed, confusing nonchalance and intensity in what T. S. Eliot once proposed as a sign of good poetry. And they were defiantly communal. In the epigraph to his book, Lomax quoted from a song called "The Jolly Cowboy":

What keeps the herd from running,
Stampeding far and wide?
The cowboy's long, low whistle,
And singing by their side.

The "folk revival" in the 1950s and 1960s owes much to Lomax and his son Alan, a reminder that songs such as these—like the border ballads of England and Scotland, and the oral performances of people all over the world for thousands of years—are an integral part of the cultural and imaginative life of nations. Including the Blackfoot, whose songs are much less well known—except to the Blackfoot, for whom they are part of their literature. This has a specific importance in Canada, where the absence of written literature has often been taken as a signal of "underdevelopment." The colonial administrator Lord Durham used it in his famous 1839 report on rebellions in Upper and Lower Canada, recommending responsible government for a united colony but dismissing French Canadians as a people who should be assimilated, since in his view they had no literary tradition and no history. Much more recently, a similar account was given of the Gitxsan and Wet'suwet'en peoples in British Columbia in a major Aboriginal rights case called *Delgamuukw* in the 1980s, where they were dismissed by the trial judge as "unorganized societies . . . roaming from place to place like beasts of the field" because they had "no horses, no wheeled vehicles, no written literature." (His judgment was later rejected by the Supreme Court of Canada on those and other grounds.)

In the late spring of 1885, the newly arrived Cowdry brothers witnessed the start of the biggest roundup that the Canadian West had ever seen, with some sixty thousand head of cattle gathered up from their winter ranges just south of Calgary all the way down to the

Montana border. The cowboys mustered at Fort Macleod and moved out from there, one group riding west toward Pincher Creek and another north to Willow Creek. There were fifteen mess wagons, each with fifteen riders, and a large herd of saddle horses from which the cowboys would choose their mounts each day for the weeks they would be out, sleeping in a bedroll covered with a tarp. At night the horses would be turned loose to graze, watched over by a young—or sometimes creaky old—cowboy called a wrangler (from the Spanish *caballerango*).

The captain of the roundup heading to Willow Creek was George Lane. Born in the United States, Lane had worked on some of the best-run ranches in Montana, where he learned about the methods of open-range "cattle drive" ranching that had been practiced for a few centuries further south in Texas and Mexico and throughout parts of South America; and he had also picked up the newer midwestern techniques, with their careful breeding and intensive feeding programs. He brought his experience of both to Alberta, where he became foreman of the Bar U ranch, northwest of Fort Macleod. The Bar U was one of the first big ranches in the Canadian West, managed in its earliest days by Fred Stimson, a character who combined a comedian's wit and an aristocrat's elegance with a rancher's initiative and a cowboy's flair—he admired and collected the regalia and equipment of cowboy culture throughout the Americas, as well as those of the Blackfoot, with whom he had very good relations; and he and George Lane and others developed a Canadian ranching compromise that drew on continental ranching experience but suited Chinook country and the conditions of its cattle industry. Stimson was a tough competitor, no matter what the occasion. In court one day, he was being cross-examined by Paddy Nolan, a Calgary lawyer known for his own quick wit, whose client was accused of stealing some cattle. The exchange went like this:

MR. NOLAN: *Your name is Fred Stimson, I believe.*

MR. STIMSON: *It is.*

MR. NOLAN: *You spend most of your time riding the range, do you not?*

MR. STIMSON: *No, sir. I spend most of my time in bed.*

MR. NOLAN: *You are very short-sighted, I believe, Mr. Stimson.*

MR. STIMSON: *No, sir, I am not.*

MR. NOLAN: *Then why do you wear glasses [actually, a monocle]?*

MR. STIMSON: *Oh, just for effect.*

MR. NOLAN: *Now, Mr. Stimson, you claim my client misbranded one of your cattle?*

MR. STIMSON: *I do, sir.*

MR. NOLAN: *Please describe the animal in court.*

MR. STIMSON: *Well, it was an ordinary, everyday steer with a leg on each corner.*

And with that, Paddy Nolan gave up.

One account of the 1885 roundup, reported in the *Macleod Gazette*, celebrated a particular cowboy with praise that invokes the combination of skill and strength and sense of humor that defined a civilized horseman on the prairies:

> *If there is a man on the roundup who keeps up the spirit of the boys more than another and who provides more amusement to break the monotony, this man is John Ware. John is not only one of the best natured and most obliging fellows in the country, but he is one of the shrewdest cow men. . . . The horse is not running on the prairie which John cannot ride, sitting with his face either to the head or tail, and even if the animal chooses to stand on its head or lie on its back, John always appears on top when the horse gets up, and smiles as if he enjoyed it—and he probably does.*

The writer of that praise song was C. E. D. Wood, the editor of the *Macleod Gazette* newspaper (and its cofounder a couple of years before). John Ware was well known to Wood, as he was to many in the community, for his courtesy, his craft as a cowboy, his love of comedy, and his courage—and newspaperman Wood was notorious for being quick with his opinions and open with his prejudices.

So it is interesting that he did not mention that John Ware was black. Because it didn't really matter, at least not in ranching country. In some of the towns (though not Fort Macleod) it was another matter; Calgary had displayed an intimidating round of racism earlier that year when a black man was suspected of murder. He was later convicted after a proper trial; but for a time both before and after that Calgary was very unfriendly to blacks. Ware had been told he was not welcome, and a black man named Henderson, visiting Calgary, had been run out of town. (He went to Lethbridge, where he apparently settled in just fine.)

The situation in the foothills was riddled with complications. Many of the white men had Blackfoot or Cree or Métis wives, so the domestic scene was reasonably accommodating—but still, like was seeking like. *Céad míle fáilte* (Gaelic for "a hundred thousand welcomes") proclaimed the *Macleod Gazette* in 1882 when news came of the arrival of a few more white women in the foothills.

In truth, there was a dog's breakfast of prejudices along lines of race and gender and religion and everything else imaginable, not only in the towns but throughout the territory, where ignorance and stupidity maintained the same time-honored hold on human behavior as it still seems to have in so many places around the world. However, what mattered most in the foothills and on the prairies was performance, and a kind of class that comes with confidence and craft. Of course, Wood's account may have been influenced not only by Ware's leadership at the roundup but also by the fact that perhaps a quarter of the cowboys on the Plains were black, freed from the curse of slavery after 1865. And although the life of a cowboy was hard, it was also free—freer than most other livelihoods available to African Americans at that time.

John Ware was born into slavery on a South Carolina plantation; and some years after emancipation he first came to Canada on a cattle drive, having been hired on the word of a friend to bring a herd north from Idaho to Alberta. With no apparent experience on the trail, he was assigned duty as night herder and pick-up man at the back of the herd—a dusty, dirty, and boring job, the lowest on the hierarchy during a trail ride. And he was given an old nag to ride, and a ragtag saddle. After several days—and cautiously, because he wanted to keep the job—he asked his trail boss for "a better saddle and a worse horse." But he wasn't looking for a lazier horse and a cushier seat. In fact, he wanted a livelier horse and a working saddle. In the way of that world, the cowboys on the trail decided on a little mischief and got him a rank horse that nobody would, or could, ride. His being black might have encouraged them; but they would typically play games with newcomers of all sorts and sizes, and dozens of cowboy songs celebrated how often the mischief-makers were shown up as fools.

As they were here. Ware knew horses, and was very strong and skillful. "Cheeking" the horse when he mounted—using the cheek strap of the bridle to pull the horse's head toward the saddle to prevent it running or bucking as he got on its back—he settled in the saddle. Immediately, the horse swapped in, spun round, frog-walked and fishtailed, went up to the heavens in one direction and came down to earth in another, and tried everything else in the copybook of an outlaw (a more or less unmanageable horse)—but Ware rode it to a standstill. From that day on, Ware's reputation was assured, and he lived up to it at every turn.

A few weeks before the roundup, newspaperman Wood had been serving as the recorder of brands (most folks served in several capacities, which confounds the purists but sustains small communities) and he was visited by Ware, asking to register a mark for his cattle. Asked how many cattle he had, Ware said he hadn't any yet, but planned to have some soon. Then Ware asked for the number nine as a brand, since he had enough money to buy nine cows. When Wood asked whether he wanted a single nine, Ware said no, he'd like four of them, because he planned to have a whole lot of cattle. And so it was. He went on to become a rancher of renown in the district, one of the very few who commanded the kind of respect that George Lane did, and whose experience and skill were widely sought after and universally acknowledged—with the brand *9999* (for "big cattle," as Wood said when he approved it).

John Ware also became known for his singing, and it was said that he could sing a herd to sleep like nobody else. Some of the most familiar songs of the period, like "Riding Old Paint," were in fact composed by African Americans—in that case, by one Charley Willis from Texas—and many others were sung by cowboys to the herds to quiet them through the night.

John Ware did not forget an insult, and for a while after his "unwelcome" he had refused to go back to Calgary. But when he died in early September 1905 (his horse stepped in a gopher hole and fell on him), his funeral was the biggest Calgary had ever seen, with news reaching far and wide even in the short two days since his death. He was celebrated as one of the greatest stockmen of his time—a rodeo cowboy and rancher around whom wonderful stories swirled, like the time he walked across a corral of range bulls by stepping from one back to another because it was the shortest and easiest way. In his eulogy, the Baptist minister in Calgary said: "To know John Ware was to know a gentleman, one of God's gentlemen. He leaves us with the thought that black is a beautiful colour—one which the Creator must have held in particularly high favour, because he gave it to His most beautiful people."

Much of the success of the Blackfoot in facing their future and securing a measure of self-sufficiency after the collapse of the buffalo herds had to do with horses. Even with the buffalo gone, the Blackfoot continued to breed horses for speed and for show but also for the new livelihoods of settlement—in which a horse's size and strength mattered—and they began to crossbreed with draft horses brought in by some of the ranchers and farmers. And the horses they had, with buffalo-hunting stamina and speed and agility, were perfect as cow ponies.

It is little wonder that the Blood, skilled at hunting buffalo with horses, took to cattle ranching without skipping a beat. The Methodist missionary John Maclean, living on the Blood reserve, estimated that there were two thousand horses there in 1887 for about 2,300 Indians.

So the Blackfoot continued to put horses at the center of their lives, giving them pride of place in their civic and ceremonial lives. And by the time Jack Cowdry arrived in Fort Macleod, many Blackfoot, including the Blood chief Red Crow and his son Crop Eared Wolf, had turned from buffalo hunting to both farming and ranching, with nearly sixty acres in potatoes and grain. Their familiarity with the seasonal round in that dryland environment put them in a good position to succeed where some of the settlers had not, and their experience with the native grass species of the western Plains and foothills, where the buffalo had grazed and parts of which (for the Blood and the Peigan at least) were now included in their reserves, provided the knowledge and know-how to build up large herds of cattle and horses, which were flourishing on their grasslands by the 1890s.

Fort Macleod was not only at the center of the ranching community but in the lead when it came to the fairs and rodeos that celebrated farming and ranching life. There had been an exhibition rodeo with local cowboys and Indians for the Marquess of Lorne at the Strong ranch just west of Macleod on his visit to the foothills in 1881. Fort Macleod then took the lead with a fall fair in October 1886, the week the Cowdry brothers opened their bank, and the bank supported the annual fairs and accompanying rodeo events for the next twenty years. They always opened with a parade of Blackfoot riders dressed in their beautiful leggings and shirts and vests and headdresses, the horses adorned with beaded saddles and bridles and blankets and breast bands and saddlebags.

But the permanence of the Blood reserve as a new homeland was hard to accept, especially for a people bewildered by the notion not of settling down, but of staying put. Nobody stays put all year, their stories told them; stay put, and you will starve. Which they almost did in those terrible years immediately following the treaty. But they had agreed to settle on their reserves; and they did, more or less. Many of them, including Red Crow and Crop Eared Wolf, kept their tipis, which were important for gathering together family and friends and were painted with spiritual designs inspired by dreams or war experiences; and they also built houses, fencing the land to corral their horses and cattle and keep them away from their crops. Being close to the land that had once been part of their seasonal routine was immensely important; and no one who has visited the country by the Belly and Old Man's Rivers around Fort Macleod could doubt that it would foster a consciousness of higher powers, especially for people who had lived there for so long. Its beauty was a rare confusion of the wild and the domestic, the sacred and the profane.

And there were always songs and stories about horses. Sanctified by the ceremonies of the horse dance and the horse medicine (that was secure in the keeping of its custodians), these helped the Blackfoot resist the pressures of a reality that might otherwise have become overwhelming. It is in this sense that so many stories are resistance stories, giving us a way of creating a center of belief from which we can move out to live in a world of events. For the Blackfoot, horses were at the heart of many of these stories, taking over from the buffalo. In Mongolia, home of one of the greatest horse cultures in the world, the word for spirit, *takh*, is also the word for a wild horse. A similar spirit shaped Blackfoot culture. And it brought together native and newcomer alike, for as the historian Lewis G. Thomas insists, "there can be little doubt that a love of horses was a most important element in the creation of a sense of community in southern Alberta." That, and storytelling, in a wide variety of forms.

8

THE UPRISING

WHILE THE ROUNDUP THAT SPRING of 1885 was full of promise, the news that was swirling around Fort Macleod was not. It came as no surprise to Jack Cowdry, though he had hoped for a better turn; but it came quickly, first by word of mouth and then by mail that there were troubles back in Saskatchewan.

The Métis had been almost completely left out of the prairie treaties, leaving them vulnerable both to the certainty of increased settlement and to the uncertainties of local influence. Language and religion, specifically the French language and the Roman Catholic faith, played a part in this malign neglect of the West, but so did ignorance (of the West by the authorities in Ottawa) and stupidity (seldom in short supply when people are in a hurry, as Canada certainly was).

It was in this setting, on March 19, 1885, that Louis Riel once again announced a provisional government for the territory. (March 19 is the feast of the patron saint of the Métis, Saint Joseph.) The declaration set in motion an uprising inspired by the Bible as well as buffalo hunting. The Cree and Assiniboine rose up on their own behalf before joining the Métis—and the "rebellion," as the government liked to call it, was under way.

After a series of military engagements the uprising was put down, and Riel was charged with treason. His trial began in late July 1885, and on August 1 the jury found him guilty of treason, yet recommended mercy; but the judge sentenced him to death. Riel was hanged on November 16.

When Jack Cowdry heard the news that Riel had surrendered and would be tried in a Regina court, he decided to go back there to support him. Because time was short, he rode on the new Canadian Pacific Railway from Calgary. He knew that the railway represented much that Riel opposed, as he himself probably did. But Jack also believed in the idea of a powerful, independent, representative government for the people of the territory, which is essentially what Riel had proposed. And Jack believed in the hopes and possibilities of its first peoples; he was quite sure the government in Ottawa wouldn't understand, and wouldn't care, and he knew that the eastern newspapers were full of malicious nonsense about the uprising.

The Cowdry brothers felt the nervousness of their fellow settlers at the uprising, but they were above all angry at the federal government's seeming disinterest in the changes overwhelming the territory, and the precarious position of the Métis in a part of the country without any kind of responsible government. Indeed, the call for a new order in the territory was widespread, and not by any means limited to Métis concerns; delegates to the territorial council (which had been established in 1876 and consisted of what one observer described as five able men disabled by limited authority) regularly demanded a shift in responsibility from Ottawa to the West.

One of the most strident, though not always the most sensible, voices was that of Frank Oliver, who had given that description of the huge gathering at Blackfoot Crossing for Treaty Seven eight years earlier. He had founded the *Edmonton Bulletin* in 1880 (the first newspaper in Alberta), and then served as a member of the territorial assembly; he would later become federal minister of the interior and superintendent-general of Indian affairs (from 1905 to 1911), but here he is in August 1885, writing in his newspaper:

> *The North-West Territories in Canada have sometimes been termed in derision, British Siberia, on account of the northern Latitude which they occupy. But the resemblance in political institutions is even more striking than in soil and climate. While Canada as a whole, and the different provinces of which it is comprised, are united under a system of responsible government, the North-West is under a despotism as absolute, or more so, than that which curses Russia. Without representation in either parliament or cabinet, without responsible local government, the people of the North-West are allowed but a degree more control of their affairs than the serfs of Siberia.*

A year earlier, he had written an even more incendiary column, suggesting that "if history be taken as a guide, what could be plainer than that without rebellion the people of the West need expect nothing. While with rebellion, successful or otherwise, they may reasonably expect to get their rights."

It was in this spirit that folks like Jack Cowdry supported Riel, but without some of the hyperbole. The Blackfoot didn't support the uprising itself, in part because they didn't like the Cree, who had led the attack against them just fifteen years earlier, but mostly because they trusted people like James Macleod and others who had seen them through times of trouble since the treaty signing. Chief Red Crow was a warrior, and he was afraid of no one. Yet war, for him, had outlived its usefulness. But he was not Métis.

Jack Cowdry was joined by a few of his settler and Métis friends at the trial, held in the recently built and still scruffy Regina courthouse before a jury of six English and Scots Protestants. (An Irish Catholic in the jury pool was rejected for not being of British stock.) Some of Jack's acquaintances did not support Riel's methods, or were not convinced by the divine inspiration he felt; others considered him unstable at best, uncontrollable at worst. Nonetheless, many in the territory felt common cause with his resistance to Ottawa's ambition to fashion the new western hinterland in a way that would do little more than serve the interests and feed the enterprises of the metropolitan East. They were proud when Riel proclaimed that even as the eastern provinces were great, the North-West Territories was greater. And when Riel insisted that he was not just a Métis leader but a leader for good in the country called Canada, they recognized that his uprising signified unfinished western business.

With faith in Catholic martyrdom and the fortitude of Métis stoicism, Riel rejected the defense of insanity which his counsel pleaded; in short order, he was convicted of treason and sentenced to be hanged despite the jury's recommendation of mercy. Jack Cowdry railed against Riel's guilty verdict and the sentence of capital punishment for the rest of his life; and he might well have agreed with some of the arguments put forward by the Catholic archbishop Taché, who in the shadow of the trial and execution called for a new kind of government and (overriding his own strong opinions) a new kind of nonpartisan understanding and commitment to peace in the North-West Territories. Taché warned (using the words of the Oblate missionary Father Alexis André in a letter to Riel's lawyer) that otherwise "we shall have in the North-West a new kind of Ireland in which the two races will cordially detest and treat each other like sworn enemies."

After the trial, which lasted only a few days, Jack stayed a week or two longer in Regina, long enough to realize that his friends from Fort Qu'Appelle—the Hudson's Bay Company manager and his Métis wife who had helped him and his brother Nat settle into the new life when they first arrived—had a surprising involvement with Louis Riel. (For over two centuries, such couples had been involved in the fur trade, and a new people, the Métis, had emerged from unions between Scots and Irish and English and French traders and [mostly] Cree women—who themselves became key players in the trade, often running it more or less as a family business.) Their daughter, a young Métis girl of thirteen, was deeply affected by the uprising and by Riel's sentence, and she made her involvement personal by somehow getting permission to visit Riel in prison while he awaited execution, traveling to Regina regularly to do just that.

How the girl managed this, and even why, is a mystery. Later, her daughter Margaret wondered whether she might have been a thirteen-year-old go-between carrying messages to the great Métis leader. Or perhaps she had a crush on Riel? Whatever the reasons, like many teenagers Margaret's mother kept a journal which she carried with her to his jail cell; and in it Riel—who imagined himself as the psalmist David, dashing down his enemies with words and music—wrote remarks like "evening prayer gives more pleasure in heaven than all the military music played by the North West Mounted Police outside my cell window." (I heard this story because Margaret became my own mother's best friend, and my godmother; and when I was growing up she would read me her mother's journal like holy scripture. And all his long life my grandfather Jack held a special affection for Margaret's mother, and for what Riel had said to her and written in her journal; and my grandfather mentioned her in the last letter he wrote to my mother just a few days before his own death.)

Instead of returning to Fort Macleod from Regina, Jack Cowdry went back to Ontario to propose to the sweetheart he had been courting, mostly at a distance, since he left to go homesteading three years earlier. Her name was Emma Whitney, though she was always called Amy; and it is a measure of their love, and her sense of adventure, that she said yes when he proposed. He had nothing arranged yet in Macleod, though he told her he was all set to start a bank. She was keen on him, but cautious about the bank. "With what?" she asked. "With my brother," he answered. But he was a good storyteller, and had almost certainly entertained her and her parents with tales of life in the foothills, and his new friends. And spoken of the territory as a homeland, not a frontier. A Blackfoot homeland first of all, he would always say; but one that he hoped to make his and Amy's as well. Even amid the unsettled economic and political circumstances that followed Riel's uprising, he believed that he and Amy could make a good life in the foothills. He believed in their future together; but "nobody has any future there if the Blackfoot don't," he would add—and then go on to say that he was sure they did.

In gratitude for their support during the Riel uprising, Prime Minister John A. Macdonald offered the "loyal chiefs" who had refused to join Riel a trip east by train to visit the capital. The chiefs of course included Crowfoot and Red Crow, who, to their chagrin, found themselves in the company of some of the Cree leaders, their longtime enemies. And there were other anomalies. Crowfoot had become a symbol of the proud and patriotic Indian to the eastern press and politicians, who lauded his loyalty during the Riel troubles; but in fact it was some of his fellow chiefs, such as Red Crow, who were steadfast in their animosity toward the Cree and refused to join the uprising, while Crowfoot wavered at first.

That said, the trip east in the fall of 1886—through Regina and Winnipeg to Ottawa and back through the Six Nations reserve near Brantford, Ontario—was a startling and in some ways inspiring one for all of them, and put them in the company of other Aboriginal leaders, especially the Iroquois of the Six Nations. Two years before, Red Crow and Crowfoot had traveled to Regina and Winnipeg, towns that were already far larger than Fort Macleod and Calgary, which up until then were the biggest they had seen—and this had made them aware that not all the white people in the world were in Blackfoot territory. Instead, as one of them commented, white people seemed as numerous as the blades of grass upon the prairie. During the 1886 trip, accompanied by their friends the Oblate missionary Father Albert Lacombe and interpreter Jean L'Heureux, they visited Ottawa and met with John A. Macdonald—called "One Spot" by the Blood, one of whom commented: "I was deeply impressed with the ability and wisdom of One Spot, who is a great friend of the Big Mother . . . there was only one chief to whom I would liken him, and that was our own chief, *Mékaisto* [Red Crow], but *Mékaisto* is a greater chief than One Spot and all his wise men."

A couple of days later they traveled to Brantford for the unveiling of a monument to the eighteenth-century Mohawk chief Joseph Brant, an occasion that had been central to the trip from the beginning. Dressed in their finest regalia, they were in the official party, leading the parade directly after Chief William Wage, followed by carriages with the lieutenant governor of Ontario, the mayor of Brantford, and other guests. The statue was unveiled, as well as bronze plaques illustrating the life of Brant, and as the Six Nations Indians began a war dance the western leaders responded with the war whoops of the Plains. At the banquet that evening, the head of the confederate Six Nations, Chief A. G. Smith (*De-ka-nen-ra-neh*), gave a speech in perfect English—witty and wise, and one of the best of the evening. That an Indian could surpass *their* "greatest chief," the lieutenant governor, in *his* language, was something Red Crow never forgot; and a decade later, on ceremonial occasions, he still wore the badge signaling his invitation to the occasion as a guest of honor. Before the Blackfoot left the East, they also visited a lumber and shingle mill at Ohsweken, on the Six Nations reserve, which was owned and operated by the Iroquois. Red Crow was deeply impressed with the possibilities this suggested for his people. He knew that they were inferior to no one; and with education and training in the new technologies (including the relatively new language of English) he was convinced they could match anyone in any enterprise—as they had on the Plains when they took up what was then the new technology of horses.

Red Crow needed all of his statecraft when he got back to the foothills and Blood territory from his trip, for all hell had broken loose. The deaths of six young men—four of them teenagers—before he left to go east were now confirmed to have been caused by Indians from the Gros Ventre tribe. The Blood braves had gone south to recover horses stolen from one of their bands, and been ambushed by a Gros Ventre war party. Over the next weeks and months, the unrest seemed certain to produce a war that could have broken the Blackfoot Confederacy. Only the winter weather stopped an outbreak of violence. Red Crow and Crop Eared Wolf took the lead in proposing the conditions for a treaty, though it was fiercely opposed by some members of their tribe. Small war parties from the Blood went down and gathered sixteen Gros Ventre horses; and a few weeks later, Gros Ventre raiders came and took forty horses belonging to Red Crow and his family. This was a blow to his economic resources as well as to his leadership, and after discussions that involved both the American and Canadian governments, a treaty expedition set out, with Red Crow and several other Blood chiefs, three North-West Mounted Police officers, the Indian agent, and Jerry Potts as interpreter. At the border, they were met by an American cavalry escort and continued on to Fort Belknap in north-central Montana, where the Gros Ventre and Assiniboine later shared a reservation. The Blood were received by both angry warriors and friendly chiefs; but after several outbursts the chiefs took the lead and a peace was secured, with Red Crow speaking to accept.

This was my country once. We used to hunt the prairies with the Gros Ventres and Assiniboines and I like visiting them. I have come over to see them, to make a treaty, and what I say I mean. . . . I hope you will stop your young men going to war. I will do the same when I get home. I am glad I have got my horses back; I feel good. We have made a treaty and we will smoke the pipe at last. . . . Now the Indians must stop fighting with each other. I will not say we do not steal horses; all Indians steal horses and the whites are just as bad.

The peace lasted only a while, but a kind of reciprocity had been reached, sternly enforced among his people by Red Crow—not because the Gros Ventre had once been allies but because it made sense. Red Crow handled the crisis in his territory better than Macdonald had the Métis uprising the year before.

Jack Cowdry in 1882 sitting on a Red River cart near Pile of Bones (soon renamed Regina), where he and his brother had just built a sod house on their new homestead. He used the cart to travel to Fort Qu'Appelle, where he would go regularly to see friends and pick up supplies from the Hudson's Bay post.

Kamoose Taylor standing in shirtsleeves in front of his hotel, wearing a bowler hat. Frank Pollinger, the masterful driver of the Concord stagecoach, is looking back toward the camera as he gets ready to urge the horses on their way to Fort Benton, Montana.

The main street of Fort Macleod in the spring of 1885 as Jack Cowdry saw it when he and his brother arrived—a wide, muddy lane on a bed of gravel. The Macleod Hotel is the first two-story building further down on the left.

Colonel James Macleod, commander of the North-West Mounted Police, was one of the two commissioners at Treaty Seven in 1877; this photograph was taken two years later in Ottawa where he'd gone to berate the government for not keeping its word, leaving the Indians without the help promised them in the bleak years after the collapse of the buffalo.

Perhaps no one epitomized the complicated character of the foothills during this period more than Jerry Potts, son of a Scots father and a Blackfoot mother. He was a legendary plainsman, a warrior with a formidable reputation, a police scout, and an interpreter who never wasted words. He knew his way everywhere in Chinook country, and, known to the Blackfoot by his Blood name, Bear Child, he was a friend to people from all walks of life.

Red Crow, head chief of the Blood, wearing his Treaty Seven medal and the ribbon given to him as an honorary guest at the ceremony in Brantford, Ontario, in 1886 commemorating Mohawk chief Joseph Brant. While a fearsome warrior in earlier days, Red Crow appears here as a peacemaker, holding a tobacco pipe.

This is Red Crow's famous Middle Painted Lodge, sometimes known as the Single Circle Otter Tipi, with sacred otters painted in black on the broad red horizontal band. Its design is said to go back to the beginning of Blackfoot religion. Red Crow transferred it to his adopted son and future Blood chief Crop Eared Wolf in 1892, probably at the Sun Dance that year.

This was taken just after Crop Eared Wolf became head chief of the Blood upon Red Crow's death. He is about to take up his warrior heritage by resisting the persistent, punishing demands from the Indian agent Robert Wilson to surrender part of the Blood reserve land. Crop Eared Wolf had promised his father he would never surrender; and he kept his word.

The Blood chiefs gathered here in 1905 include (left to right), back row: the interpreter Joe Healy and Chief Running Crane. Front row: Blackfoot Old Woman, whose ambitions troubled Red Crow; Day Chief, whom Red Crow had instead promoted as chief of the bands downriver on the reserve; and head chief Crop Eared Wolf.

The Blackfoot visit to Ottawa in 1886 was sponsored by Prime Minister John A. Macdonald in gratitude for their not participating in Riel's uprising. Left to right, back row: Father Albert Lacombe, an Oblate priest who mediated between the Blackfoot and the government, and the interpreter Jean L'Heureux. Middle row: chiefs Three Bulls and Crowfoot (both Siksika) and Red Crow (Blood). Front row: North Axe (Peigan) and One Spot (Blood).

In 1894 Jack Cowdry took a trip to Ontario with his children Gus and Mary, after Amy's death the previous year, to see their grandparents. The picture catches something of Jack's life as a single parent, for both his young wives—the second being Gussie—died soon after childbirth. He spoiled his children, because he could; and he gave them his spirit of fortitude and his sense of fun, because he knew they would need them.

The new Cowdry Brothers Bank is on the left halfway down the street, just past the telegraph pole doubling as a barbershop sign. Other shops include Charles Reach's greengrocer and dry goods store and Chow Sam's restaurant.

John Ware's ranch, northwest of Macleod, with John on horseback on the right and his wife, Mildred (known to all as Mother Ware), standing on the verandah. He was a celebrated figure in the foothills, a respected cattleman and one of the best rodeo cowboys.

One of a sequence of photographs of the construction of the Sun Dance lodge by the Blood in 1893: the pole is in place and the people are coming together in praise. The Sun Dance was the most important spiritual ceremony of the year, and, like religious occasions around the world, it was a sacred as well as secular gathering.

In August 1897 John Black put an advertisement in the *Macleod Gazette*, mischievously welcoming "the white subjects and red allies of her Gracious Majesty" to his new store.

The classic rodeo picture from the 1912 Calgary Stampede, with the Blood rodeo cowboy Tom Three Persons riding the notorious outlaw Cyclone to a standstill, making an Indian the first to win the competition.

This remarkable photograph taken in 1912 catches the promise of Chinook country at the time, the Packard Model 30 touring car signaling a new era for all its passengers. The driver is the provincial treasurer Malcolm MacKenzie; sitting beside him in the front seat is the Peigan head chief Leans Over Butchering; behind are Bull Plume and their friend Ned Maunsell; three Peigan fellow travelers are in the backseat.

9

SETTLING INTO THE FOOTHILLS

JACK COWDRY AND HIS NEW BRIDE were part of a long line of settlers in the foothills. Newcomers had been arriving in southern Alberta for centuries: from the east and north, following the beaver and the buffalo; from the west across the mountains, hunting and fishing in summer and fall; from the south, seeking the shelter of the wooded coulees and benchlands in the front range of the Rockies in fall and winter. And all of them were looking for new opportunities.

Jack Cowdry didn't have a trade or a profession, and although he knew horses he didn't yet know the cattle business. But he had some modest funds, a brother whom he trusted, and a fiancée who believed in him. So when he returned to Fort Macleod in late August of 1885, with a wedding date set for December, he turned to the task at hand. A house for him and Amy could wait until the fall; right now, he had to decide about the bank.

The town itself expanded considerably in the late 1880s, with I. G. Baker one of the main shops, selling not only groceries, dry goods, and hardware but also ranching supplies such as saddles and harnesses and wagons. Tony La Chappelle's candy and tobacco store and billiard saloon continued to be a local gathering place; a former trader started another blacksmith's shop, while a former boatbuilder for the Hudson's Bay Company in the north opened a carpenter's shop, and an ex-policeman a bootmaker's shop, the second in town. More gambling establishments opened up, with faro and poker the preferred games and high stakes the preferred limit—Jack Cowdry liked cards, and certainly had a gift for numbers, so he was a regular—and over the next couple of years more lawyers arrived, a barber shop opened next to the shoemaker's, and a dentist came to town for ten days each month. Soon there were several more hotels and saloons and grocers, as well as stores offering a wider range of horse tack and wagon rigging and general agricultural supplies, as well as household appliances and homemaking goods.

Jack and Nat chose a site between the Queen's Hotel and the Athletic Saloon on Main Street, and built a small banking shop with boards from the river bottom (where some of the timber from the old fort had ended up) which they hauled up on foot, or hitched onto any wagon that passed by. They had help on the building from the local tinsmith and hardware merchant Al Grady, the jack-of-all-trades D. W. Davis, and Ned Maunsell, who brought along a couple of his friends from the Blood reserve. They were joined by the North-West Mounted Police surgeon George Kennedy and Big Swan, the Peigan chief, whom Jack had met on one of his rides to the country around Pincher Creek (where many of the ranches were located). By the following summer they were ready. They opened the bank in the fall of 1886, with advertisements soon appearing in the *Macleod Gazette* for "Cowdry Brothers: Bankers and Financial Agents. Drafts Issued on and Collections made on all Available Points. Drafts, Cheques and Sterling Exchange Bought."

They began their loans in town with the local livery stable (as crucial back then as a gas station and car mechanic are in a small town now); Jack had checked out the stable carefully long before the bank opened. And soon they extended their business not just to ranchers—who became their mainstay—but to grocers, auctioneers, hardware merchants, saddlers, builders, undertakers, lawyers, and pharmacists, among others, many of whom brought money in as well as borrowed it. These relationships continued even after the arrival of the chartered banks in the foothills later in the 1890s; they could sometimes offer lower rates—but not better service, or the flexibility that was Cowdry Brothers' trademark. Loyalty and friendship played a part in their business, of course; but their hardscrabble customers would not have stayed with them if it put their livelihood at risk. The bank had a few fairly secure institutional customers, lending funds to the government-run Indian agency on occasion; and during the 1890s they routinely underwrote the payroll of the North-West Mounted Police. But most of their business was with ranchers and merchants and the men and women holding households together.

As for the Blackfoot, Fort Macleod was substantially dependent on them, for the treaty had given the town as much life and purpose as the police and the ranchers did. Treaty payment day in November was a special occasion. After bonus payments the first year, payments of five dollars were made annually to each man, woman, and child on the reserves, with the minor chiefs and councillors receiving fifteen dollars and chiefs twenty-five dollars; and then, as David Laird had said in his address to the tribes during the Treaty Seven gathering, "you can spend as you please [and] buy what you think proper." Which they did, with pleasure and to the delight of the town merchants, as a description in the *Macleod Gazette* in 1888 confirms.

> *One of the important annual events in this part of Alberta is the treaty payments to the Blood and Peigan Indians, or rather the trading in town which follows. . . . The Peigans came first. On Saturday the Blood procession began, and all day Sunday they arrived in droves of hundreds. . . . On Monday morning it was estimated there was close onto 2000 Indians in town. The stores*

were simply packed with men, women, children and dogs. During almost the entire morning it was absolutely impossible to get from one end of I.G. Baker and Co.'s store to the other. It is safe to say that no city in the Dominion of Canada presented the same stir as Macleod did on Monday last.

The merchants and the Blackfoot both looked forward to the treaty day trips to town: the local newspaper announced payment days with great enthusiasm despite the occasional grumble about the small-town inconvenience of large crowds. The local ranchers also benefited from the treaty, for its ration commitments (now that the buffalo had gone) gave them a reliable local market. In normal times, the Blood and the Peigan (whose reserves were near town) consumed over two thousand head of cattle in a year, along with 3,700 sacks of flour—1½ pounds of meat and ¼ pound of flour per person per day; and when ranching and farming became well established on the reserves, Fort Macleod continued to be the main center for their agricultural supplies. There was provision in the treaty for an annual purchase of ammunition, and rifles and suits of clothing were provided for chiefs and councillors, along with axes, handsaws, augers, files, and whetstones. A few cows were given to families who wanted them, or hoes and spades and scythes and pitchforks, along with a plow and harrow, for those who wished to take up farming. And teachers' salaries were to be paid.

There were Department of Indian Affairs buildings on both reserves, the construction of which enriched the town and its trades, and the department provided settler employment to a number of trades and professions as well as to the Indian agents. As employees of the federal government, responsible for the application of the repressive Indian Act, the Indian agents were insulated from local influence, but they were far from headquarters in Ottawa and had to manage relations with the Blackfoot, as well as with other federal authorities such as the police, on their own—which fostered some very personal and occasionally pernicious conduct. The presence of some of these agents greatly disturbed the Blackfoot; but there were exceptions, and even in the darkest hours some bright lights.

Of course the North-West Mounted Police also represented a significant presence in the town, spending a good amount of money from government funds for supplies, and for goods and services from their own salaries; and like the ranchers and merchants they too often found themselves onside with the Blackfoot. During the latter part of the 1880s, it was estimated that over $100,000 (around two and a half million dollars in today's currency) was spent annually from these sources in and around Fort Macleod.

Overall these revenues (treaty payments aside) benefited the newcomers to the territory. As for the Blackfoot, reserve life and broken promises hardly seemed a fair exchange for having "ceded, released, surrendered, and yielded up" to the government of Canada the rights, titles, and privileges to their hunting grounds—language that was not appreciated by them at the time, and nearly a hundred and fifty years later is still not accepted as representing the spirit of the treaty. But they had agreed to keep the peace, an agreement they have kept. The treaty may have been a good deal for the town, but it became clear it was not a good one for the Blackfoot.

Jack Cowdry was well aware that if there had been no Blackfoot there would have been no Fort Macleod. And thus no opportunity for Cowdry Brothers Bank to play a significant part in the success of ranching in the foothills, and of the businesses in that part of the territory.

Jack Cowdry was an enabler by instinct, and relied on a word and a handshake. And he was seldom disappointed. He listened to the talk of the town, often providing funds for ventures written off by others, or to individuals whose reputation was down. Nobody's perfect, he would say—and go ahead, if he felt, well, confident (or at least cautiously optimistic). That was one advantage of a private bank—you had nobody to answer to except yourself . . . and your brother. Over the twenty years that Jack ran the bank, very few of the bank's loans went bad; and there were only a couple of occasions when he found himself in court. One was almost comical: it was to accept a proposal, called a "discontinuance," from Ned Maunsell to cancel a legal action that Maunsell himself had started, in a bad mood, having to do with a loan. When it was done, Jack Cowdry turned around and loaned him some more money. The other time involved a lawyer who, as one contemporary observer remarked, "found a quibble and dwelt on it." It came to nothing.

Of course, some of his clients were a bit slippery . . . but not with Jack. Probably one of his favorites was Dave Cochrane, a successful rancher and renowned maker of mischief. He had been notorious as a whisky smuggler, and continued his craft long after the police had shut down the trade. He knew the routine of the North-West Mounted Police well, since he had joined the force in its early days; and after he left he would frequently fool the officers by drawing attention to himself after making handoffs to others, so that he would be arrested and distract the police until his associates could make their way to market in town (often selling to the very same police officers).

Dave Cochrane also liked taking things, "liberating" anything that wasn't tied down . . . and untying some things that were. There was a story that he once took the shingles off a neighbor's house while the owner was inside; but an even better one, and unquestionably true, involves a stove—a North-West Mounted Police stove. It seems a new stove had been delivered to the barracks, and was sitting out back while the police did some renovations inside to make room for it. Cochrane liked the looks of that stove. But it was very heavy, and much too close to the building for anybody to move without being seen, even someone as experienced at "moving" merchandise as Cochrane. So he devised a plan. Every few days, while passing by the fort on some made-up business or other, he would take one small item from the stove—a grate, a lifter, a damper, or a door—until soon the stove was looking pretty broken up, but still bright and clean. But Cochrane had a solution for that: water. He doused the stove with water, and within a short time it was rusty, and impressively decrepit. Then one day Cochrane drove up to the fort in his wagon, and said he was cleaning up some junk around town and had noticed some behind the fort. He went to look with one of the officers; and there, amid some broken-down rigging and remains of wagons and such, was a rusting shell of a stove. The officer said they'd be glad to get rid of it all, and would be very happy if Cochrane would take it away . . . and off went the stove in the wagon. A few weeks later, one of his friends on the force was visiting Cochrane in his home and noticed a beautiful new stove there, all cleaned up bright and shiny and working just fine. "Just got it," said Cochrane to the officer, who thought he recognized the stove but said nothing. They all knew Dave Cochrane.

But he didn't mess with Jack Cowdry, and their dealings were clear and clean. And for anyone who thought the Blackfoot were not quick to pick up the principles of the market, Cochrane himself had a story about the early days in town, before the railway was through to Calgary, when almost all the supplies were still coming from Fort Benton by bull train. Groceries were always at a premium, and store-keepers would corner the market in the fall, with prices for sugar and bacon sometimes rising substantially in spring until a new shipment arrived. One November, after treaty payment, a young Blackfoot came to town to spend his money, and was told that some groceries were in scarce supply. He knew the folks well, and assumed they were saying this not because he was an Indian but because they were scheming storekeepers hoarding their goods until spring; but he was angry. He was also smart. Fighting fire with fire, he went around and bought out all the sugar he could purchase from every store in town, paying twenty-five cents per pound. He held it until spring, and sold it for fifty cents. He was Cochrane's hero.

A few years later, when Jack Cowdry's bank was up and running, C. E. D. (or Charlie) Wood published the following story in the *Macleod Gazette* under the heading "No Bank in Town" in a section devoted to lighthearted and good-humored stories from various parts of the world. This one was from the western American frontier, set in a town like Fort Macleod.

The Colonel had the freighting of all the provisions over the trail from Silver City to Johnsonville, and also owned the only stage line, and one day he called the boys together at the White Wolf saloon and said:

"Boys, what this town needs is a bank, and I'm thinking of starting one. I thought I would call you all together and see how you would take it. Joe Henderson, would you come in and draw a check, same as other folks do in the east?"

"Not if the sight of a gun would answer just as well," replied Joe.

"And how about you, Tom Smith?"

"I feel like I'd kinder want to clean out the shop, colonel."

"And you, Bill Johnson?"

"I wouldn't fool with no checks, as you call 'em."

"Well, the crowd seems to be ag'in me," sighed the colonel, "but I'd like to hear from Pete Green."

"How much money would there be in that 'ere bank, Kurnel Taylor?" asked Pete in reply.

"I'd start it with $5000."

"And who would handle it?"

"I will myself."

"And you'd be right thar ten minits after the bank opens for bizness?"

"Of course I will."

"Well, then, kurnel, there ain't no need of guessin what I'd do. I'd be right on hand with two guns, and them guns would be ready fur shootin, and I'd lay the bar'ls on the counter and say:

"'Good mornin, Kurnel Taylor.'

"'Good mornin, Pete Green.'

"'Is this bank open fur bizness?'

"'She are.'

"'Then hand me over them $5000 as quick as ye kin handle money, fur my fingers hev got the cramps and will be pullin on these triggers if ye wait to catch your breath!'"

The colonel treated the crowd and decided to keep out of the banking business.

Jack Cowdry must have been amused to see it in the *Gazette*, for there, on the front page, was the advertisement for Cowdry Brothers Bank that had appeared every week since it opened.

His own local "Kurnel," Colonel James Macleod, had been enthusiastic about the bank, but he became even more encouraging when Jack told him about his fiancée, Amy. There weren't many women in the settler community in those early days, and Macleod knew that his wife, Mary, would be delighted; and when Jack went for dinner with the Macleods the following week, Mary assured him that Amy would have a warm welcome and good company in the territory. When she herself arrived, Mary told him, she had hired a woman she met on the boat going up the Missouri River to Fort Benton as a housekeeper. Her name was Annie Saunders, and she lived with them the years they were in Fort Macleod, helping with the children, and then, when James Macleod left the police force, moved with them to Pincher Creek and set up for herself. Annie used to say that when she and Mary arrived they were the first white women in the foothills; and the humor wasn't lost on anyone who knew them. Annie Saunders was black. Known as "Auntie" (a name *she* chose to call herself, perhaps partly as a way of preempting any other names that new settlers might bring to town along with their prejudices), in Pincher Creek she ran a laundry operation; welcomed guests to her boarding house (with "good accommodation for ladies"); and had a dining room that catered to everyone from the policemen after a baseball game, the Anglican church choir, costume parties with dancing through the night, and the Marquess of Lorne. One posh visitor noted that Auntie's establishment was "of a much higher character than Kamoose Taylor's," but nobody else was making comparisons. She was one of a kind, like Kamoose and many others in a place full of characters and contradictions.

After their wedding in December 1885, Jack Cowdry settled with Amy into the new house he had built—he liked building things—and for Amy he had designed one with two stories and a shingle roof, bought from a new mill close to town. They found a neighbor, Marie Cumming, to help with the housework, and with the children they hoped to have. "Sweet Marie" she was called by everyone in town; and she continued to assist the Cowdry family through Jack's time there, later marrying a North-West Mounted Police officer who had come to Macleod the same year Jack did. Amy and Jack's first-born, Mary, came along early in 1887; their son Fred was born the following year, but died within weeks; and then Augustus, or Gus, was born in 1890.

The buffalo had gone, cattle and cowboys—and horses—were roaming the Plains, and the Blackfoot were settling by the rivers and on the benchlands of their old territory, taking up ranching and farming and entering each season with a new sense of surprise, though without the possibilities for hunting and gathering that had sustained them for generations. Meanwhile, new settlers were moving along the trails and rails and into the scattered homesteads and small towns of the foothills. It was a new way of life for everyone; and they were making it up as they went along, making friendships and finding common cause as well as making trouble and finding fault.

Crop Eared Wolf and his father, Red Crow, had been among the first to take up farming, storing their potatoes in a root cellar they dug, and distributing them to band members over the winters. Red Crow had been gathering and breeding horses for a long while, and by the time the Blood settled on their reserve in 1883 he had a large herd, which made him a wealthy man by any standard, his stature measured by the fact that he paid a hundred horses to acquire (in an exchange sanctioned by traditional practice) a medicine pipe that was one of the most sacred items on the reserve. Crop Eared Wolf himself became one of the first Blood Indians to start raising cattle, trading fifteen horses for the same number of cows and a bull; and Red Crow had turned horses to the plow by 1889. In 1890, he built a large stable, putting up twenty tons of hay for the winter while his wife, Singing Before, bought a milk churn and a sewing machine for their home, bringing venerable Blackfoot skills to work with settler technologies. By the 1890s there were substantial herds of farm and ranch animals and rodeo and racing horses on the Blood reserve; and by the end of that decade, cattle ranching had taken its place among the Blood, with band members owning over two thousand head. They took to ranching easily, for managing great herds had always been an aspect of hunting buffalo. Indeed, the Blackfoot understood the management of herd animals, especially in their foothills home-land, better than many of the newcomers. And they continued to amass large horse herds, selling some of the stock to local ranches and the North-West Mounted Police.

Horse races brought together the Blackfoot and the newcomers more than almost anything else. The races at Fort Macleod were on a track laid out for the purpose at the edge of town: one mile for the fastest horses, a half mile for the cow ponies, and slow races for mules and plodding ponies, with good prize money. The Blood and Peigan brought their horses to run against the others, and that mix of Indian and settler participation became the norm in the foothills. (There were also quarter-mile races, a quarter mile being the rough distance down the main street in many towns in the Old West; and what we call a "quarter horse" got its name from the races that were run there. The considerable width of these main streets, on the other hand, was designed to leave room for a mule team or an ox train to turn around.)

Horse races were usually straight, rather than on a circuit; and although this reflected the British practice, it also copied the Plains Indians, who held races that sometimes covered a distance as far as the eye could see on the open plains—which, interestingly, made them about the same length (four miles or so) as the racecourses that were common in England in the eighteenth and nineteenth centuries. Races of this distance were often run in the foothills in the early 1880s. George Murdoch, the first mayor of Calgary, describes in his journal a race meet just after he arrived in the territory in 1883. "Attended races. One five mile race between the Police, One Blackfoot, One Sarcee, One Stoney . . . Blackfoot won. I bet on Blackfoot."

Fort Macleod had put on the first fall fair in the foothills in 1886, the year after Jack and Nat arrived, with vegetable, flower, and livestock exhibitions, along with horse races and a rodeo—and of course a parade (the staple of such gatherings for thousands of years around the world) along the dusty main street that ran through the small town. Those parades quickly became an important part of all the town fairs in the territory, with Indian riders and their horses and travois decked out in their finery to the delight of the crowd. And from early days the North-West Mounted Police set another precedent for collaboration by joining the parade ritual with their Musical Rides, later parading in London for Queen Victoria's Jubilee in 1897. The first Musical Ride was performed in Regina in 1887 (though Fort Macleod claims precedence, with a training ride there in 1876). Not only were cowboys and Indians competing together in the rodeo, as they were on the range, but they were fellow travelers with the police on the parade circuit.

In 1891, a rodeo at the end of the Fort Macleod fair had marquee billing, and is often said to have been the first "real rodeo" in Alberta, though riding and roping competitions had been around for a couple of decades. Two of the best bronc riders in the territory were competing: Johnny Franklin against Billy Stewart. Jack Cowdry said that both Franklin and Stewart rode their pitching, bucking, wriggling, spinning horses to a standstill in such sensational style that the competition was declared a tie. A couple of years later, Calgary held its first rodeo, organized by George Lane to settle an argument about who was the best roper in the territory. Lane took four minutes before he was able to rope and tie his wayward steer. Then John Ware, riding a horse without a bridle, threw a loop as the steer came out of the chute, sprang off his horse, and had him tied in fifty-one seconds. The crowd, who knew and loved Ware first of all as a bronc rider in Johnny Franklin and Billy Stewart's class, went wild with delight. (As for Johnny Franklin, he went on to become a successful rancher as well as one of the greatest bronc riders of his day, and when the first Calgary Stampede was held in 1912, he was asked to judge the bronc-riding events.)

Other activities on horseback were also popular, including an unlikely game—polo. Indeed, one of the earliest polo games played in North America (some say the very first, though New York probably deserves that honor) was in the mid-1880s at Pincher Creek, with equipment ("real sticks and balls," according to the local newspaper) brought back from England by a local rancher. And in another unlikely setting, John Ware "rode to hounds," chasing coyotes and rabbits with a pack of dogs (in a hunt modeled after the Quorn Hunt of Leicestershire by the English syndicate that bankrolled the Quorn ranch northwest of Macleod).

Beginning in 1880, the Canadian government issued grazing leases to large ranching enterprises—up to a hundred thousand acres, at one cent per acre per year—for twenty-one years. In some cases, the ranchers didn't own any property at all; the Bar U, for instance, only secured deeded land in 1891, nearly ten years after the ranch began operation. Not surprisingly, many of these leases went to individuals and groups with good contacts in Ottawa; but most were serious about ranching. If they weren't and didn't meet their "hoof and home" obligations, they had their leases canceled.

Ranching *was* a favored enterprise, even though many of the smaller ranchers didn't feel very special. Many of them had to work at other jobs; and they were vulnerable to forces that felt even more unpredictable than the weather, such as the practices and priorities of the railway for transporting their cattle to market. But even if ranchers didn't have large leaseholdings, they benefited from a land lease system that inhibited piecemeal farm settlement, and that sustained the grasslands in a way that would be the envy of many contemporary environmentalists.

Ranchers were committed to responsible land use for the next generation. But this raises a question. Whose land were they looking after? Rangeland in the United States was deemed "public land"; in Canada, it was "Crown land." The idea of Crown land—the Great Mother's land—may have offered the Blackfoot some comfort as being closer to their understanding of territory. But it involved turning land that was Blackfoot by covenant with the Great Spirit into land that was in the constitutional safekeeping—and special giving—of the Great Mother's government. A sleight of hand; and as soon as they took stock of the treaty, it didn't fool the Blackfoot.

One thing that made some difference to them—especially the Blood and the Peigan—was the richness of the rangeland on their reserves, which allowed them to build up and graze large herds of cattle and horses. For the ranchers, the open range of Crown land under lease gave them what was sardonically referred to by farmers and others as "free grass"—albeit within a long-range strategy that required attention to environmental principles, which is to say to its carrying capacity in a region where drought was the norm. As the Blackfoot knew well, overgrazing the open range in summer meant there would be no grass for winter, and that meant the ranchers would soon be out of business.

Still, the land lease system privileged the large ranchers; in addition, large ranchers were able to pay cowboys to round up their herds from the open range in the spring and move them about all summer, while those with smaller herds couldn't afford those labor costs, needing instead to keep the cattle close at hand and supplement winter grazing with hay and grain. And even if their cattle were ranging with the large herd, at roundup and branding time the cattle of small-holders ran the risk of being absorbed, willy-nilly, into the large herds.

Most of all, the open range created tension between the ranchers, both large and small, and the settlers, who wanted to break up the range into small parcels protected by the newly invented, relatively cheap barbed wire. When John Lomax published his *Cowboy Songs and Other Frontier Ballads*, he struck an elegiac note when he said, "The nester [the small farmer] has come, and come to stay. Gone is the buffalo, the Indian warwhoop, the free grass of the open plain."

Homesteaders were able to settle in the foothills only on those Crown lands that were not leased by ranchers under the twenty-one-year leases; it wasn't until 1896 that the government canceled all the big leases (notice of the change had been given in 1892), allowing ranchers to buy back 10 percent of the land they had originally leased and reapply for leases on the rest. This leveled the plains for small and medium-size spreads, though water rights continued to be contentious as farmers and ranchers and townsfolk, as well as the Blackfoot on the reserves, competed for scarce water resources on the semi-desert land. In order to provide some protection for the ranchers, settlers couldn't block access to streams and springs for the cattle; and the reserves were strictly off-limits to settlement. Unregulated squatters, on the other hand, settled wherever they could, though seldom for long on reserve land, and continued to be described with generalized contempt.

The barbed wire fences were easy to set up and hard for the cattle to get past. Fences and farmers would ultimately choke the open range, or at least severely compromise it. "Don't fence me in" became a catchy refrain for good reason. In the words of an Alberta cowboy, "Barb wire is what ruined this country. At first we could keep it cut pretty well, and use the posts for firewood, but it got so, after a while, they were putting up the damned stuff faster than a guy could cut it down. Every homesteader has his little bit fenced off, and there was that whole stretch between Standoff and Fort Kipp . . . When I saw that I said to myself, I says, 'This country's done for'—and you see now I was right."

10

CHINOOK COUNTRY

ALTHOUGH THEY HAD SEEN EACH OTHER several times since their first meeting on the main street in Fort Macleod in 1885, Jack Cowdry made a visit to Crop Eared Wolf at his home on the Blood reserve at Stand Off, southeast of Fort Macleod, in March of 1887. It was a surprise, in more ways than one, to both of them.

The winter had been brutally cold, thirty to forty below every morning for six weeks, and once it went down to fifty-one below. On March 10, Jack left Fort Macleod on the way to Lee's Creek, south of the Blood reserve. A local rancher's description of riding out in winter to check on the herd gives a sense of the dress code back then.

> *I have a good buffalo skin cap, made to my own order, which covers my ears and has a strip across the nose, then I have a woolen comforter round my neck, then a buffalo coat, buckskin mitts with knitted mitts inside them on my hands . . . then buffalo trousers, and on my feet a pair of woolen socks, over them a pair of thick lined German socks and over these a pair of buffalo moccasins, hair side in and wrapped over these and the bottoms of my buffalo trousers to keep the wind from going up the legs, I wrap horse bandages.*

There was an unusual amount of snow on the ground this winter of 1886/87, up to a foot and a half on the low-lying land; and there had been only one brief Chinook since before Christmas. But Jack was feeling good, turning thirty in a few weeks, and he and Amy were happily settled. When the weather was cold, travel was easy; and he started off expecting to reach Lee's Creek in a couple of days. He had heard about a proposed Mormon settlement there, and the first large group did indeed arrive by wagon train later that spring; and he may have had in mind some banking opportunities. But this trip was about something more personal. His oldest brother, William, had died in 1855 (at the age of sixteen) back in Ontario, in a tragic hunting accident. Jack never knew him, since he had been born two years after William's death; but the tragedy—and that terrible year, when two of his other siblings had also died—marked his family in ways he had never really understood. They all took some comfort in the "mysterious dispensations" that the preachers talked about; but then each of them, father and mother, three sons and the one daughter still living, found their own ways of coming to terms, inevitably awkward terms, with their family's lives and deaths. One of the reasons Nat and Jack got on so well was that they respected each other's ways.

In Jack's case, this involved Lee's Creek, which flowed down from the sacred Chief Mountain, the towering spirit of the foothills and Fort Macleod. The creek had been named after Lee Kaiser, a bullwhacker who accidentally shot himself in a hunting accident in 1872; and Jack had the idea that going there might be a way of paying respect to his brother, and to the dreadful wonder of his death. A curious way, perhaps; but Jack's ways were often . . . well, let's just say unusual.

He had been down in that direction, south of Fort Macleod, several times the previous fall before winter set in, so he knew the trail. Earlier snowfalls had filled many of the coulees, but the weather had been dry for a week or two, and the snow covering the short grass on the higher ground was blown thin. The cattle had scraped and snuffled their way through but some had died from the bitter cold, their carcasses scattered across the winter range or piled in the coulees; and since many of them were carrying calves, the spring count did not look promising. From what he saw around him, Jack knew the bank would be in for a rough ride later. The ranchers would not be able to pay off their loans, and some of the merchants in town wouldn't either—like his friend Al Grady, who had opened a hardware store a couple of years before and expanded last fall—because they relied on the ranchers for their trade. But at least this ride would give him a chance to see what shape some of his customers' cattle and horses were in after the past terrible winter, and what to expect.

Charles M. Russell, one of the great painters of the Old West, had done a watercolor that winter of a skeletal starving cow surrounded by several wolves in Judith Basin in Montana, called *Waiting for a Chinook*, which had brought him his first recognition. Russell came to southern Alberta the following summer, his experiences with the ranchers and the Blackfoot there helping to shape his career. He would do a painting of his friend George Lane (of the Bar U ranch) being attacked by a pack of wolves in the foothills, one of which bit off the toe-cover on Lane's stirrup before he shot him; and while the story was often told (mostly by Lane himself) in the foothills, it is a measure of the role of visual images in storytelling that it was Russell's painting *George Lane Attacked by Wolves* that made the incident famous.

Traveling was easy for Jack Cowdry that first day, and he expected to reach Lee's Creek the following afternoon. He made camp in a little coulee, fairly free of snow because it caught the wind, but with enough shelter for his horse, which he tethered in the cottonwoods down by the frozen creek. (I still have the homemade sleeping bag my grandfather Jack used during those years, with no zipper or buttons but a heavy sheet and blankets sewn into what we would now call a mummy bag, on top of which he would throw a wrap of heavy canvas and the horse blanket from under the saddle, still steaming and warm.)

The next morning, after a breakfast of johnnycakes and bacon that Jack cooked on a little fire fed by some cottonwood and serviceberry branches (instead of the old standby, buffalo chips), he rolled up his bags, saddled his horse, and continued south. It was clear and cold; but in an hour or so he saw the unmistakable Chinook arch of cloud and a belt of blue in the western sky, and could feel the temperature rising. And then he began to notice the small splashes of water as he rode across another little creek up onto the benchlands above the Belly River.

Chinooks work like a refrigerator in reverse. When westerly winds carrying moist air from the Pacific hit the Rockies, the air cools as it rises, dropping rain and then snow. If the conditions are right the air—nicely dried—will slide down the eastern slopes of the Rockies several thousand feet to the plains below. Cold air heats up when it falls, because the air is denser and the pressure higher at lower altitudes; and dry air warms twice as fast as moist air. The warm air pushing out the cold creates the wind called a Chinook, raising the temperature dramatically. Chinooks were always welcome in the middle of winter, but they came with a warning. If they melted the ice, a traveler could be stranded on the wrong side of a river for days, maybe weeks. This one came with a vengeance, and within hours there was flooding everywhere. At Fort Macleod, three of the new telegraph poles on the west shore of the Old Man's River and two on the east side were broken in two by enormous blocks of ice smashed into them by the floodwaters; and all the southern rivers were impassable with the crushing ice floes sweeping by.

The cattle weren't paying attention to the rivers, at least at first. They sensed a change, a new lease on life. They wouldn't have to scuffle and scrape anymore. They looked up to the sky in a moment of faith, and stumbled on through the crud and the crust in a mellow mood. The temperature, which had been well below freezing that morning, was up into the fifties by now. The snow started to melt; and before long they could see the grass underneath the water that covered the land.

But this Chinook was breathtakingly short-lived. The cold weather came again, hard and fast, and within a very short while the water covering the grass was frozen so hard that the cattle couldn't break through. It was much worse now than it had been with the snow cover.

Late February to early March was known as the Uncertain Moon in the Blackfoot calendar, and it was the most dangerous time for snow blindness, with the intense glare of the sun, still low in the sky, on the snow and the ice. Snow blindness could be deadly, and Jack Cowdry had heard about it; but even Jerry Potts got caught a couple of times. So did Jack this day, with the glaze of water on the snow and ice dazzling his eyes. But he trusted his horse, and let him have his head. The horse, for his part, wondered what on earth was the matter with the old boy, but wasn't complaining because with his big ears and big nose and big eyes (with big lashes to keep off the sun), he could hear and smell and soon see the horses of Crop Eared Wolf and his band, where he found a warm welcome for both himself and Jack.

Crop Eared Wolf greeted Jack Cowdry, and praised the sorrel— the horse—for getting him there. He took Jack into his house, and saw him through. Jack's eyes eventually recovered, though he couldn't see for a couple of days, and he had a fierce headache, for both of which Crop Eared Wolf had remedies; and he had sent a rider to Amy to let her know that Jack was all right. When he was feeling a bit better, Crop Eared Wolf took him to his tipi, where a good fire had been laid in the hearth, and they smoked a pipe, which kept them in a conversation when words ran out. But then the Methodist missionary John Maclean came by, and thanks to his fluency in Blackfoot the three of them talked for hours together about their lives, and about the challenges they were all facing now after a hard winter, though it seemed the Blood horses at least had come through well.

Maclean told Jack Cowdry and Crop Eared Wolf about a reprimand he had received from Medicine Calf, the former war chief and one who initially opposed Treaty Seven. Maclean had put out new ropes to tether his horses one night . . . and woke up to find the ropes gone. He told Medicine Calf (of whom he said to Jack on another occasion, "His word was true, and promises were never broken, and I was glad to number him among my friends"), and shortly afterward Medicine Calf came to return his ropes, and to give him a dressing-down. "I thought you were a wise man," he said to the missionary. "Would you put new ropes on your horses and turn your animals out to graze in the white man's town? No, I would not do that. Would you expect to find your ropes again? No! And you tempt our young Indians. Do you think we have no bad men in our camps? You are not very wise if you expect our people to be perfect, and different from white men." (In a journal note from around that time Maclean identified for himself several "noble men—orators—dignified statesmen" among the Blackfoot, listing Crowfoot, Red Crow, Medicine Calf and White Calf [his successor as war chief], and Crop Eared Wolf.)

Knowing that Jack Cowdry had started a bank, Maclean said he was glad because he had just lent one of the Blood some money to buy a wagon and another young man some cash, and he wasn't sure how to handle the paperwork because it was money he had from the Methodist headquarters in Toronto, and he didn't like asking his friends to sign pieces of paper when he trusted their word. Jack said he would go with a handshake for something like that. And then they listened to Crop Eared Wolf tell them about sacred Chief Mountain.

Wonder comes in various guises, which need to be factored into our understanding of Aboriginal life, as well as our own. Ironically, and despite what may be our skepticism about the wonders they were promoting, some of the missionaries in Blackfoot territory were ahead of their time in recognizing this. John Maclean, for example, described how he was sternly corrected, as one might correct a child, when he questioned why food and implements left for the use of the dead (placed on a platform in a tree or raised on a scaffold) were still there years after. "These are spirits and they live on the souls of these things," he was told. "We are material, and we live on the matter of these things."

Maclean was a refreshingly independent spirit, and he had the respect of many Blackfoot friends, some of them among the angriest over what was happening to them. In 1889 he received a letter from the Methodist Committee in Toronto, which employed him, asking how it was that after nine years he had not converted a single person. (In fact, many of the missionaries of various denominations had very few conversions to record among the Blood and the Peigan during these years . . . but many friends.) A few years later Maclean published a popular book in which he gave his answer. "We wish to make them white men," he wrote, "but they desire to become better Indians. They believe the native culture is best suited for themselves, and having developed under it, and enjoyed it so long, they care not to give it up for an untried system. There is a danger of educating them away from their real life." For Maclean, the "real life" of the "real people" was part and parcel of their imaginative life—their stories and songs and Sun Dances and medicine bundles that confirmed who they were, and where they belonged; their knowledge of the land, the weather and the plants and animals that told them how to live there; and the spirits of place and power that spoke to them.

———

With Crop Eared Wolf's warm welcome never far from his mind, Jack Cowdry thought running a bank should be like running a hotel such as Harry Taylor's; he too would be in the business of hospitality—credit hospitality. And he believed in Jawbone credit, in a person's word and a handshake. Foolish familiarity would get you gone; but genial hospitality and good judgment would get you business, and keep business going.

Jack's approach clearly reflected the hospitality that was widespread in the foothills at the time, where everyone's latchstring was out—doors were never locked—and passing strangers were free to come in and help themselves to a meal or stay the night, as long as they left the place tidier than when they came. The I. G. Baker store in Fort Macleod routinely offered blankets off the shelves to ranchers who were in town for the night, saying, "It's your fault if you sleep cold; we only ask you to fold them up in the morning and put them back on the shelf." And John Maclean told about visiting one of the Blood tipis where he found a cowboy from one of the local ranches, seriously ill, being tended by the Indian family . . . just as Jack had been.

Jack Cowdry obviously loved the risks involved in banking, for almost every loan was a risk in that time and place; and he loved the fact that the skills he put to use managing risk at the bank were also useful playing cards at Tony La Chappelle's saloon, and betting on racehorses—which he also loved to do, even winning some blankets from Crop Eared Wolf. In any event, the Cowdry brothers seem to have managed their risks, and the responsibilities to their depositors, remarkably well. Certainly others admired their style and appreciated their support; Jack was routinely involved in all the affairs of the community, and later competitors such as the Bank of Commerce even appointed him as director for southern Alberta later in the 1890s. No other bank was as heavily involved in financing ranching operations in the foothills, even though that brought with it the ups and downs of the cattle business. Seasonal surprises, patterns and problems of family as well as commercial life, illness, all influenced business; and so did what could be the biggest surprise of all, the weather.

And it was the weather that winter of 1886/87 that put Jack Cowdry's tolerance for risk to the test, for the brothers almost lost the bank. It was, as Jack had expected after his trip in March, a disastrous season for the ranchers, and the roundup that spring became known as the Big Die-Up throughout the northern Plains. Whether clustering in the coulees or huddling out in the open, animals died in staggering numbers, often piling on top of each other as they crowded close together for warmth. The country around Pincher Creek suffered the fewest losses—which is to say thousands of cattle, not tens of thousands—and the cattle ranging on the Blood reserve came through fairly well, but the numbers of Blackfoot cattle were still small in comparison with the bigger ranches in the district, several of which lost half their herds, and some more. One of the most experienced cattlemen in southern Alberta, Tom Lynch, had brought in two hundred and ninety "dogies"—scrubby orphan calves—the previous fall and rounded up only eight in the spring. To quote L. V. Kelly, praising the resilience of the ranchers in *The Range Men*,

> *No business in the world can recuperate from losses that the cattle industry receives and recovers from. No known legitimate undertaking could meet the blows that the best ranches of this province come smilingly and hopefully through. No business, without insurance, could within three or four years be wealthier than it was before half its capital stock was utterly lost. What business, other than ranching, could have survived such damages as were experienced by the stockmen in 1886–87. . . .*

Well, Cowdry Brothers Bank, for one. But it was a close call. On top of the catastrophic losses, beef prices fell in Canada and the United States (for there were many more cattle going *into* that winter than the year before, and even though losses were high so was the inventory of cattle). For the Cowdry brothers, it was not a good start. Nat and Jack's experience in Saskatchewan had helped them judge the needs of farmers and ranchers, but there was no telling about the weather. Still, they took on the losses with the same resignation that their customers and the community displayed; and very few folks went under in Fort Macleod, kept afloat by the credit the bank extended, along with some interest-free loans, which helped almost all of them make it through. For there was still optimism in the midst of the wreckage, and some of the optimism must have been nourished by the bank's backing, and the Cowdry brothers' belief in the future. They were treading water themselves, but they made it to the next season all right, counting on local businesses in Fort Macleod as well as the North-West Mounted Police and the government Indian agencies—less immediately vulnerable to the weather—to have money on deposit that they could put back to the ranchers, and some cash in reserve. And they all learned some lessons about maintaining supplies of feed for cattle that could not find grass beneath snow cover, or could not get to the coulees and benchlands where feed was sometimes available. Cropping hay and grain became more common, and Jack and Nat supported such ventures, but farming in such a semi-arid region was always marginal. Some ranchers brought in sheep to replace cattle, but few of them had yet turned to "stock farming"—finishing cattle for market on hay and grain rather than raising a herd on the open range; and Ned Maunsell, who had been farming crops for a couple of years to supply the small-parcel settlers as well as the North-West Mounted Police, gave it up and made cattle ranching his principal business that summer on the heels of that terrible winter. He was undoubtedly encouraged by the contrarians Nat and Jack, for he quickly became one of Cowdry Brothers' biggest customers. Keeping cattle on the open range in winter under minimal supervision was still part of life, and from that year on Jack rode out frequently in winter to get a feel for the situation—though fortunately never again into the conditions he encountered on that trip to Lee's Creek and Crop Eared Wolf.

The first years of the bank were, to say the least, interesting ones, quite apart from that disastrous first winter. Fires were always a problem on the prairies, and fearsome stories of their spread haunted everyone who lived there. The railway had added a new threat with their "fire wagons," mitigated somewhat when they plowed an eight-foot fireguard alongside the tracks. But fires would continue to be a menace, especially with a wind that sometimes seemed to blow forever. So was liquor smuggling, which had never fully gone away, and everyone realized that it would probably be around until judgment day.

Jack and Nat Cowdry had developed a good trade with many ranchers, mostly small and medium-size, though by the 1890s they also had business dealings with Pat Burns and George Lane and Archie McLean and A. E. Cross, the big four who bankrolled the first Calgary Stampede; and with Ned Maunsell, who was building up a large herd and diversifying, buying up the old butcher business of I. G. Baker in 1892. Start-up costs for a ranch were substantial, but manageable with help from the Cowdrys. For a ranch of two thousand acres, the cost would be somewhere between fifteen and sixteen thousand dollars: $10,000 for the stock, including saddle horses; $2,500 for buildings, fencing, and equipment; $3,000 for incidentals; and $165 for a lease and homestead of a hundred acres. Some of the bank's customers had herds of fewer than a hundred and fifty head, such as the spread owned by Dave Cochrane; but they had many customers with larger herds, up to six hundred head, including William and John Black's. The Black brothers were stalwart supporters of the town as well as the countryside, where they had settled in 1884, and few enterprises in the foothills succeeded without their sometimes mischievous participation (often in concert with a banker named Jack Cowdry . . .). But their ranch was a serious venture, and Jack was delighted when they brought in a Devon bull from a famous breeder in England to beef up their herd. It was not only an ancient breed, from his father's home county, but its color was chestnut. Another sorrel.

The Cowdry brothers had counted on the success of local businesses in Fort Macleod, like the government somewhat less vulnerable to the weather, to have money on deposit to lend back to the ranchers; and in keeping that line clear, they protected their depositors and ensured the continued availability of funds to the community. And they had a strict agreement between themselves never to use bank funds to underwrite any of their own adventures (such as several rather doubtful mining enterprises in British Columbia that intrigued Jack Cowdry). They certainly saw their success as the community's. They had to earn their good names, but earn them they did. They secured the trust of the national banks from whom they needed to borrow money if Cowdry Brothers Bank were to grow; and during the 1890s their credit rating was remarkably high, especially for an unregulated bank.

In a familiar move, some of the ranchers—even those who had substantial spreads, like the Blacks—took other jobs to make ends meet. William Black hit the ground running when he first came to the territory, starting the ranch with his brother and at the same time joining in late 1885 with other folks in Fort Macleod to build a town hall. Since the modest property tax revenues all went to the

North-West Territories government, he and his newfound friends formed a joint stock company to fund the building. The shares sold out before the prospectus was printed, and the town hall was built within a few months, functioning as a school, a courthouse, and a very popular place for dances and concerts and public meetings. William Black also worked for Jack Cowdry in the bank for several years, before going to the Blood reserve to do the Indian agency accounts there.

His brother John started a business in town right opposite the Hudson's Bay Company, for which he had worked for several years, and his announcement of the opening of his store is a reminder that the sometimes rough-and-tumble folks in Fort Macleod were much more aware of things than we might expect. Recalling the distinction between "allies and friends" and "subjects" made by William Johnson in the 1700s, and the casual misrepresentations of Treaty Seven and its Blackfoot signatories that were voiced by some in town who cast them as "uncivilized" and "dependent wards," consider John's advertisement for his new general supplies store that he put in the newspaper:

> *John Black, the gentleman adventurer into Fort Macleod and the Belly River, authorized by low prices and popular satisfaction to do business with the white subjects and red allies of her Gracious Majesty.*

White *subjects* and red *allies*. With this cunningly contrary phrasing, he neatly turned things around for some of the townsfolk; and while no doubt this was lost on a few of them, we can also be sure that others would have enlightened them.

11

HOMELAND AND FRONTIER

NAT COWDRY HAD ALWAYS PLANNED to return to Ontario after they got the bank business going; but he stayed in Fort Macleod for a while longer, and in 1887 he married and brought his Bermuda-born wife, Anna, there. During that time, both he and Jack also nourished other interests—Jack in horses and cattle, as well as local and territorial politics and public service; and Nat in history, both natural and national. He gave a talk to Fort Macleod's newly formed Literary, Scientific and Historical Society in November 1887; and he published a long article—unusually long for that newspaper—in the *Macleod Gazette* the following January on local plants and trees, drawing heavily on local (which is to say Blackfoot) knowledge. He seems to have spent a good amount of his time there out and about the countryside.

Then, with the birth of their son, Vincent, in 1888, and Anna's health uncertain (she would die two years later), Nat took his family and went back east, giving Jack power of attorney over the bank and its business. It must have taken considerable faith in his brother for Nat to leave him in charge, since Jack was not as experienced as the older Nat, and almost all of Nat's money was bound up with the bank. But Nat trusted Jack. Over the next seventeen years (until the sale of the bank), they kept in close touch by telegraph and later telephone, and by frequent family visits.

After Nat left to go back to Ontario, he started a grain business and took a position in the local bank in Waterford, eventually managing it until it was taken over by the Bank of Commerce. He obviously played his part in that community too; and his interests in the natural sciences flourished. Much later, between 1919 and 1921, Nat spent time in China visiting his son, Vincent, who was there to establish a medical school in Peking funded by the Rockefeller Foundation, bringing traditional Chinese medicine into conversation with Western techniques. During the relatively short time he was in China, Nat collected and classified and described over 2,200 plants from the northern coast and mountains in a monograph, published by the Peking Society of Natural History after his death in 1925 as the *Cowdry Collection of Chihli Flora*.

In some of his letters to Nat, Jack writes how much he misses him and how he is now working twice as hard on his own, expanding the bank—cautiously—to the small towns close by, such as Pincher Creek, and trying to take on a central role in the southern Alberta ranching and business and civic communities. He seems to have had remarkably affectionate relations with his customers. There is the story about a North-West Mounted Police officer finding himself in difficulties after buying some stock in a gold mining company that went broke, and then facing dismissal from the force for being drunk on duty after an all-night wake for a friend. Even in this unfortunate state the officer felt moved to say to friends in the barracks, "I feel very sorry for Cowdry," because he had taken out a loan to buy the stock against his future salary. It all turned out well—after an inquiry he was "retired" from the force with a small pension.

But life was not all business for Jack, and maybe that contributed to the genial relations with his customers. He loved to get old and new friends together over a good meal to tell stories and listen to the music of what happened . . . and talk about what might happen next.

One of his dinner parties featured a summer feast of "tomato soup with bread in a napkin on the left; roast ducks with parsley garnish, gravy and apple sauce; scalloped potatoes, creamed celery and peas; and deep plum tart and sliced peaches for dessert, along with individual jellies with wine, whipped cream and macaroons." If asked about how all this gracious living, straight out of Victorian England or southern Ontario (there was little difference), fitted with being in Blackfoot territory, Jack probably would have said that Red Crow and Crop Eared Wolf often told him how important it was that he not give up the traditions of his people, because they would help him keep a sense of honor and humor and home—just as it was important, they would always add, that he not ask them to give up theirs. And he took that to apply not only to sacred ceremonies, sacrosanct as they were, but also to traditions of clothing and cooking and entertainment. This suited Jack just fine, for he was a bit of a dandy and liked dressing well and eating well and smoking cigars and drinking port of an evening and keeping up with the stories and songs and music and painting from his eastern Canadian and European heritage. He said holding on to such habits made him relish the ceremonies of the Blackfoot even more, which may have been an excuse, but he always brought it back to the Blackfoot and their horses dressed up in their wonderfully beaded and woven rigging. The men spent hours brushing and braiding the horses and as much time preening themselves, using tweezers to pull out any hairs on their face, for they prided themselves on their hereditary smooth faces, and their long, braided hair. As for Jack, he always took trouble trimming his sorrel-colored beard, which he sported all his life.

In the foothills during Jack Cowdry's time, one form of specifically Blackfoot storytelling irritated the white custodians of civil society —specifically the police, and sometimes (but not always) the missionaries. They were relatively comfortable with Blackfoot stories about war, because that sort of boasting was familiar to them; they had grown up reading about Achilles and the Trojan War, and the pages of the *Macleod Gazette* were full of news about whatever war the British happened to be engaged in, from the Afghan War that had just ended in 1880 to the African Boer Wars that began in the 1880s.

What bothered them was storytelling about stealing horses. They could see that horse stealing was a way of exalting the virtues of courage and cunning and conspicuous consumption, but they worried that it was also a way of exacerbating old conflicts, especially between tribes who had long been in competition with each other for territory and trade, and of engendering a proliferation of small but often deadly feuds. The authorities complained to the government, to each other and, in a completely futile gesture, to the Blackfoot chiefs about how ceremonial and social occasions like the traditional sacred Sun Dance gave warriors an opportunity to tell stories about old raids and their feats of bravery and achievement—including the number of horses they had gathered in from their enemies. "This," said Mounted Police Superintendent Sam Steele in 1889, "has a pernicious effect on the young men." Possibly it did—at least insofar as it inspired some of them to do what young people have done since the beginning of time: seek opportunities to match their elders' achievements by replicating their adventures. But it also gave these young men a sense of pride that was hard to come by in those days, and stories to share.

But the risks of retaliation were beginning to tell; and the chiefs of the Blackfoot did their best to discourage, and by 1890 to prohibit, raids against the Crow and the Assiniboine and the other Plains tribes south of the border, going so far as to return stolen horses and turn over the horse thieves to the police—though often misplacing evidence that they knew would be necessary to convict in court. Still, the stories kept coming, and helped to keep the Blackfoot together, proud and positive even when they were feeling oppressed. That, after all, is what stories do. Oscar Wilde, the great Irish trickster, once suggested that "we should live our life as a form of fiction. To be a fact is to be a failure." To be fully human, we need to both surrender to a story and separate ourselves from it; live in both grief-stricken reality and the grace of the imagination; believe the stories we are told, and not believe them too. The Blackfoot knew this— and by holding on to their stories they reminded the settlers that they did too.

Since the beginning of time, storytelling has inspired people to do things—or to imagine doing them. One story that was soon to capture the imagination of many people in the United States and Canada was Owen Wister's novel *The Virginian: A Horseman of the Plains*. It was, it is generally agreed, the first authentic western novel, and certainly the most popular; its hero displayed fierce pride and stubborn independence by heading west to make his way in the world. In the words of the writer Teresa Jordan, such heroes were "absorbed into so many family stories that one would think the trails west were blazed by armies of homeless fourteen-year-olds." And it became a kind of history of the West, with both American and Canadian connections, shaped by a storyteller's imagination of how people were assumed to live in the western territories, their destiny and doggedness so interwoven that they become indistinguishable. It was dedicated to Theodore Roosevelt; and when it came out in 1902, it was a bestseller across the continent.

As it turned out a rancher whom Jack Cowdry knew well, who had come to Canada from the United States in 1888 and taken over as foreman of the famous Bar U ranch from George Lane, was believed to be the *real* Virginian. His name was Everett (Ebb) Johnson, who had gone out to Wyoming from his birthplace in Virginia; later he guided Owen Wister on a trip he made to the West and inspired the novel. In the copy he inscribed to Johnson, Wister wrote "to the hero, from the author," and that's as good as it gets from a writer.

There was another part to the story that interested Jack Cowdry, especially with the attempted robbery of his bank in mind. Ebb Johnson had a couple of young cowboy friends back in Wyoming, where he had started his career at the famous "76" ranch in Powder River country. One was Robert Leroy Parker, though he gave his name as Butch Cassidy; the other was Harry Longabaugh. The three of them remained close for years. As mentioned, Longabaugh got himself into trouble (stealing a horse) and spent eighteen months in the jailhouse in the town of Sundance (Wyoming). When Longabaugh got out, Johnson wanted to help him, so he brought him up to the Bar U and gave him a job breaking horses. Unfortunately Longabaugh wasn't very good at it; next Johnson put him to work riding herd, which by all accounts he did fairly well. But Longabaugh was restless, and after a year he left the foothills and returned to his old habits and haunts in the United States, soon joining Butch Cassidy, finding a home with his Wild Bunch gang, and becoming notorious as the Sundance Kid. The Wild Bunch became some of the most famous outlaws, credited with a very large number of bank and train robberies, on the continent; but when Jack Cowdry had met Longabaugh along the bar in the Macleod Hotel, he was simply good-natured Harry, an amiable cowboy. Or maybe Jack just knew how to handle bank robbers.

Around this time, many people on both sides of the border were talking about the frontier and its meaning, the Canadians looking south for a cue and the Americans just looking around. In 1893, from May to October, the city of Chicago hosted a great fair called the World's Columbian Exposition, held (a year late) to commemorate the four-hundredth anniversary of Columbus's arrival in the Americas. During the fair, two notable storytellers took different stages and offered their different perspectives on the frontier. One was the historian Frederick Jackson Turner, who came to deliver a paper at a congress of historians on what he called "The Significance of the Frontier in American History." The other was the legendary Buffalo Bill Cody, and his show—twice a day opposite the fairground in a covered grandstand accommodating eighteen thousand people—was titled Buffalo Bill's Wild West and Congress of Rough Riders of the World. Together, Turner and Cody established markers for the mythologizing of the American West that continues to this day. But indirectly, they also offered a crucial perspective on the West in Canada at that time. In the United States, this moment was said to mark the closing of the frontier of so-called "empty Indian land" for the "taking" and "wilderness" for the "taming." In Canada, it marked a moment in which the national dream took over the native domain.

In Turner's account to his scholarly audience at the Exposition, the frontier in America was definitely over. (Though nobody told that to Butch Cassidy and the Sundance Kid, for whom the Wild West continued until the turn of the century; Jack Cowdry, for his part, believed that the frontier as Turner and Buffalo Bill Cody understood it had never really existed in Canada, and certainly not among the settlers he knew.) Turner proposed that "the existence of an area of free land, its continuous recession, and the advance of American settlement westward, explain American development"; and he suggested that—with the census of 1890 having concluded that all land available for "frontier" settlement within the United States had been claimed—the frontier was gone. Closed. History. Behind Turner's enormously influential account was the assumption that this so-called "free land" had been available for the "taking," an assumption that ignored not just the abstract idea of Indian sovereignty but the very real and unmistakable Aboriginal use and occupancy of most of the territory—unmistakable because, as Cody would insist, the Indians were *there* when the settlers arrived, attacking them at every turn to defend *their* territory (but Cody would skip over that last part).

On his stage, Turner argued that American progress (or what he called "development") required new settlers to experience the "prairie primitive" before they recapitulated the essential stages of Western civilization—from the primary phase of subsistence hunting and commodities trading to homestead farming and then farm communities, and eventually to secondary industrial production and sophisticated cultural practices. But in Turner's story, instead of the land that had been made available to settlers through several Homestead Acts beginning in 1862—one of which had been the Dawes Act (also called the General Allotment Act) of 1887, which displaced so many Indians—"education" was to be the key agent of progress now that the frontier days were done, and it would provide a new kind of freedom from the Old World chains of inherited power and privilege. Education was the way to move *beyond* the frontier, and also *beyond* being Indian—and here the storyline crossed the northern border, not with regard to the settlers but to the Indians, with school becoming the instrument of "advancement" and assimilation.

Not so many years earlier Chicago had been a fur-trading center and had only recently grown into a metropolitan city, so Turner's account had purchase with his audience. His image of the West before settlement was of a territory inhabited by a few Indians, roaming over "idle" land that belonged to no one. The fact that this was contradicted by maps of the West circulating through the nineteenth century, depicting a continent filled with people, did not distract Turner. Now that there were so many settlers (and fewer Indians) it was time to get on with Western civilization, and to redefine the frontier as a place of agricultural and industrial enterprise.

The sheer idiocy of this attitude toward indigenous peoples who had been living there for hundreds and in many places thousands of years is astonishing in itself, but it is a measure of the power of storytelling that the myth of an uninhabited land without social structures or civil governance was believed by so many people (even—or perhaps especially—by those who also believed that the western frontier was "teeming with Indians ready to pounce on unwary settlers"). For this story, while terribly wrong, was the one that Buffalo Bill peddled in his Wild West extravaganza, first mounted ten years earlier, and he always insisted it was not a "show" but a recreation of the "real thing." Conquering the Indians was at the heart of Cody's immensely popular story. Turner joined the chorus, using the language of "common danger" and "resistance to aggression," but his main storyline was about the conquest of nature by the civilizing energy and enterprise of the settler, and by the surveying of the land. Indians, it was assumed by people like him, would follow the lead of the conquering settler society.

The story of an uncivilized and possibly empty frontier has always had an appeal for newcomers; and if it wasn't in fact empty, then the people who were there must themselves be uncivilized—like nature, benign or malignant as circumstances revealed. It was a place to start, or to start again; and in a breathtaking, quintessentially storytelling contradiction, both a place to bring civilization to, and a place to be free of civilizing influences. It was also a place to turn "idle" land, roamed over by "primitive" hunters and gatherers, into useful production, a place to test yourself with the challenges of adaptation and innovation and to bring human ingenuity and Christian instruction into play. And for the metropolitan masters advertising pioneer settlement, it was a place where people with the "right stuff" (a phrase actually used by Canadian government officials in the mid-twentieth century to promote the surrender of Indian reserve land for soldier settlement) could make the desert bloom and develop resources for metropolitan needs, or for recreation.

But for many of those who came to the foothills of Alberta, it was none of those things. It was a time and a place of contradictions, to be sure—but one imbued with hope, epitomized in the opening lines of the American frontier song "Home on the Range." It is perhaps the best-known western song of all (composed by a medical doctor in Kansas in the 1870s): "Oh give me a home where the buffalo roam," it begins. *Home*, and *roam*: bound together in rhyme by their similar sounds, their senses pull in completely opposite directions. Wandering—and settling down. It's hard to imagine a more fundamental contradiction affecting (and inspiring) the condition of settlers wandering onto the range of the buffalo. Our imaginations take this contradiction to heart every time we recite this rhyme, imagining the amazing grace of those stars in the prairie sky at night. We don't remember these lines because they tell one truth about ourselves, but because they tell two contradictory truths about our human condition and about the idea of "home": we are all both "bound to go" and "bound to stay." And when we try to eliminate this contradiction, we are not only trying to straighten out a curve at the heart of being human, we are discounting a condition that is *not* as contradictory as it seems. It was a condition the Blackfoot understood fundamentally in their way of life before treaty, roaming freely throughout their homeland; and it is closer than we realize to the heritage of all people who have moved widely—and still do—within and beyond the tribal or national territory they call home.

12

THE BLACKFOOT QUIRT

IN 1889, AN ATTEMPT WAS MADE to bring the railroad to Fort Macleod. Jack Cowdry—with D. W. Davis (the sometime whisky trader, store manager, and rancher who had been elected Alberta's first member of the Canadian Parliament in 1887 when the district became a federal constituency), along with the mayor of Calgary and the manager of the I. G. Baker store there—had secured a contract to run a railway from Edmonton through Calgary and Fort Macleod down to the Montana border. It was a good idea, which they thought would benefit everyone in the territory by expanding trade beyond the monopolistic eastern markets. But the Canadian Pacific Railway, with a monopoly of its own, thought otherwise, and Jack and his friends didn't have the kind of capital that railways require to get them rolling. And so, not wanting to go broke, they sold their option to the Canadian Pacific Railway.

In those days, cities like Toronto or New York, and towns like Fort Macleod, seemed like different worlds: the metropolis and the hinterland. But both of them were experiencing changes unlike any that the world had seen since the domestication of the horse or the invention of gunpowder or the printing press. And just as printing provided a new currency for thoughts and feelings, the late nineteenth century brought a new kind of illusion into the world, the illusion of being there when you weren't, of happenings that weren't happening right then and there, but seemed to be. This was both brand new and as ancient as storytelling. A virtual reality.

Growing up, Jack Cowdry had watched Upper Canada become Ontario, Canada become a Dominion, and the Canadian West become a land of opportunity. In the early 1880s, he had ridden on a Red River cart at Pile of Bones, a unique and stalwart and very noisy contraption (someone said it sounded like a horde of devils filing saws) that all but defined travel in the early days of the Canadian prairies—no iron was used, the frame was held together by wooden pegs, and the wheels bound with strips of *shaganappi* (fresh raw skin of buffalo or cattle, which shrank as it dried and formed a hard rim). A few years later, he took the Canadian Pacific Railway from Calgary to Regina (to attend Riel's trial). So he knew all about change. (It was said that he had even listened to his family's friend Alexander Graham Bell make the first telephone calls from his summer home in Brantford, Ontario.) And shortly before he died in 1947, Jack Cowdry flew on a Trans-Canada Airlines DC-3 from Vancouver to Calgary. It didn't have a pressurized cabin, so the passengers had to put on oxygen masks. He was very proud to have lived to travel in all these ways, and he said it helped him understand what the coming of the horse meant to the Blackfoot.

New transportation and communication technologies changed many things during Jack Cowdry's lifetime—for better, for worse, and forever: the railway and (by 1901 in the foothills) the automobile; the typewriter, the telegram, and the telephone; photography and film; wax recording cylinders and tape and disk recording, and then radio and television—these all came quickly, and came everywhere (with computers and the Internet now taking up the challenge of these changes). They brought people closer together—but in a paradox that we still haven't resolved, they also set them further apart. They changed people's sense of space and time, and they changed their sense of themselves and each other. Managing this has been the most important challenge of the past hundred and fifty years.

As the politics of regional autonomy in the North-West Territories rose higher on the political agenda of the nation, Fort Macleod came to embody a cultural and commercial character quite distinct from the rest of Canada. In the opinions of Fred Haultain and his friend D. W. Davis, their hometown remained a place that credited the intelligence and imagination of all those, Indian and non-Indian, who were trying to make the foothills flourish. Though he started his career as a lawyer in Fort Macleod, Haultain was first elected to the North-West Territories legislative assembly in 1887 and won the next five elections by acclamation, becoming the territory's first premier in 1897; but he always maintained close ties to the town, and for him and Davis it was a place where most people discounted any easy classification of folks according to race or color or class, respecting the Blackfoot heritage that held together the first peoples of the foothills and dealing with dissent and disruption cautiously and according to the customs of the communities (interpreted by the chiefs and the North-West Mounted Police, often in concert). In other words, it was a good place—not perfect, but full of promise. However, it would be a mistake to think that such noble thoughts were all that preoccupied the folks in and around Fort Macleod. As Haultain's biographer noted, "names like Eagle Plume [a bay thoroughbred brought to the territory by the Quorn ranch into the keeping of John Ware] and Marcus [a dappled grey Percheron, one of the first in Alberta] were about as well known as those of Frank Oliver and Frederick Haultain, who were making platform pleas for self-government in the new northwest."

It was not a simple time or place; it was a medley of complicated relationships and allegiances. When Jack Cowdry arrived, many of the men in the foothills were married to Indian women, some of them from important families in the Blackfoot community. D. W. Davis, for instance, married Red Crow's sister Revenge Walker. The marriage produced four children, and Revenge Walker herself cut a dash on the social circuit. There are some wonderful descriptions of her—at Fort Whoop-Up in the early days, for instance, in "a dress of a very light coloured and well turned buckskin. It was made to conform to the shape of the body. It was trimmed with the usual buckskin fringe, but also had a double row of elk's teeth in a semi-circle beneath the neck and quite a number on the sleeves. Taken all in all, it was quite a spectacular looking dress, and one that would have attracted attention anywhere."

Women took on many responsibilities and played many parts in the West, though they are mentioned much less often than the men—and when they are, it is often only as partners or spouses. But their importance was recognized at the time. Five settler women were among the sixteen non-Indians who signed as witnesses to Treaty Seven with the Blackfoot, and they included Mary Macleod (the wife of the commissioner) and Annie McDougall, married to a trader and sister-in-law to the well-known Methodist missionary John McDougall. There were schoolteachers such as Lillie Grier; owners of lodgings and restaurants, like Annie Saunders; and women ranchers such as Mary Inderwick and Mildred Ware (her husband was John Ware), to whom the cowboys all paid respect since their well-being depended on them. One rancher's wife, Agnes Skrine, took to verse—fondly quoted by many at the time—under the name Moira O'Neill.

The community in those days brought everyone, young and old, together; and so when the earliest public school in Alberta was started by Elizabeth Bishop in Fort Macleod in 1878, the students included the son of one of the North-West Mounted Police officers;

the son and daughter of Jerry Potts; Jeff, John, and Julia Davis, children of D.W. and Revenge Walker; and Bobby Gladstone, from the Blood tribe.

But marriage is never easy in any society, and as settlement increased so did the strains in some of those mixed families, with several of the Indian women leaving their marriages and returning to the Blackfoot circle, and some of the white men taking up new wives from the settler community. The percentage of bad marriages was probably no greater than in any other community, but breakups were easier. That said, many of the men continued to support the children of those first marriages: Kamoose Taylor sent two of his sons by his first (Blackfoot) wife to the private Trinity College School in Port Hope, Ontario (where Charlie Wood had taught before he came to Fort Macleod); and when Revenge Walker returned to her people and D.W. married Lillie Grier, he sent his children by Revenge Walker to the same school back east.

Sadly, some of these mixed family relationships later played into the negative stereotypes of Indian women and white men and "half-breeds," stereotypes that were becoming as common in Canada as they were in other parts of the world, and that took hold of some of the newcomers in the foothills, especially those who had no continuing contact with the Blackfoot. It was not for nothing that at the annual New Year's Ball put on by the North-West Mounted Police (the most important social occasion of the year for the settlers and ranchers in the early days of Fort Macleod), Colonel Macleod always took the first dance with an Indian woman—a mark of respect from a man who knew, whatever the treaty said, that they were in Blackfoot territory.

And although it was often discredited by outsiders, the Blackfoot family structure was time-honored, and equitable—certainly as equitable as the family structure in most of the rest of Canada. (And when it became an issue in the 1880s, the federal Department of Justice issued a directive that marriages according to tribal custom should be treated as legitimate.) Adoptions were common, an adopted child immediately becoming a full part of the family, and open to the same rights of inheritance. Traditionally, Blackfoot men had several wives, the number depending on wealth and status as well as responsibilities, for women took on a number of the tasks in a camp. As the historian Sarah Carter notes, "they enjoyed more options and autonomy than Canadian women of the nineteenth century married under English common law," and an anthropologist who worked with the Blackfoot noted that a Blackfoot woman of that time "could lead a war party; she could own property, receive and exercise medicine power, and give names. She was a necessary part of every ceremonial transfer; she was the custodian of the [sacred] bundles that her husband bought . . . the wife receives the power from the seller. Her husband could only gain possession from her."

A few of Fort Macleod's prominent figures (such as D. W. Davis) had political party loyalties, but the town, like the territorial government at the time, was surprisingly nonpartisan. Still, politics was a favorite topic of conversation for both men and women, though in what was still a traditional Euro-Canadian custom it was men who usually took the public roles. In the case of Fort Macleod in those early days, all of them seemed to be a candidate for everything. During the town's first municipal elections in 1892, one wiseacre said that the only people who weren't running for council were those who were running to be its first mayor—which included Jack Cowdry, age thirty-five.

He won the election, took the town through incorporation, and became its first mayor in January 1893. The first council meeting was held in the Macleod Hotel, and the first year's business was mostly taken up with by-laws, one declaring that there should be no drunkenness in public places, no fighting or use of profanity, and no beating of horses or cows; another required an outdoor toilet for each house. The townsfolk also decided to drop the tag "Fort," as Calgary had done when it incorporated in 1884, and Fort Macleod became simply Macleod, in a gesture of civic independence from the frontier. (Later, in 1952, it changed back to Fort Macleod as a tribute to its beginnings, and to attract tourists.)

Jack Cowdry for one had never felt like he was in a garrison community, a "fort," protected from either the Indians or the environment; and he didn't want the name of the town to suggest anything like that. For him, there was no protection against life, and life in Macleod and the foothills included the Indians, who had faced devastating loss with courage and conviction. Macleod was an Indian town as much as it was a settler town, or a North-West Mounted Police town, or a ranch supply town. It was a town in Chinook country at the crossroads of the old Blackfoot Confederacy and the new confederation called Canada. "This territory and this town are not the frontier," he would say to anyone who would listen—especially over a meal at Taylor's Table in Kamoose's hotel, when they had no choice—"but a homeland we are trying to share with the Blackfoot, with whom we have signed a treaty. Macleod is a treaty town."

Also in January 1893, Jack Cowdry's wife, Amy, gave birth to a little boy, whom they joyfully called Jack. Two months later, in March, Amy died at the age of thirty-one. A long obituary in the *Macleod Gazette* offers a heartfelt remembrance, reflecting how much she had given to the town in the seven short years she had been there; the pallbearers included James Macleod and Sam Steele and other close friends. Jack Cowdry was shattered. And then six months later, in September, young Jack died from infantile cholera. Medical care was not enough to save either of them, or not good enough. The doctor in charge was their friend and neighbor George Kennedy, who had much experience from years as the North-West Mounted Police doctor, was dedicated to the most up-to-date care, and was the one who put Macleod in the lead in Alberta for hospital facilities. But knowledge of infectious disease was limited in those days, and women were especially vulnerable after childbirth, and children in their first year. Kennedy was among Amy's pallbearers.

To no one's surprise, Jack stepped down after his first year as mayor was over, though folks said he could have stayed for twenty years if he had wanted. In this time of devastating grief and loss, the friends Jack had made since coming to the West helped him pull through. And others shared his sorrow. The same week that Amy died there was a notice in the *Gazette* that a son of Jerry Potts had passed away.

The next couple of years, with a young daughter and son to raise and a bank to run, must have been a blur. Three telegrams that Jack had sent to Nat in 1893 relayed the tragic news. The first said that Amy was "weaker but holding strength well as possible." The next, three weeks later: "Amy gone home. We will meet again." And in September: "Dear little Jack died this afternoon."

One day, Crop Eared Wolf came to visit Jack Cowdry with a gift, something which he had carved and painted. It was a ceremonial riding quirt—a wooden crop or whip about eighteen inches long and two inches wide, with a braided leather tail about two feet long, and ornamental buffalo hide bound in at the end. It told—it still tells—the story of Crop Eared Wolf's life, or at least the audacious spirit he displayed when he was younger and proving himself, a spirit that sustained him when he got wounded and as he got older and lived through even more dangerous times after the buffalo had gone and the treaty had come. It was, Jack Cowdry later said, like the weapon or the shield of a great warrior like Achilles. He knew Crop Eared Wolf had a reputation for "bringing home" horses with craft and courage and in the most unlikely circumstances, and for breeding horses that were fast as well as ones that could turn on a biscuit and never break the crust, horses with grace and strength and skill. He told Jack, another time, that when he rode horses, or watched them running, he felt the spirit alive in him. Whose spirit, he didn't say. But he would say there was a moment when he felt one with both the earth and the sky. *Ponokaomitai saam*—horse medicine—Crop Eared Wolf called it, the most powerful medicine among the Blackfoot.

Jack Cowdry knew that Crop Eared Wolf was well known for his artistic and historical craft. He had recorded his exploits capturing horses across the Plains and raiding other tribes as far away as the Yellowstone—exploits that secured his high status among his people and respect from many others—on a buffalo robe commissioned in 1882 by an Indian agent (later a rancher) named Charlie Geddes. The painted robe eventually found its way into the care of the North-West Mounted Police; and it provided the ethnographer Marius Barbeau with a defining story and an image for the colored frontispiece of his landmark book, *Indian Days on the Western Prairies*. Later, the robe ended up at the Royal Canadian Mounted Police (successor to the North-West Mounted Police) headquarters in Regina, to be used as a training text for recruits, and to recognize Blackfoot traditions.

Crop Eared Wolf had gone on his first raid in 1865, when he was about twenty, together with his father, Red Crow. But since Crop Eared Wolf (like his father) was also a great peacemaker, the quirt has both a gun and a pipe on one of the flat sides, and below them two men carved and colored in blue and red and rendered in traditional Blackfoot style. One symbolically represents Crop Eared Wolf; the other is an enemy . . . or a friend. There are eight marks in the shape of large staples on the narrow sides of the quirt, each colored blue or red or yellow and signifying raids or other excursions, the number perhaps arbitrary but the enterprises certainly not.

At the top of the other flat side is a curved line in red, and three wavy lines perpendicular to it below, two of them blue and one yellow. They would have signified scouting expeditions, with several raiders waiting hidden at the top of a hill overlooking the enemy camp while the scout—Crop Eared Wolf—slipped down and after checking out the camp came back in a zigzag course to survey the countryside, and avoid detection. His comrades would have made a pile of buffalo chips or stones or small sticks, and the scout would scatter them on his return to symbolically indicate that a raid would be successful. His action would also represent an oath that he was telling the truth. Jawbone.

Finally, there are three finely rendered horses and a mule below the scouting figurations; they would have been "gathered in" from enemy camps, and they celebrated both the virtues of the horse thief and the value of horses and mules, as well as the imagination and skill of the person who gathered them up and rendered them on the quirt. The horses are colored differently—two are shades of yellow-gold, one is red—and the mule at the bottom is blue. Two of the horses have reins running down to the ground, signifying that they were particularly prized and would have been attached by their reins at night to the ankle or wrist of the chief as he slept in his tipi. With that, and several dozen dogs outside, the horse thief would have had to have exceptional skill to steal them. The mule is interesting, for mules were relatively new to the West around that time; and they were valued, among other things, for leading horses across rivers in flood, when the horses would typically balk.

Gerald Conaty, an ethnographer at the Glenbow Museum in Calgary who was widely respected by the Blackfoot, "read" the quirt some years ago and said, with disarming matter-of-factness, that

Crop Eared Wolf must have had help stealing horses and a mule that were so highly valued and carefully watched. He did not mean help from within the enemy camps—but help from the spirits.

The Blood elder and tribal historian Frank Weasel Head also "read" the quirt, and he told the same story as Gerald Conaty—with one exception. He said it may have been—indeed he believed it was—the record of a dream, not a set of real events, and that the dream made these things (the raids and the horse and mule thefts) happen.

Was it a dream carved on the quirt, preceding and predicting the reality? Or the record of an extraordinary reality, still celebrated in Blackfoot territory? And what exactly is the difference anyway? The quirt (to use categories that are part of European literary training) is narrative, lyric, and dramatic all at the same time. It is both a riddle, whose meaning needs to be interpreted, and a charm, making something happen. And all those uncertainties are what makes it so compelling.

However we interpret it, the quirt is a ceremony of belief as well as a chronicle of events; and the interpretation of it—requiring belief as well as knowledge—represented a crucial part of its power, then and now. At *Áísínai'pi* (Writing-on-Stone Provincial Park) there are ancient paintings and carvings of animals and humans on the rocks, and many see the place as a kind of auditorium for a certain kind of storytelling, and a certain kind of history. This quirt belongs in that company.

Crop Eared Wolf gave no reason for the gift of this quirt to Jack Cowdry, except that was what he called it. A gift. It was a token of friendship, to be sure; but receiving it as a gift, Jack accepted that he had an obligation, a promise to keep. It was up to him to figure out what that was. When he asked Crop Eared Wolf, his friend said, "You will know."

The gift signaled something, Jack Cowdry thought, something about respecting the promise of the past in order to redeem the future. It marked a moment when he realized his friend knew that the future they believed in was in danger of being lost; and the gift was a reminder that together they not forget the promise.

13

"HOW CAN WE SING OUR CREATOR'S SONG IN A STRANGE LAND?"

IN THE EARLY 1890S FORT MACLEOD was flourishing, ranching had been on a roll the past couple of years, and since no other bank in southern Alberta was as heavily involved in ranching, Cowdry Brothers Bank was doing fine. But Jack Cowdry was concerned about the impatience of the editor of the *Macleod Gazette*, C. E. D. Wood, for increased settlement in the foothills. He was worried that Wood, and others, including a few of the missionaries, were becoming too fond of saying that the Indians were not "progressing" fast enough—by which they meant that they weren't getting on with losing their Blackfoot identity and becoming white Christians, which some other people in the mixed-race and dubiously devout town of Fort Macleod weren't either. And Jack was increasingly worried that the party politics of the East would infect the West.

Since many of the ranchers he supported lived in Peigan territory to the west of Macleod, he went there often to visit. His good friend James Macleod had died in 1894, but he kept in touch with Macleod's wife, Mary, their children, and with Annie Saunders; and he had friends throughout that part of the foothills. One of them was the Peigan chief Big Swan. He had a reputation as a great hunter and warrior. In 1877 Big Swan had been on the way to Montana for one of the last buffalo hunts when Treaty Seven was called, but he returned in time to sign. After the treaty, like many other Blackfoot, he had taken up some new "adventures," as he called them, planting potatoes so that within a few years he had a substantial farm in operation. Big Swan, like many in that time of transition, was full of contradictions: deeply traditional in holding on to the annual Sun Dance, but—drawing on his tribe's experience with newcomers to the territory—shrewdly aware of new opportunities. His people had been traders and travelers for centuries, and Big Swan was an entrepreneur as well as an imaginative leader. So he established a staging post, with a log house and stables, at Scott's Coulee, where he lived with his wives and family, welcoming travelers on the stagecoach between Calgary and the foothills around Pincher Creek and Fort Macleod. While the coach changed horses, the passengers could buy some food and knick-knacks and take a rest—not unlike a modern bus and truck stop; and it was supported by the local banker. (Big Swan, along with his fellow chiefs Leans Over Butchering, Bull Plume, and Running Wolf, painted their war exploits on a single buffalo robe completed in 1909 for the artist Edmund Morris [son of Alexander Morris, commissioner for several of the early prairie treaties], who painted a number of portraits of prairie chiefs.)

The next federal election in Canada was scheduled for June of 1896. For Jack Cowdry it was time to ruffle some establishment feathers, and he came up with a plan to start a newspaper with a few friends. Its ambitions were clear: "to expose the shams and frauds and rampant hypocrisies that surround us on every side." Sometime in the winter of 1895/96, he went out to see Chief Big Swan about using his place at Scott's Coulee as a base for their newspaper, which they planned to call *The Outlaw*. Big Swan was delighted. They made plans to publish weekly, beginning the first issue in May, figuring out whom they would approach for good newspaper copy and how much they would write themselves—a lot, as it turned out; they met at least once each week at Big Swan's to put the issue together.

It ran for six glorious weeks, from May 19 to June 30, 1896. In that short time, it claimed to have outstripped the *Macleod Gazette* in sales, and was hilarious in its description of that paper even though it was in fact printed on the *Gazette* press. It also boasted that it had the largest circulation of *any* paper in the territory, noting that "its exclusive news franchises make it the most widely read and influential journal in the West." Its journalistic ambition was made from a singular vantage point—the top of the fence, of course, on which the editors promised to remain,

> not because we want to see which way the cat jumps before jumping ourselves, but for the reason that from the higher elevation it will be the easier for us to watch the struggling mobs below, and point out the foibles and vanities, the vices and tricks, that will make up the contest [the upcoming federal election] on which the people of Alberta have entered. "Spare none, praise none" will be one of our mottos for the next few weeks, and if politicians don't like its application, they had better get under the barn.

The Outlaw was probably partly inspired by the great British tradition of satirical journalism going back to Jonathan Swift. But it had a distinctly foothills sense of satire and the liberating value of serious, scandalous fun. Its name represented a nod to horses, for "outlaw" was (and still is) a term not only for someone who breaks the law but also for a really difficult horse that no cowboy would want to ride, and that any good bronc rider on the rodeo circuit would want to try.

The editors did not advertise themselves, though Jack Cowdry and his colleague at the bank, William Black, were identified in the last issue: Jack as "first assistant to the chief editor," one Chollis Miller, who had been a close friend for a while. Jack's neighbor, the town doctor George Kennedy, was also party to this scurrilous venture. William Black's job seems to have been to offer entertainment in the paper in the spirit of the "decadent nineties" that were being alternately celebrated and censured in England at the time, since he was routinely described as wearing lavender pants and writing poetry. He was joined by his brother John Black, the storekeeping "gentleman adventurer" who had advertised to "white subjects and red allies." Jack Cowdry came in for all kinds of genial joking in its pages, including being called a "chump" for asking what the difference was between the Liberals and the Conservatives at a candidates' meeting; and in another issue he was described, in a piece on political affairs in Pincher Creek, as "Sorreltop Jack."

In the first issue, they described Big Swan's staging post, the head office of the enterprise, as "Hotel de Log," declaring, "Big Swan, the genial proprietor, has thrown open the doors of his hospitable mansion" for performances by the local candidates. The motto of the newspaper was *Cultores Veritatis, Fraudis Inimici*, which they translated as *With Malice Towards All and Charity to None*—though it might be rendered more literally as "supporters of truth, enemies of deceit." Its politics were manifestly bipartisan and moderately incomprehensible, and the proprietors were as good as their word, lampooning everyone within the territory, and anyone who came by to interfere in its affairs. They expressed editorial contempt for both the Liberals and the Conservatives, and indulged in all kinds of libelous commentary. They included expressions of respect and declarations of praise—made up, needless to say—from newspapers such as the *Globe* and the *Mail and Empire*, the eastern establishment organs of the Liberals and Conservatives respectively. From the

Macleod Gazette came a special "tribute": "*The Outlaw* should have been named *The Outrage.*"

Throughout every issue, and through the mischief, one theme is clear. The 1896 federal election in distant Ottawa was almost comically—but would become cruelly—irrelevant to the communities of the foothills; and the partisan obsessions of the candidates were damaging to the compelling interests of the territory. Behind the banter in *The Outlaw* was a nervous concern that Indians and new settlers might both be buried by the government's increasing drive toward more settlement and trade, both of which were about to get an eastern booster in Ottawa in Clifford Sifton, a man dedicated to "settling the West." He had moved to Manitoba from Ontario, and would become the minister of the interior and superintendent general of Indian affairs in Wilfrid Laurier's soon-to-be-elected new Liberal government. Sifton was an evangelical proponent of dramatically expanding immigration to the West—offering "free homesteading" to European farmers and "stalwart peasants in sheep-skin coats, born on the soil, with a stout wife and a half-dozen children"—and of centralizing the administration of everything (including Indian affairs) in Ottawa. His was the writing on the wall that would affect the Blackfoot for the next hundred years.

In its final issue, the loud little newspaper published its obituary: "DIED: At Scott's Coulee, Alberta, at 4:00 p.m. Tuesday June 30, 1896. *The Outlaw*. Deeply Regretted." Two weeks later Wilfrid Laurier became Canada's first francophone prime minister.

In the early 1880s Jack Cowdry's friend John Maclean had been invited, as a well-known Methodist missionary fluent in the Blackfoot language, to give the inaugural lecture for Fort Macleod's newly formed Literary, Scientific and Historical Society. Maclean's topic? "Indian Literature." He believed that the Blackfoot stories and songs offered insight into their way of being in the world, a world out on the prairies that they understood better than the newcomers, and constituted their "real life" as surely as their actions. These were both national literatures as well as spiritual texts, and included stories that rivaled those of the European traditions in which Maclean had grown up and the Asian traditions in which he was well versed, having turned to wider reading early in his life and becoming a comparative literary scholar as well as a correspondent with the leading anthropologists of the day. For the Blackfoot, he came to understand, some stories were more than textual codes to be deciphered; rather, they were cultural codes, determining destiny. In them, the Blackfoot realized themselves as "chosen," bound as a people into a place by ceremonies that fortified them in a world that was always more or less unstable, and filling them with obligations to each other, to the Creator, and to the wider world. Every culture has its own version of this, which is why the poet Samuel Taylor Coleridge called the Bible a "science of realities"; the Blackfoot, the real people of the Plains, would have understood what he was talking about. They would also have understood Coleridge's fierce resistance to the kinds of institutional pressures that were imposing themselves on the Blackfoot. "No power on earth," wrote Coleridge, "can oblige me to act against my conscience. No magistrate, no monarch, no legislature." Jack Cowdry could see that the Blackfoot were coming to a time of resolute resistance.

Their voices of conscientious objection were first and last spiritual voices, just as they were for Coleridge; and they were collective voices, cherishing the institutions that defined *their* society. There was, and still is, an essential conservatism behind much Aboriginal dissent, a determination to protect values that transcend the sum of individual preoccupations and which are enshrined in the institutions of both secular and sacred significance in their communities, their tribal lore and their tribal law.

———

Many Blackfoot, when they saw newcomers arriving, must have been convinced that only the continued presence of the Blackfoot would ensure a truly civil society in the foothills. Maclean titled a passage in a journal (in which he was drafting essays and stories) "The White Savages: As the Indians see the white man." Keeping the foothills civilized was everyone's concern, and caused more conflict and confusion than almost anything else. For some, the terms had been laid down by the poet and cultural critic Matthew Arnold in his widely read book *Culture and Anarchy* (1869). Arnold had tried to redefine the categories of rich and poor, social and economic categories that he believed were mutilating England. Instead, he proposed a set of dichotomies—between order and chaos, civilians and barbarians, those with culture and those without—that shaped (or warped) nineteenth-century British colonial expansion. Few debates about cultural relativity or discussions of national identity in the past hundred and fifty years have been able to ignore Arnold's formulation, or discount his celebration of ceremony and tradition.

The specter of anarchy that haunted Arnold was both secular and spiritual, and was embodied in an excessive materialism—what he scornfully referred to in one of his chapter titles as "Doing As One Likes." He was dismayed at the subversive pluralism to which he felt his society had surrendered, which for him meant the disintegration of a sense of shared, permanent values, and a corresponding collapse of cultural standards.

But while it was impossible to agree with Arnold's dream of a unified national culture in the foothills, his apocalyptic vision of anarchy was immensely compelling to many people in a time of worldwide demographic changes. And we misunderstand the encounter between natives and newcomers in the Americas if we think that the anxiety was all one-sided. On the Plains, at precisely the same time as Arnold was pronouncing on culture and anarchy, the Aboriginal peoples were doing the same thing, shaping their politics and their statecraft around a core belief in the importance of maintaining a continuity of cultural values in the face of the incursions and innovations taking place all around them. They believed, no less than Arnold did, that every culture must maintain an orderly balance between the stabilities of convention and the energies of change, or else anarchy will take hold. That was why the Blackfoot entered into treaty; and that was why they kept the promises they made, despite pressure from some within the community to break their word even as the other side had broken theirs.

Aboriginal peoples had lived side by side with other peoples for centuries, making all sorts of arrangements to get through the season, or the territory, or the dispute, but maintaining their distinctive languages and customs. New technologies and customs were often incorporated into old cultural practices without causing a loss in their core meaning and value, as the Blackfoot and other Plains tribes had done with horses and guns and networks of trade and commerce. And while the Blackfoot refused to give up spiritual practices such as the Sun Dance, they took to farming and ranching and to speaking English alongside their own language. James Macleod understood, and supported Red Crow's stern admonition, often repeated, that he and his people must be allowed to pray in their own way. "There is praying all over the world," Red Crow said at the time of a dispute over the Sun Dance. "Red Crow believes in his own praying. This next month is the time." That said, he converted to Catholicism in the course of his later life and married his youngest wife in a Catholic ceremony (using the new legal protocol to ensure an inheritance for his baptized Catholic son Frank). And he was close friends with several of the Protestant missionaries. But he would not give up his traditional forms of praise and prayer. He would just accompany them with others.

Treaty Seven was supposed to establish new coordinates for maintaining Blackfoot cultural integrity against pluralistic anarchy; and the Blackfoot did their part, accepting the challenge of translating their covenantal relationship to the land—their belief that they were a chosen people—into the constitutional offer of a reserve, a small piece of the domain that had once been vast and varied. They did so with the conviction that this offer represented another covenant, this time with the Great Mother. She would be their protector, if they would be her people. The promises made under that covenant were at the heart of the treaties. Break them, and you have broken much more than a commercial "deal." You have broken faith. Failing to keep your word was for the Blackfoot the quintessentially uncivil, and uncivilized, act. It was also, to use a word with ancient spiritual associations, a form of pollution, poisoning the wells. And they were right. It would produce for them the very anarchy that Arnold was chronicling.

But keeping your word was inconvenient for administrators trying to manage the bipolar pathology of "separation" on the reserve and "assimilation" into white society (which morphed into "protection" and "advancement" early in the twentieth century), and they were bewildered by the impossible choices it offered. Some grim regulations were piled on to cover their confusion, but they had brutal consequences.

None were more devastating than those caused by the residential school system in Canada, set up to destroy the imaginative and spiritual integrity (what Arnold called the "culture") of Aboriginal communities for generations, until the painful process of truthtelling and reconciliation in recent years.

The residential schools began here and there in the second half of the nineteenth century, and took on a brutally widespread role in the twentieth century. These schools were set up to separate children from their parents, obliterate their language, replace their traditional spiritual beliefs with those of Christianity—the schools, though government-sponsored, were run by Christian religious orders—and assimilate them into the ways of "civilized" society, disabling their relationships with things of value in their lives and corrupting their reality by discrediting their imaginations. Some of the schools were cesspits of criminal abuse of children by the staff, but many of them were devastating simply because they were in the control of men and women who liked to be in control.

In a sense it had all started some time before the treaties, but the institutional conveniences that treaties introduced and the iron fist of the 1876 Indian Act (which established a uniform system of wardships rather than a network of alliances and friendships) made it easier to undertake the program of cultural genocide that it truly was.

It begins in the Americas with the earliest encounters between Aboriginal peoples and settlers over five hundred years ago, and a poem tells the story. Written by one John Rastell about twenty years after Columbus made his first landing, it reads as follows:

> *And what a great and meritoryouse dede*
> *It were to have the people instructed*
> *To lyve more Vertuously*
> *And to lerne to knowe of man the maner*
> *And also to knowe of god theyre maker*
> *Which as yet lyve all bestly.*

Oh, that such a strangely simple-minded sentiment could unleash such a deadly plague as the residential schools. But it did, not directly of course but over time in various guises around the Americas, and with startling ruthlessness in Canada. This poem presented the orthodox missionary problem, and proposed what became its orthodox solution. "To live more virtuously" requires people not to "live all beastly," which is to say less like "primitive savages" and more like "civilized citizens." And to know "of man the manner" and "of God their maker" was to receive instruction in the "blessings of civilization"—that is to say, of Culture (with a capital "C") and of Christianity—and thereby to become compelled and converted by their specific truths and beauties and goodnesses. The only question that literally bedeviled the early compellers and converters was which should come first, Culture or Christianity; and the history of the cultural and religious coercion—a.k.a. "education" —of Aboriginal peoples in the Americas shuttled between these alternatives.

Until, in a stroke of demonic institutional madness, the Canadian government decided to combine the two, and at first sanction and then wholly support church-run schools in which Indian students were removed from the influence of hearth and home, sheared like sheep, forbidden from speaking their language, and forced to behave in the ways of settler society—except that it wasn't always the settlers' ways they learned, but the ways of some strange sociopaths.

And along with the horrendous pain and suffering the residential schools caused Indian children separated from their families, they also did one thing that was designed to make the damage permanent. They changed the stories, and the storylines, that had held First Nations communities together for generations and had been hard won by their ancestors and hard-wired into their consciousnesses. To change the story was to change the languages and the lives and the livelihoods and the lands—and to replace them with ones they couldn't believe. That is a deadly legacy.

The residential school system was started in the middle of the nineteenth century, often in the form of what were called "industrial schools" that taught some valuable new crafts and skills to the young Indian boys and girls—but in doing so relentlessly discounted the knowledge and the experience of the faithkeepers and scholars and scientists and storytellers in their own communities and the culture their parents held dear. It was to one of these schools—St. Joseph's Industrial School built by the Roman Catholics in 1883 in Dunbow, south of Calgary—that Red Crow sent his son Shot Close, convinced by his visit to the Six Nations reserve in Ontario of the importance of education and training. There were schools on the Blood reserve, but Red Crow was not impressed with the results, and he felt that a break from the distraction of family and friends would be good for his son, by whom he set great store. He knew this would mean long periods away from home, but he saw it as a kindred sacrifice to that of the warriors of old, giving up much for new knowledge and experience. When he arrived at the school, Shot Close was given the name Frank Red Crow, number 166. His hair was cut short, he was dressed in a grey uniform, his traditions were routinely discredited, and he had to speak English—but at least, unlike many less fortunate children, he kept his Blackfoot language and later returned to become a chief in his Blood tribe.

The name "industrial school" also reveals another purpose behind the schools: to imbue in the students those habits of industry and thrift that were *the* Victorian virtues, and which in the prejudiced view of the newcomers did not seem evident in their parents. Thrift had been pretty well looked after by the treaties, you might think; but Indians still loved dressing up, and parades, and spending money in town. Just like everyone else. However, their joy on such occasions seemed to be particularly irritating to the white crusaders for industry and thrift.

Not everyone was caught up in this system of Indian "improvement" during Jack Cowdry's time in the foothills, for it was just gathering steam, and schools had not been established everywhere, certainly not enough of them to make them compulsory, as they would become by the 1920s. And the Blackfoot, for their part, refused to accept the alternatives of assimilation or separation and countered some of the effects of the changes that followed the treaty, and the loss of the territory that followed the disappearance of the buffalo, by maintaining a sure sense of their place, literal and figurative, in the foothills; and of that place as a homeland, however diminished. The stories, old and new, that sustained the Blackfoot became part of the ceremony of belief around which they lived their lives, an imaginative center. Some new neighbors recognized this because it mirrored their own convictions about community and culture. But even the most sympathetic had trouble comprehending all that was happening to the Blackfoot, especially after residential schooling, when some of the youngsters moved to the cities and their sense of dislocation and dispossession became different from anything their parents had experienced, and devastating to both.

"How can we sing our Creator's song in a strange land?" some Blackfoot youth may well have asked their elders, quoting Psalm 137's lament for the exile of the Jewish people by the waters of Babylon. Just watch and listen, said their leaders, singing their songs and dancing their dances even as they made peace with the newcomers and fenced their land, raised cattle and potatoes, and bred their beloved horses to win races and herd cattle, and showed their spirit in the rodeo, and then rode in parades with traditional trappings. Parades and pageantry, like stories and songs, have provided ways in which communities define their identity for thousands of years, all over the world. This has sometimes been mistaken as being simply for show, and it is that. But it is also the "essential gaudiness" of the imagination—the extravagance celebrated in all cultures even when it is frowned upon by the agents of utility and morality—pushing back against the everyday. In that sense it is something that all human beings in all societies cherish, whatever their circumstances, and express in ways that convey important elements of meaning and value in their lives.

The Blackfoot celebrations had their counterpart in settler society, with its formal dances and social dinners and church rituals and cowboy displays of skill and style. And such displays, such extravagances, often do provide common ground between native and newcomer, for the simple reason that they give pleasure. Pleasure has been a moral test for a long time around the world. In the old rationalist crossroads of Europe, the Roman poet and philosopher Lucretius based his theory of the *Nature of Things* (*De Rerum Natura*) on the relationship between pleasure on the one hand and pain on the other. Francis Bacon, at the beginning of the seventeenth century, insisted that "all knowledge and wonder (which is the soul of knowledge) is an impression of pleasure in itself." In the eighteenth century, the philosopher David Hume insisted on the equal importance of feelings and thoughts in civilized society, especially feelings of pleasure. That may sound revolutionary; but it is ancient, and Aboriginal. And among many other things, it is at the heart of parades—making everyone feel good. This delight in display, bringing out your very best and putting it on show, was something Jack Cowdry and Crop Eared Wolf would often talk about, the importance of show for its own sake. For Jack, it was pleasure for pleasure's sake in defiance of the utilitarian urgencies and moral strictures of Victorian life. For Crop Eared Wolf, it was being Blackfoot.

In 1898, Jack Cowdry ran for mayor once more—perhaps because of his ability to balance the books, perhaps because of his rebellious turn, perhaps because *The Outlaw* had been very popular—and he was easily elected. (A few years before he had been appointed a justice of the peace, joining 439 others in the North-West Territories in the enforcement of territorial ordinances and municipal by-laws, passing judgment for summary offenses, and holding preliminary examinations in cases destined for the Supreme Court of the territory.)

Another factor heavily influenced Jack Cowdry's decision to take on the mayor's job again. He was becoming fed up with the ignorant, negative attitude of some of the newcomers in the 1890s toward the Blackfoot, and their ambition to keep Indians out of town on the grounds that they were . . . well, they were *Indian*. Because, as new settlers moved into town and the countryside around, the attitude toward the Blackfoot started to change, and there were more grumblings about Indians crowding the streets and stores.

This was also an attitude fueled by a Canadian immigration and settlement policy that identified the "best sort of people" by their occupation. The occupation of an Indian, in this accounting, was simply being an Indian—an "idle Indian." But in Fort Macleod the merchants at least had a different view: they certainly didn't mind Indians in town. As far as they were concerned, their occupation was being "good customers," and shopkeepers continued to welcome them and give treats to their kids, many of whom they'd watched grow up. And most of the established merchants did so not just because the town depended on the Indians for business, but because they genuinely felt that they were part of the community, as worthy of respect as anyone else (and more than some, they might have added). When Jerry Potts had died in 1896, the town had come together to honor him, with a large funeral and full military honors. "His memory will long be green in the hearts of those who knew him best, and 'faithful and true' is the character he leaves behind—the best monument of a valuable life," proclaimed the *Macleod Gazette*. Jack Cowdry, who treasured the photograph that Potts had given him, picturing Potts and his wife, Long Time Laying Down, the daughter of the Blood chief One Spot (he had married her in the late 1880s), was not sure anything like that would happen now, just two years later, in the town he loved so well.

For there were displays of what was beginning to plague many western towns, setting Indians into a kind of civil competition with newcomers. C. E. D. Wood, who had peddled the stereotype of "primitive savages" and "civilized citizens" in the *Gazette* (rebuked time and again by Fred Haultain and Jack Cowdry), was adept at misrepresenting the showiness of the Blackfoot on parade or at market as a refusal to become "civilized"—even as he celebrated their "civilized" spending of money in town and participation in community activities, and even had some grudging praise for their gloriously "uncivilized" and highly successful participation in horse races and rodeos. Also, he had to admit that the horse parades were becoming very popular, just like the Mounted Police Musical Rides.

Jack Cowdry believed that the Blackfoot were what made Macleod different from Calgary and Lethbridge and Edmonton and Regina. This was not because he had many Blackfoot friends; indeed, perhaps it was exactly the opposite. He had many Blackfoot friends because he believed this. The Blackfoot were the future of the foothills. Townspeople sometimes got irritated when hundreds of Blackfoot came by cart or on horseback and took over the town on treaty payment days, but they also brought blessing and beauty and business to Fort Macleod and all its residents.

Jack Cowdry wanted to bring the town's ambitions into line with Blood and Peigan aspirations. He also wanted to be sure that his Indian friends were always welcome in town. He never wrote much about all this; he believed it was what he did that mattered. But he probably said a lot on this subject at the time, especially around Taylor's Table. And we do see traces of it in *The Outlaw.* Another upstart newspaper, less mischievous and more municipal, began publication in 1899. It was called *The Advance* and it raised the issue bluntly, encouraging old-time consideration

> *for the Indians themselves [rather than merely for their money] and not [being] tight-fisted in the matter of expending a few dollars for the people whose trade they seek to cater to. . . . Macleod was a thriving town years before [when] the merchants were in the habit of brewing large quantities of strong tea, which would be placed in some convenient spot in the store where the Indians could get at it readily. A barrel of biscuits would be left uncovered close beside the tea. . . . Money would also be subscribed and this would be spent in furnishing . . . sport in the way of horse racing and other kinds. . . . Our businessmen held the confidence of the Indian populace and if they have of late years lost their grip, they must blame themselves for it.*

For Jack Cowdry, that advice needed to be directed to everyone in town—and he decided to see what he could do about it as mayor once again, full of ambition for a town that he knew could not compete with Calgary for metropolitan appeal but was a better model for the West he was trying to nourish, and was calling home.

14

WHEN CROP EARED WOLF BECAME CHIEF OF THE BLOOD TRIBE

IT WAS IN AL GRADY'S HARDWARE STORE that Mayor Cowdry fell for the schoolteacher Miss Thompson. They had met several times during the past year or so—her name was Augusta, though everyone knew her as Gussie—and she had come from Ingersoll, Ontario, to teach at the Macleod school. Shortly after she arrived, she was taken in hand by Lillie Grier, who had been the first teacher at the new school organized in town the year the Cowdry brothers had come. With Lillie Grier as her mentor, and Al Grady (who was on the school board) as her friend, Gussie would have gotten to know the town well, and Jack had seen her at several dances and a horse race; but he tumbled into love while watching her choose some glazed redware flowerpots for the school's spring fair.

After that, they moved quickly, almost as though they knew they didn't have much time. During the summer they were back and forth from Ingersoll, Jack telling stories to her family and Gussie giggling, and they got married in December of that same year, 1898.

By early in the new year Gussie was pregnant; but the pregnancy was not easy, and after several months of feeling more than usually poorly, and on the advice of their doctor, George Kennedy—who had seen Jack through his earlier losses, and maybe doubted himself a bit this time—they decided that Gussie should go back to Ingersoll to have the baby. Neither of them wanted that so they waited a while, and she was soon feeling much better; but as the time got closer Jack got worried, and they both thought the comfort and care of her Ingersoll family might be a good thing. So he went back east with her on the train, stayed a few weeks, and then returned to Macleod in late August.

In mid-October, he got the good news that a baby girl, Edith (my mother), was born, and healthy. He was getting ready to go to Ingersoll to see mother and child when a telegram arrived saying that Gussie was seriously ill. She died just after he got there.

Men have had no monopoly on courage in the history of the world; and it isn't for nothing that in the Book of Common Prayer (which was part of Gussie's Anglican upbringing) there is a service for women who have given birth to a child, thanking God for "safe deliverance" and preservation "in the great danger of child-birth." It was indeed a great danger, next to which even the rough-and-tumble of North American frontier life was fairly secure. At the time Gussie gave birth, for some time afterward, and indeed in many parts of the world to this day, childbirth has challenged available health care, with infection, bleeding, and convulsions the most perilous threat for women, and digestive and lung disorders and virulent diseases often taking the children. One in ten children would die before the age of one in Canada in the late nineteenth century, better than in many European countries at the time but devastating nonetheless.

After the funeral, Jack Cowdry returned to Fort Macleod, arriving back on December 6, a day before what would have been his and Gussie's first wedding anniversary. Pole-axed by grief, he went around town with a box of Cuban cigars that he had ordered to celebrate Edith's birth; and he resigned as mayor. Then he had to face a grim reality. He had two children—Mary and Gus, age twelve and nine—in Fort Macleod, and little Edith in Ingersoll. With a heavy heart, he agreed that his baby daughter would stay for the time being in Ingersoll with Gussie's parents and her three sisters: Bertha, Edith, and Elizabeth. (Elizabeth was always called Diddy by my mother; and Diddy, bless her, gave up her own engagement to raise my mother as her daughter . . . and to tell her about Gussie.)

Jack Cowdry's resignation brought much sympathy and some consternation in Fort Macleod. A good mayor had never been more needed, and the editor of the *Gazette* was anxious to take charge and turn Macleod over to the new settler reactionaries. The Canadian economy was going up and down, as economies do, during the 1890s, with the costs of the railway stretching capacity, and familiar conflicts over language, education, and religion causing unease not only across the territory but also back east. Federal party politics had been fairly ramshackle until Wilfrid Laurier came to power. But the period unleashed a cohort of belligerent bureaucrats in the Indian service both at headquarters back in Ottawa and in the field, some of whom did their best to brutalize many First Nations communities. (John Maclean had to face war chief White Calf's contemptuous diatribe one day against him and his people, upholding their warrior virtues of resistance and valor—which Maclean agreed were admirable—in response to the barbarities they were enduring.)

Underlying everything was the blunt and brutal fact that during these times both the spirit and the letter of the treaties were being dishonored throughout the West: rations were intermittently reduced on instructions from Ottawa, and sometimes completely withheld by Indian agents who treated rations—promised under treaty—like gold stars for good behavior, or as incentives for the Indians to get out of the way of the railway and move onto their reserves. The respected Methodist missionary John McDougall, familiar with conditions throughout the prairies, denounced "the almost despotic power of the ration house." Things were a bit better for the Blackfoot, since their move to reserves, however constrained, had been made by them with both the railway and their traditional territories in mind. But there were confrontations with agents who did not like the idea that Indians had rights as well as responsibilities, and who did not see themselves beholden to the treaty promises. A "pass system" designed to keep Indians on the reserves had been introduced on the Canadian prairies in 1885, partly as a "crowd management program" and partly in response to the uprising of the Métis under Louis Riel. It was deeply offensive in principle, as well as intermittently irritating in practice. But it was also illegal, a fact that was recognized by the North-West Mounted Police (at least throughout Blackfoot territory, though inconsistently in the rest of the North-West Territories), with Macleod's stern instructions about the rule of law ringing in their ears. It was, however, convenient for autocratic Indian agents, anxious to exercise their authority (and what some of them under-stood as their righteous responsibility) to "protect" Indians from "backsliding" or "wayfaring." There were occasional injunctions from senior officials condemning the system; and at the end of the 1890s a letter from David Laird, during another term as commissioner of Indian affairs, laid it out bluntly to the Indian agent on the Blood reserve. "The pass system as it stands cannot be enforced by law." Still, it continued to be used, and abused, and represents one of sev-eral regimes that menaced and marginalized First Nations peoples across the prairies.

Some of the agents tried to break down the authority of the chiefs, convinced that the traditional structures of order and good governance in the tribal communities—where consensus was care-fully balanced by the varying levels of authority of chiefs in the band and the tribe—represented one of the major obstacles to the "civiliz-ing" of the individuals and fostered resistance to whatever objective the agent might have at that particular moment. And they would use dissent and discontent within the band or tribe as evidence of immature politics rather than democratic openness.

In many ways nothing did more damage across the country than this attitude on the part of the Indian agents, often working under direction from both politicians and bureaucrats in Ottawa. In the foothills, the Mounted Police generally sought to maintain the authority of the chiefs, which inevitably produced some awkward moments; but it sustained a structure of governance which during that time worked well. And some of the agents did defend the rights of the Indians, opposing among other things the infamous pass system. One of them, William Pocklington—who worked closely with Red Crow and Crop Eared Wolf on a number of difficult occasions—resisted an attempt by the impatient Mounted Police superintendent Sam Steele to tidy up the territory and keep the Blood in their place, responding bluntly that "the Indians are not confined to the reserve by any law or regulation . . . and [they] know they have the right to go and come as they please." Steele got slightly better at working with the chiefs during his ten years in charge, which made the job of his officers easier. In 1898 he was transferred to the Yukon, where he was in his element, managing a volatile situation with greedy gold miners.

What motivated these actions were familiar ambitions. The first was practical: exercising despotic power with arbitrary ruthlessness made life easier for the agents. The second was what we might call theoretical, and it was the deadliest, for it was part of a deep-seated determination described by John Maclean when he said, "We wish to make them white men, but they desire to become better Indians." This was social engineering on a national scale, and it involved First Nations whose lives and livelihoods were as different as the woodlands and the lakes and the mountain valleys and the coastal waterways and the tundra and the prairies they had called home for centuries, often millennia. It was a concept that had immense appeal to the authorities as a way of tidying up the territory for "development"—which is to say, for the agricultural and industrial enterprises, and the urbanization, that were associated with "civilization." And before we feel too superior to this, we need to recognize that this idea has infected much of our own international enterprise to "help" and "improve" many struggling societies around the world, destroying indigenous cultural traditions and viable harvesting practices by identifying them as insignia of "underdevelopment," to be replaced by models of "development" that are not only inappropriate but often economically, socially, culturally, environmentally, and spiritually toxic.

For the Blackfoot, it all came to a head in 1900, and at the center of it was the one ceremony that had become a flash point for the Blackfoot and the Indian agents: the Sun Dance, held in summer when the saskatoon berries were ripe. It was the great sacred gathering of the year; but it also had a secular component, as sacred gatherings often do, bringing the tribal communities together—consolidating the status of the confederacy, sustaining its material well-being, and celebrating spiritual presences and the power of prayer as well as the knowledge of medicine and ritual vested in particular individuals. And it confirmed the Blackfoot understanding of the seasons and of home, not unlike pow-wows and green corn ceremonies and thanksgivings and national holidays. This made some of the Indian agents and a few of the police officers angry, because they thought that the Sun Dance encouraged the "progressive" Indians to go "back to the blanket" when instead they needed to get on with becoming "civilized" and give up their "primitive" nomadic habits. And as Sam Steele noted grumpily, it was also a forum for boasting and toasting about the old days and the old ways, reimagining and rediscovering the past.

The Sun Dance was celebrated by almost all the Plains buffalo-hunting tribes, though many referred to it by other names such as the sun-making dance, the lodge-making dance, the thirsting dance, and the sacrifice lodge. Preparations for the Sun Dance began long before its celebration; in the case of the Blackfoot, a woman would have vowed to give the dance (in order to secure the benefit of its sacred medicine) and then told the chief, who spread the word to all the bands, who would then come together when the buffalo were gathered in large numbers. As both a spiritual and social occasion, the Sun Dance was a time for political discussions and family reunions and the recounting of successful raids, with gift giving, the transfer of songs and medicine bundles, and the trading of goods. Bull buffalo tongues, given into the care of the presiding medicine woman, were a crucial part of the ceremonies in buffalo days, replaced in the late 1800s by the tongues of beef cattle. There were meetings of sacred societies; and for a time the Sun Dance included a ritual of self-imposed sacrificial flesh-wounding by some men to keep vows made earlier, usually before going to war or on forays to gather horses from enemy camps.

The cutting of the central pole of the Sun Dance lodge initiated a series of ritual activities, including the placing of the pole in the ground with willow branches tied in its forks and supporting poles attached to construct the ceremonial lodge. The movement of the gathered bands to the selected location was traditionally in the nature of a "dress parade" when (in the words of one observer) "the Indians wore their finest clothes, decorated their horses with the best trappings, and the men rode with their weapons and shields exposed to view."

The last war party raid—at least the last to get attention from the authorities—was in 1889 against the Assiniboine, in which one scalp was taken. Crop Eared Wolf led a protest against the subsequent attempted arrest of the raiders at the Sun Dance that year, precipitating a scuffle in which the guns and clothing of the police were ripped from them. Red Crow managed to calm things down, and in doing so highlighted the sanctity of the ceremony itself. In this, he was supported by James Macleod, who said that intruding on a Sun Dance was like trying to arrest people in a church. Even so, conflicts with the government and church authorities over its celebration continued, especially during the 1890s when a particularly belligerent Indian agent among the Blood became determined to stop the Sun Dance, punishing those who were planning one with reduction of rations and treaty payments. But he had no real authority to stop it, since the Indian Act did not prohibit it.

The agent tried to have one of the chiefs, a leading ceremonialist, deposed for incompetence, stating that "any head man who so persistently refuses to obey the wishes of the Department cannot be said to be competent." The local Anglican bishop, William Cyprian Pinkham (called Chief Holy Rest by the Blood), intervened; Canada's Governor General Lord Minto took up the issue, advising that the Sun Dance should not be prohibited; and the police were mostly onside. But the agent was stubbornly opposed. He impaired the ritual, first by cutting the beef tongues in two and then by withholding them entirely from the rations, effectively putting a stop to the Sun Dance for several years.

The summer of 1900 threatened to turn the conflict into a crisis. In the winter, Yellow Buffalo Stone Woman had promised to sponsor a Sun Dance that summer to restore her sick husband to health. Red Crow took a major role in resisting the efforts of the agent to stop it by supporting the preparations, seeking the help of the superintendent of the police and, when he heard that the agent was refusing to provide the necessary beef tongues, offering to slaughter some of his own herd. But that turned out to be unnecessary when the North-West Mounted Police arranged for their police scouts from the Blood tribe to take their treaty meat allotment in whole tongues. The Sun Dance that year was the biggest in a decade, and was never again denied to the Blood. The year was remembered in the winter count as when "Yellow Buffalo Stone Woman put up the Sun Dance by force."

Even with all his achievements in leading his people toward material self-sufficiency, securing the place of that spiritual ceremony in the life of the Blackfoot was perhaps Red Crow's greatest triumph. And it was his last. Later that summer he died, having indicated that he wished his adopted son Crop Eared Wolf to succeed him.

Crop Eared Wolf consoled Jack Cowdry on Gussie's death in the fall of 1899, and Jack comforted Crop Eared Wolf when his father, Red Crow, died the following year—and also congratulated him as the new head chief of the Blood tribe. Jack never remarried, and for the rest of his life he grieved the loss of Amy and Gussie, and of those of his children who never made it past their first year. But he also believed in getting up and keeping going. Crop Eared Wolf's friendship helped. And they both kept their mutual love of mischief alive a few years later when a survey was being done to appraise some reserve acreage bordering the Mormon settlement in Cardston that the government wanted the Blood to surrender for sale.

Jack Cowdry had done a fair bit of banking in the community of Cardston by then, opening an office there so he had a comfortable association with the Mormon community—more comfortable than Crop Eared Wolf, who was engaged in a dispute with them over their "occupation" of land bordering the Blood reserve that he believed was Blackfoot. He was about to send a letter to Commissioner Laird—but Jack Cowdry said no, wait a bit . . . and the next week, wait a bit more . . . and a week later, wait a bit more . . . until Crop

Eared Wolf got completely exasperated. But just then, Jack (who knew something about surveying from his uncle and Ned Maunsell's brother George) came down to Crop Eared Wolf's home at Stand Off to say that the survey was all done—which was the last thing Crop Eared Wolf wanted to hear—and that they should go and see . . . and to bring a shovel and a big potato sack. Now Crop Eared Wolf trusted Jack, and was sure he wouldn't have done anything wrong deliberately. But he thought that he himself had done wrong in taking Jack's advice . . . until they got there, and he found out what Jack had in mind. The survey stakes stood about a foot above the ground, numbered in red crayon, with stakes (for positioning the transit that was used to measure angles) driven flush to the ground whenever the direction changed. Beginning at the boundary where the surveyors had started, Crop Eared Wolf rode and Jack walked along and carefully picked up every stake they came to and could pull or dig out, which was nearly every one, and put it in the sack that Crop Eared Wolf had tied to his saddle. It took them half the day, made more interesting by the stories Crop Eared Wolf told about "surveying" the terrain as a scout on raids, using the reflection from a looking-glass to signal from one hill to another, but they eventually came to the other boundary line, and had the survey stakes safely in the sack. "Now," said Jack, "let's go and take this to the Indian agent's office (where his old friend and former clerk William Black was working) and tell them we were riding down at the southern boundary and came across these stakes, and I said they were government survey stakes and you couldn't figure out what they were doing there and I said they must have misplaced them on your reserve land and we should bring them back in case they were wondering where they got to." The agent wasn't there; William Black couldn't speak, he was laughing so hard; and nobody ever said a word about what had happened, because the surveyors had not asked permission to come on the land, and they had been out-smarted by the Blackfoot and the banker. (The story has never been told before because everybody had a reason to keep it quiet—including Crop Eared Wolf, for some members of his tribe were keen on selling land they weren't using.)

Along with the ranchers, many in the foothills community felt their lives, and those of their families, were enriched and illuminated by living with and learning from the Blackfoot. Farm instructors and medical officers often brought their own expertise and intelligence together with Blackfoot experience and wisdom to serve the communities. One of them, Dr. Oliver Edwards, was for a time medical officer on the Blood reserve. He had begun his career in the Indian service as medical officer at Indian Head, near Fort Qu'Appelle, in 1883, just after Jack Cowdry arrived thereabouts. So they had known each other in Saskatchewan, and they were delighted to renew their acquaintance when Oliver Edwards and his wife, Henrietta, arrived at Stand Off in 1902.

Henrietta (also known as Hettie) Edwards became the more renowned of the two. A formidable presence, she was instrumental in establishing both Canada's National Council of Women and the Victorian Order of Nurses. In 1927, she was one of the "Famous Five" women from Alberta who fought to have women recognized in the constitution—which was then called the British North America Act—as "persons." At that time only "qualified persons" were eligible to be appointed to the Senate of Canada, and the phrase was widely accepted (by men) as referring only to them. The case was officially designated as *Edwards v. Attorney General of Canada* but is now better known as the "Persons Case," and it has become one of the landmark cases in Canadian legal history. The "Famous Five" took advantage of a provision in the Supreme Court of Canada Act that said that five persons acting together as a group could petition the court for an interpretation of any part of the constitution; and so they took the case first to the Supreme Court— which ruled against them. But Edwards and her co-petitioners were not so easily put off, and went to the Privy Council in England, at the time the court of last appeal for Canadians—which decided in their favor in 1929: women were persons.

Some of Hettie Edwards's determination may have been encouraged by her close contact with the women of the Blood community around Stand Off. She had close associations with many Blood women, and was honored with the name "Otter Woman," after an animal sacred to the Blackfoot. With tuberculosis common in the hospital and maternal mortality high on the reserve, she lobbied (sadly unsuccessfully) for a separate maternity home for the women; and she wrote several texts on the legal status of women that addressed some of the particular inequities facing First Nations women. (She was also an inveterate collector of Indian artifacts, but unusual back then in that she took the trouble to identify their provenance and purpose, as well as the stories and beliefs associated with them. She commissioned paintings from the First Nations communities, as well as becoming a painter herself.)

Jack Cowdry continued to raise his older children, Mary and Gus, in Fort Macleod. (There are receipts in his diary for the purchase of a doll's house and a tricycle, and a little later a sidesaddle and tack and a regular saddle and bridle from Harry Litle, who ran a saddlery store in town.) Jack's daughter Edith was still in Ingersoll, and he went there more and more often as the years went by, and as she got older he brought her more and more presents, and more and more stories.

Edith later said that one thing she noticed about her father was that he was shorter than the farmers she knew in Ingersoll; but he had a beard just like they did, and his hair was the color of the horse that pulled the wagon that brought the milk every other day. He always wore wonderful hats when he came to visit, a different one each time, and as soon as he arrived he would take it off and place it upside down on the side table. She asked him why he did that, and he said it was so the brim wouldn't flatten out like a johnnycake (which was a kind of pancake, but tasted better). Then he would ask her to hold St. Bruno, his tin of sweet-smelling tobacco, while he filled his pipe and lit it with a single match and started telling stories. He would always start with a story about the long pipes of the Blackfoot Indians who lived near Fort Macleod, telling her how they smoked them in their tipis, and when favorite guests came they would share a pipe. And to show her he gave her a puff on his pipe when the aunts weren't looking. She said it smelled better than it tasted.

Every few months Jack would send Edith clothes from the Eaton's catalogue: on her birthday when she was eight she got a green Ulster coat, double-breasted, with a high storm collar trimmed with fancy braid; and at Christmas that year, a pair of single-strap slippers made of chocolate-colored kid leather. She had fond memories of her life as a little girl in Ingersoll with Diddy and the aunts, especially tea time, when the crocheted doilies would be brought out to put under cups and saucers with pretty designs, and a spoon would be put in the cup before pouring in tea to draw off the heat so the cup didn't crack. They lavished their stern, sentimental Victorian attention on Edith, and engaged a tutor to come and teach her about the world as far away as, well, Woodstock, down the road a full ten miles.

During those early years all Edith really knew about her father's life out west was from his stories, and from Uncle Nat, who came to visit every month or so. And from her own imagination, which Diddy and her aunts told her was what brought stories to life. She wasn't sure where her imagination was, but they said it was what they relied on for their sense of Jack's life in the foothills. That and the novel *The Virginian*, which they had bought when it came out in 1902.

On one visit when Edith was nine, Jack brought her a gold nugget and some flint made into an arrowhead from the mountains to the west of Fort Macleod, and a piece of rock called ocher that he had picked up just a few miles from town, with which she wrote her name in orange in the front of the journal he gave her. He told her how he had got the nugget from a stream in the mountains by taking a pan and swirling the stream water around in it until everything had swished out except the heaviest bits of sand—and if you were lucky some of those were gold, and sometimes big pieces of gold like this nugget. He said the people who lived in the mountains had traded flint to the Plains Indians to make the spears and arrows they had used to hunt the buffalo in the old days; and the Blackfoot had found ocher in the hills close by and used it to paint on the rocks near Fort Macleod for a very long time, and sometimes to paint their horses or themselves.

A year later around Easter, Jack brought Edith a jade pendant shaped like a tear and attached to a gold chain, which she wore around her neck every day for years afterward. He told her it had been Gussie's favorite piece of jewelry.

15

FOR SALE: COWDRY BROTHERS BANK . . . NOT FOR SALE: LAND ON THE BLOOD RESERVE

POLITICAL CLOUDS WERE GATHERING over the town and country Jack Cowdry loved; and he and Nat (who was consulted at every turn back in Ontario, and heard a fair bit of cursing from Jack over what was happening) started to think it might be time to close the book on the bank. Canada's national institutions, including the national banks, were buying up local businesses in the West, bringing them into line with national priorities and reinforcing a frontier ideology in which Indians were mere distractions. Also, Alberta ranching and Saskatchewan farming interests were both demanding separate roles in the Dominion, and forming a single new province was looking more and more unlikely. And no one was thinking seriously about the First Nations except as wards who were constantly on the verge of being betrayed.

Jack Cowdry always thought of Fort Macleod and the foothills as the center of a new kind of conversation between the old nations of the territory and the new nation of Canada. It would be too easy to say that provincial status for Alberta and Saskatchewan came in 1905 and undermined the need for any conversation at all, but certainly it played its part by creating a new set of metropolitan ambitions in which the First Nations did not directly figure.

Whatever the reasons, and probably there were several, Jack and Nat decided to sell Cowdry Brothers Bank to the Canadian Bank of Commerce in 1905. They had excellent relations with the Commerce—Jack Cowdry was one of their directors in the territory—and the Commerce (along with a couple of the other nationwide banks) had provided good lines of credit for Cowdry Brothers through the years. The deal went through at a price of $105,904.88, with the Bank of Commerce taking over nearly half a million dollars in loans, and Jack Cowdry personally guaranteeing a little over fifty thousand dollars for six months—at the end of which he was only a couple of hundred dollars short. Everyone had paid up on unexpectedly short notice, even in that uncertain time, to make sure Jack Cowdry was not out of pocket. As L. V. Kelly, the author of *The Range Men*, put it in his history of the ranchers and Indians in the territory, that was "an astonishingly pleasing average for any banker." Or anybody at all. Jack, for his part, was both very pleased and not surprised. "They just kept their word," he said.

What was not so pleasing was how some things changed for the community when the Canadian Bank of Commerce bought the local bank. The Agricultural Society of Macleod asked the new management if they would sponsor horse racing at the annual fair, as Cowdry Brothers had done from the beginning in 1886. The big bank said no.

Jack Cowdry took his portion of the proceeds of the sale of the bank and put it, along with some savings, into a ranching venture with Ned Maunsell, who had a lot of experience both with cattle ranching and with Jack Cowdry. The Cochrane ranch, which had been staggering along for a number of years, had decided to sell off both its cattle and its land holdings. The ranch, which was one of the first in the territory—it had been established in 1881—owned

67,000 acres in the area around Cardston which the Mormons were anxious to purchase. A deal was soon reached for the Cochrane ranch to sell the land and ranch buildings to the Mormons for six dollars an acre, with the cattle—about twelve thousand head—to be removed as soon as possible. Enter Ned and Jack, with an offer for the herd. The cattle needed to be counted to confirm the price; so in due course the count was completed and a check for nearly a quarter of a million dollars signed on the seat of Ned Maunsell's saddle. Family gossip has it that Jack went in on the deal because the Cochrane brand was "C"—just right for Cowdry; and that has his hallmark sense of humor. But he also wanted to turn his twenty years of banking back into a local business; and for him *the* local business was ranching.

That said, there were some things to be sorted out . . . among them the fiery personality of Ned Maunsell. He already had about six thousand cattle in his herd and seems to have seen this as his chance to be *the* big rancher in southern Alberta, rivaling George Lane and Pat Burns. Pat Burns was a very good friend of Jack Cowdry's, and thrived on competition; but Jack had no such ambitions. By this time he did know the cattle business, however, having been banker for most of the ranchers in the foothills, including Burns, through thick and thin and roundups and die-ups for the past twenty years. And he had also spent time listening to Crop Eared Wolf. The only things he didn't understand about ranching, he used to say, were the cows and the weather. The horses he could figure out.

With the days of the open range numbered, one urgent issue had to do with leasing more grazing land for such a large herd. Leases were hard to get, given the changes in leasing arrangements in the 1890s, and Ned Maunsell had already had some unpleasant run-ins with the government about canceled or amended leases. So Jack Cowdry went to Ottawa to see Frank Oliver, who had just been appointed minister of the interior and superintendent general of Indian affairs. Maunsell had singled out Oliver for some of his less courteous invective, so it would have been hopeless for Maunsell to go and see him, or even to come along. But Oliver liked and trusted Jack Cowdry, and he helped him acquire a 60,000-acre land lease, a rare treasure since it was one of the few that was still irrevocable for twenty-one years. The cost was something over $22,000, which was substantial—but so were twelve thousand head of cattle.

With his name on the line, Jack Cowdry also secured five other leases with a total acreage of nearly 126,000 acres. These five were subject to cancellation on two years' notice if required for settlement, but they were valuable for now, and might well be renewable. Also, Jack (and Ned Maunsell too) had very good relations with the Peigan, close to where the new leases were, and Jack was optimistic they would be able to lease some reserve land for grazing if they needed to.

In many ways Jack Cowdry and Ned Maunsell were like chalk and cheese; but they had worked together for many years, in good times and bad, and were old friends. So they worked things out. And ranching in the foothills was never the poorer for having two people with different temperaments and talents in partnership, even though it might cause sparks to fly from time to time.

Jack sold his house in Macleod and moved with the kids to a ranch near Pincher Creek on the long-term leased land. He stayed in very close touch with the town of Macleod, which was just down the road a ways, and was there often. He also kept up other interests, helping out a friend in Calgary who was starting a business there. The leasing arrangements worked well, and Ned Maunsell was a good cattleman, the equal of any in the territory when it came to stewardship of the grazing lands, and that (along with their friendships on the reserve) served them both well when it later came to leasing land for the winter from the Peigan.

———

But as so often in the ranching business, and especially in the foothills, the weather was about to take charge. The winter of 1906/7 was as bad as 1886/87, and took over the tag as the Big Die-Up. Cowdry and Maunsell lost over half their herd; the numbers are inevitably a bit sketchy, but Maunsell put the losses at $120,000. They had seen this before, from both sides of the corral—banker and rancher—and both times they got through it. It was a tough way to start a new business, but so had it been for Cowdry Brothers Bank and the Maunsell Brothers ranch when both were set up.

Other ranchers also took heavy losses, some catastrophic. Discouraged by the closing of the open range with the withdrawal of large, long-term leases, many turned into stock farmers rather than herd ranchers as they "beefed out" their herd, spaying cows and selling off breeding stock to stay in business; but that in turn created an oversupply that brought down the price of beef. Some, like George Lane at the Bar U, diversified, maintaining as much of a commitment to open-range ranching as was possible while developing crops and a very successful breeding program with Percheron horses. And Pat Burns moved to integrate ranching with food marketing, understanding the need to find common cause with the farming communities. Both Lane and Burns continued to believe that the best livestock was the least pampered, but they were practical about the decreasing availability of winter range; and all the ranchers had an independence of spirit that served them well in bad times, though sometimes not so well when times were good. They shared a reputation for honesty and hard work and a sense of humor, and for putting in hours that would make most of us melt.

For their part, Cowdry and Maunsell Brothers ranch took its losses, bringing Jack's credit and Ned's craft together to manage the next season, with Jack working from his base near Pincher Creek and arranging to sell some of the Cowdry Maunsell cattle to Pat Burns the next fall at a better price.

The years after 1900 were challenging ones for the Blood, as they were for all the Blackfoot tribes. The Blood, having won the Sun Dance fight, now faced a new threat with the rush of settlement encouraged by the Canadian government, which increased homestead entries from just over 7,400 in 1900 to nearly 31,000 five years later. And to top it off, or bottom it out, there was the appointment of an Indian agent on the Blood reserve who was determined to secure a surrender of some of their land. When he met with opposition and a blunt refusal from Crop Eared Wolf, who rallied the tribe against the proposal, the agent became determined to destroy him.

Bad idea. And a hopeless one. The agent's name was Robert Wilson, and he knew the territory well. He had begun his time in the foothills with the North-West Mounted Police before becoming a trader and then signing up with the Department of Indian Affairs, posted first to the Peigan and then to the Blood reserve. He was knowledgeable about Blackfoot life, to the point that he fancied himself something of an ethnographer, in touch with the anthropologist and naturalist George Bird Grinnell, who visited him regularly on the reserve; and he was a photographer of considerable talent and tenacity, one of the very few to have received permission to photograph some of the ceremonies. He also had entrepreneurial agricultural ambitions first for the Peigan and then for the Blood (when he became their agent in 1903), designed to create the conditions of self-sufficiency which leaders like Crowfoot and Red Crow envisaged. But they were *his* designs, not those of the Blackfoot—his "wards," as he would later describe them—and they masked an impatience that was brutally uncontrolled.

A couple of years before Agent Wilson took on the responsibility for the Blood reserve, the Mormons in Cardston had asked for more land to be opened for settlement. There was little question where that land might come from, since the Cardston community bordered the Blood reserve, and those trespassing survey stakes were obviously intended to map out the sale. Before he died in the summer of 1900, Red Crow had already been disputing with Cardston about what he perceived as encroachment on the reserve, a dispute in which he was awkwardly implicated because some in the Blood tribe blamed him for not paying attention to decisions made when the reserve was surveyed back in 1883. Knowing that the issue, and the grasping ambitions of settlers, would not go away easily (and they still haven't), Red Crow had secured a solemn promise from Crop Eared Wolf that as chief he would not sell any of the land on the reserve, a promise that was also kept by Crop Eared Wolf's son Shot Both Sides and by his successors. Thus Crop Eared Wolf and Shot Both Sides (who served as chief from 1913 until 1956), along with the chiefs of the Blood bands, became what the Aboriginal rights lawyer Leslie Pinder once called "the Carriers of No."

Keen on increased settlement, the government put considerable pressure on the Blood to surrender some of their land to the Mormons, and eventually forced a tribal vote in 1907 on the sale of 2,400 acres near the southern border of their reserve. Crop Eared Wolf went to every family in the tribe arguing against the sale—it was reported that he "scared some, coaxed others, and still others he persuaded to abstain"; and when the vote was taken, to the surprise and dismay of the agent and the government, who had predicted a landslide in favor, the surrender was rejected by a margin of over three to one.

Agent Wilson was furious; and for the next four years, with compulsive energy, he tried to humiliate Crop Eared Wolf and terminate his tenure as chief. Exercising his role as "warden" of his "wards," he also tried to prohibit the Indians from participation in local fairs and rodeos and other events—even though by this time the Blackfoot parades had become a star attraction—on the grounds that it interfered with their harvesting of hay to secure revenue to pay for reserve expenses. Writing to the secretary of Indian affairs in Ottawa in the spring of 1908, Wilson complained that Indian parades, with their paint and feathers, represented "a revival of barbarism under the direction, and with the substantial encouragement, of municipalities or similar organizations of wealth and influence. . . . At Macleod the Indian show was practically the whole thing, the ordinary fair of the white people being quite insignificant." Certainly Jack Cowdry, ambling among the crowd of admirers, was delighted. Later that season, Wilson tried to stop the Blood participating in the Dominion Day pageant in Calgary by refusing them permission—commenting that "the Indian Pageant business [has] been so much overdone in late years in neighboring towns as to become a distinct detriment to the progress of the Blood Indians." Fortunately, his refusal made no difference. Among those who pushed back was the Methodist missionary John McDougall, who wrote bluntly, "the Indians being the original dwellers in this country should take a leading part."

Wilson had set his store by agricultural production on and off the reserve, and his reaction to these setbacks was pathologically vindictive against Crop Eared Wolf. He thought he was smart, and certainly he was devious; but he was no match for Crop Eared Wolf, and soon the wheels started to come off the agent's wagon train. He cut off rations for those who participated in the fairs; in response to which, the fair committees butchered steers for the Indians. And he refused to approve the chief's annual treaty payment. But Crop Eared Wolf was not sitting this out. Unwilling just to react to Wilson's actions, he went on the offensive, making the rounds of the hay camps to persuade the Blood not to work on contracts with one particular cattle company favored by Wilson, saying that if they withdrew their labor—a time-honored strategy for those who control little else—it would be easier for him to get Wilson discharged, and then they would get a new agent. But even then, the old warrior was not through. Wilson had tried to get him deposed as "incompetent"; Crop Eared Wolf turned this back on him, and was almost certainly behind a letter from the secretary of the department in Ottawa chastising Wilson for "neglect of duty" for not reporting on the number of cattle owned by that same favored company on the reserve—a very serious charge for what was a fairly routine lapse. And taking up new legal technology, as his people had taken up horses and guns and ranching and farming, Crop Eared Wolf filed a formal complaint of harassment through a Macleod lawyer; and as an extra measure Crop Eared Wolf complained about the actions of the agent to the commissioner of Indian affairs. It was a mistake to push him and his people around. And Agent Wilson was gone by 1911.

It is the unique character of each First Nation that gets lost in many accounts of their past and much accounting of their histories and hopes, which are jumbled together into something called "the Indian question" and applied to every indigenous community in the Americas in countless European reports and commissions and inquiries going back to the beginning of the sixteenth century. They effectively homogenize the situations of peoples from widely different cultures living in widely different geographies and communities and speaking many different languages, peoples whose histories of dislocation and dispossession and disillusionment and despair are stunningly similar but whose hopes and dreams and possibilities and beliefs are specific to their situation. There is no single answer to "the Indian question," because there is no single question.

———

The Blackfoot, even when they resisted most fiercely and said no most firmly, were always looking for a way of also saying yes—their peacemakers and peacekeepers waiting for the warriors to finish their task so they could begin theirs. But woe to anyone, such as Agent Wilson, who tried to harass or humiliate them. One of the things that characterized the foothills during the late 1800s was that, in most situations when there was a discussion, a disagreement, or a showdown between the different attitudes and ambitions—and the often unpredictable personalities—of the Blackfoot and the newcomers, the Mounted Police and the Department of Indian Affairs, the politicians and the citizens, the warmongers and the peacemakers, everyone recognized that they needed to find common ground.

It was an unsettling time of change for everybody, so it produced some uneasy relationships that occasionally appeared quite contradictory but allowed a path forward for a lot of people. For example, the missionaries had to seek the alliance of the chiefs for permission to establish churches and schools on the reserves; the chiefs in turn listened courteously to them, and analyzed the vagaries of both Catholic and Protestant fortunes in the territory. The men of the North-West Mounted Police, for their part, while supposed to be maintaining law and order quite often engaged in their own "disorderly conduct," and some of them had relationships with Indian women—which often caused bursts of convenient outrage from the missionaries (and others). And at the same time the police in Blackfoot territory generally refused to enforce the prohibitions against Indian spiritual ceremonies that were intermittently proposed by Ottawa and by some Indian agents.

And while the authoritarianism of the agents was one of the most wretched legacies of the past for many First Nations peoples, there were exceptions. For instance, agents determined to use the letter to fulfill the spirit of the treaties were in office fairly consistently at the

Siksika agency in Gleichen, and cooperation was the result. The Gooderhams, father and son, served as successive Indian agents, mostly based there, for nearly seventy years, balancing habitual paternalism with capable peacemaking, and facilitating moves toward self-sufficiency that the tribe approved. Their style was not by any means always welcomed; but they were respected, and when George Gooderham retired he was made an honorary chief of the Blackfoot.

In 1911 Jack Cowdry sold most of his interest in the ranch to Ned Maunsell, bid farewell to his friends in the foothills where he had lived for the past twenty-five years, and moved to Vancouver. He had visited often over the preceding few years and knew folks there; and his two older children, Mary and Gus, were also looking to the West Coast. (Gus had learned some of the elements of trade and commerce from his father, and was hoping to go into the import-export business in Vancouver.) Jack Cowdry rented a house on Nelson Street, bought land in what is now Jericho Beach and West Point Grey, built a home for Mary (who had become engaged) and then one for himself, and made plans to bring his family together.

So he called for Edith, who was going on twelve by this time, to come from Ingersoll and live with him. And Diddy too, if she would. He said he had found a young girl about Edith's age named Margaret, whose parents and grandparents he knew, and they could go to school together just down the street from where Edith and he would live.

It's hard to imagine what it must have been like for Edith to travel several thousand miles away from the only home and the only family she'd ever had, to live with a man who brought chocolates and smoked a pipe and told stories. But she did. Or what it must have been like for Diddy to follow the niece she had raised since birth to resettle in a strange town called Vancouver on the other side of the world. But she did. Or for Jack Cowdry to pick up where he had left off a dozen years earlier with Gussie, and make a new home with memories of marriages and births and deaths like the hinges on every door in the house. But he did.

Later, when Edith was thirty-one, she opened a little shop on Howe Street in Vancouver. She called it The Jade Box; and in photographs from those days one can see she was still wearing her mother's tear-shaped jade pendant.

During those years, the early 1930s, Edith heard a song recorded by the Carter Family which she remembered overhearing her father sing when she came to live with him in Vancouver. It had first been recorded by others in 1901, she found out later; but her father never sang it to her. Just to himself. The song was called "Hello, Central, Give Me Heaven."

Papa, I'm so sad and lonely,
Sobbed a tearful little child
Since dear mama's gone to heaven
Papa, darling, you've not smiled
I will speak to her and tell her
That we want her to come home
Just you listen and I'll call her
Through the telephone.

Hello, Central, give me heaven
For my mama's there
You can find her with the angels
On the golden stair
She'll be glad it's me who's speaking
Call her, won't you please
For I want to surely tell her
We're so lonely here.

———

Ranching had been changing with the closing down of the open range and the parceling up of the foothills with settlement fences, and the first Calgary Stampede in 1912 was conceived and bankrolled by Burns and Lane and McLean and Cross (to the tune of $25,000 each) as a "final celebration" of the ranching heritage they had helped nourish, and in which Jack Cowdry's bank had played a significant part. But the reason Jack found this Stampede interesting wasn't just the riding and roping and other events that brought the skills and storyline of ranching to the wider public, or the nostalgia of his friends among the ranchers, but the prospect of wide participation by the Indian horsemen and the tribal communities of the Alberta plains, whose courtesy and hospitality he had enjoyed for a quarter century. He knew that Guy Weadick, the promoter of the event, had approached Crop Eared Wolf about this; and that his friend was very keen, and had come up with several ideas on how to highlight their participation in the event. (Another elaborate display of foothills First Nations traditions, Banff Indian Days, had begun in 1894 and became a major attraction just after the turn of the century, continuing through the 1970s.)

Crop Eared Wolf, among other leaders, saw these occasions as offering an opportunity to educate as well as entertain; and he fiercely dismissed the attempts of some of the Indian agents to discourage participation. So with Crop Eared Wolf's encouragement, Weadick's energy, and the support of the four ranchers of the range, Indians from the Blackfoot Confederacy along with Stoney Indians led the parade at the opening of the Calgary Stampede on September 2, 1912, followed by the old-time traders, the North-West Mounted Police, some of the early stagecoaches and drivers and settlers, and the ranchers and cowboys with their chuckwagons and cavvy of horses. The Indians camped with their traditional tipis on the rodeo grounds to signal their presence at the heart of this life on the prairies, and the celebration of ranching, with over eighteen hundred Indians there for the occasion and for genial conversation between them and other participants and spectators (along with considerable education for some of the citizens of Calgary who had never met an Indian or talked with one).

In the Blood agency files, there is an item for the treaty payments in November 1900, identifying 261 persons in Crop Eared Wolf's Fish Eaters band. After payments to him and his family, there is one to "Tom Three Persons," listed simply as "boy." Five years later, he is listed again, this time "aged 15." The involvement of the Blood in fairs and parades and pageants—and in rodeos—may have nourished a dream in this young Blackfoot. Tom Three Persons went to that first Calgary Stampede, riding a notorious unconquered outlaw called Cyclone, who had thrown off all 129 cowboys who tried to ride him in rodeos throughout the West, twelve of them that very week. (Tom almost didn't make it to the Stampede; he was being held in the police cells in Macleod for some minor offense and not due to be discharged until after the rodeo. But Ned Maunsell heard about the situation, went to the sympathetic inspector of Indian agencies, and secured Tom's early release for the competition.)

Tom Three Persons rode Cyclone to a standstill (which was the routine in rodeos back then), thus winning the premier event—the bareback bronco competition. So the star cowboy at the Stampede that year was an Indian; and Tom Three Persons would soon become one of the most famous rodeo riders of his generation.

Crop Eared Wolf declared himself very proud; though sadly he missed the Stampede because he was also very ill. In 1917 Tom Three Persons incurred the wrath of the Blood Indian agent when he voted against a land surrender. The agent, W. J. Dilworth, was so angry that he somehow forced Tom Three Persons off the reserve; but Dilworth was gone by 1919, and when Tom Three Persons returned he became one of the wealthiest, as well as one of the most generous, men on the Blood reserve.

Jack Cowdry had gone back to the foothills from Vancouver for the Calgary Stampede in 1912, and he said to Edith that he also had some ranch business to attend to. But his real reason for the trip was to see Crop Eared Wolf.

From 1900, when he succeeded his father Red Crow as head chief of the Blood, until his death in 1913, Crop Eared Wolf had led his people with a sternness of purpose that has inspired the tribe for over a century since, maintaining their reserve as the largest in the country. He lived his life bravely. Though wounded at an early age in that raid against the Cree, he was one of the most renowned "custodians" of horses on the northern Plains, and one of the best storytellers. In his younger days he could ride like the wind, was renowned as a scout, and throughout his life he understood people and horses so well that he could be in and out of an enemy camp gathering horses—or interfere with an Indian agent's belligerent scheming—without interrupting their dreams. He had an uncanny gift for knowing what was happening before it happened, and for seeing new possibilities in the old ways. Like his horses, he hardly slept; he was a fighter, and a dangerous one; he was a peacemaker, and a good one; and he was proud. And pride was a saving grace for the Blackfoot then and now.

Jack Cowdry had gone back to the foothills because he wanted to say goodbye to his friend. Crop Eared Wolf died the following year. They never met again. Until now. And anytime that quirt is brought out, especially in Blackfoot territory.

In Vancouver, Jack Cowdry was never without an adventure in hand; first he bought a ten-ton yawl to sail up and down the coast, and later he purchased a sturdy west-coast motor launch on which he and

Edith traveled the islands and channels and up the fjords that make up the Northwest coast, navigating the gloriously beautiful passages studded with sovereign First Nations communities.

Later, when he was in his mid-seventies, Jack took his son Gus through western British Columbia to Alaska—not on a cruise but riding on horseback from Garibaldi up through the Chilcotins to Anahim Lake, making camp along the way until they reached Stuie in what is now Tweedsmuir Park, then down to Bella Coola and the ocean, where he borrowed a Tlingit canoe and they headed up the inside passage—or inland passage, as he always called it—to Prince Rupert and onward to the Alaskan Panhandle, just the two of them most of the way.

He lost Gus to cancer in 1935, and Mary passed away in 1942 after a courageous struggle with tuberculosis. My mother, Edith, married my father, Edward Chamberlin, in 1939, and my grandfather Jack came to live with my parents and my sister and me and Diddy. He wrote wonderful letters, including one to me—addressed to "Master Teddy"—in a firm and steady hand, written a week before he died and hoping I had recovered from a cold.

Jack Cowdry died in Vancouver in 1947, at the age of ninety, after taking friends to the Yacht Club for tea and returning to the nursing home for a whisky.

Listening to others is the first courtesy, and a custom which Jack Cowdry and Crop Eared Wolf both rendered and respected. They are the presiding spirits of this book. They opened doors; and they also shut doors against the bullies and the breakers of promises. They left us with a line of credit, to be used in building a world of customs and courtesies. And most of all they left us with some promises to keep, and a couple of questions. What have we done? And what do we do next?

ACKNOWLEDGMENTS

I could not have written this book without my beloved wife, Lorna Goodison. She has been with me every step of the way, picked me up after each misstep, and put up with my whinging and whining with remarkable grace and generosity and good humor. And she has given me consistently wise advice, drawn from her lifetime's experience as a writer and from her celebrated memoir of her mother and her people.

My children—Sarah, Geoff, and Meg—asked me all the right questions, and (bless them) never expected sensible answers; their good wishes have meant the world to me. And their great-grandfather would have been as proud of them as I am. Meanwhile Fin and Thomas giggled and called me Grampy, catching the spirit of this book; and Nica nuzzled.

Some of my old friends are mentioned in the text. Others belong right here. George and Dianne Laforme have been with me for most of my life; and George, a master storyteller, helped me more than he knew, and probably more than I realize—this book is dedicated to his memory. For many years I rode in the foothills with John Burns from the home ranch of his great-uncle Pat Burns, where he grew up and I grew to love the country; his stories are part of this book. The friendship of John and Barb Murray has been both a rock and a touchstone, for which I am forever thankful. Neil Sterritt honored our home with a Gitxsan name, *Wilp Skimsim*—the House of the Golden Eagle.

This book is about friendship, and it would take another book to do justice to the many other friends who have helped me along the way; I hope they know how grateful I am. For now, I can only mention some who have played an important part in the writing of this book. First of all, Kate McAll from the BBC, who started me off with a radio program about my grandfather produced on location in southern Alberta in 2002. Others followed with advice and assistance and books and contacts and inspiration: Michael Asch, John Borrows, Arni Brownstone, Paul Chartrand, Hugh Dempsey, Simon Evans, Jennifer Glossop, Janet Irving, John Jennings, Tina Loo, John Lutz, Gordon MacIvor, Ian MacRae, Val Napoleon, Don Smith, Meg Stanley, Jan Reeves, Jim Tully, Graeme Wynn.

Louise Dennys, my Knopf Canada publisher and editor, believed in me when I began thinking about this book, and worked with me on it from the start. Her enthusiasm kept me going, her friendship kept me comforted, and her editing kept me on track.

It is to Jan-Erik Guerth of BlueBridge that I owe this edition, and this opportunity to reach readers south of the border. He is a publisher of rare diligence and dedication, and I am deeply grateful to him for his imaginative, intelligent, and wonderfully well-informed suggestions, his lovely sense of humor, and his editorial judgment. I have been a much favored fellow traveler.

PHOTO CREDITS

SOURCES AND ENDNOTES

Many of my grandfather Jack Cowdry's personal notes and banking records are in the Glenbow Museum archives in Calgary, as well as in papers and letters and journals held by the Cowdry family. And in his stories, held in the memory of family and friends. I remember his storytelling; but I was very young, and many of the stories I tell come from my mother, Edith Cowdry, who was born in 1899 and lived until 1986, and some from my father, who shared my grandfather's banking heritage. My debt to them goes beyond words. The widespread Cowdry clan has also been indispensable: Jack Cowdry's other grandson, also named Jack Cowdry; his granddaughters, my sister Liz Food, and Nancy Tinning—and her son Ret; Nat's granddaughter Margie Park; Jack and Nat's brother Ned's granddaughters Mi Haas—and her grandson Adam Shoemaker—and Marnie Ovens—and her son Peter who, along with his father, Frank, prepared and updated the Cowdry family genealogy. On Gussie Thompson's side of the family, Edith Crichton and her son Ted Boon; and my godmother Margaret Williams. I am also grateful to Annabel Crop Eared Wolf for a conversation about her great-grandfather.

There are records relating generally to this period, as well as specifically to my grandfather, in Lethbridge and Fort Macleod, as well as in the Methodist (United Church) archives in Toronto. Record Group 10 (Indian Affairs) and Record Group 18 (for the North-West Mounted Police) in Library and Archives Canada are major sources for documentary evidence; but they always need to be complemented, and sometimes corrected, by historical accounts, both amateur and professional, and by the oral traditions of indigenous peoples. The Glenbow Museum is a treasure house for anyone interested in the history of the West; and Doug Cass and his colleagues made working in the archives a pleasure.

There are some excellent academic and popular histories that I have relied on, but many of the details in this story are to be found in reminiscences published locally, catching the voice and much of the spirit of those who lived in these remarkable years. It is storytelling—mine and theirs, both in writing and in "writing without words" on quirts and buffalo robes—that shape this book, anchored in the realities and celebrating the imaginings of the people living in this brief period and this particular place. The stories of the Blackfoot, unique in both their forms and their functions, are at the center of my account; but I have been careful, because they are Blackfoot stories, not mine. And while my account of the *Niitsítapi* draws on a wide range of written sources and oral performances, the permanent exhibition *Niitsitapiisinni: Our Way of Life*, developed collaboratively by the Blackfoot and the Glenbow Museum has been a constant inspiration.

INTRODUCTION. There are excellent and wider-ranging perspectives on this fascinating time and place in Richard White's *"It's Your Misfortune and None of My Own": A New History of the American West*; Patricia Limerick's *The Legacy of Conquest: The Unbroken Past of the American West*; Hugh Dempsey's *Red Crow: Warrior Chief*; Richard Slatta's *Comparing Cowboys and Frontiers: New Perspectives on the History of the Americas*; and John Jennings's *The Cowboy Legend: Owen Wister's Virginian and the Canadian-American Frontier*. Their work, along with that of many others acknowledged in the following notes, has been indispensable. The legal system on the prairies is described in *Laws and Societies in the Canadian Prairie West, 1670–1940*, eds. Louis A. Knafla and Jonathan Swainger; and in *Law and Justice in a New Land: Essays in Western Canadian Legal History*, ed. Knafla. The comments on Sitting Bull are taken from a number of historical accounts, including Alvin Josephy, Jr.'s *500 Nations*; James Olson's *Red Cloud and the Sioux Problem*; and an article by Garrett Wilson, "Refugee Crisis," in *Canada's History* (Febr.-March 2017).

CHAPTER ONE. William Johnson's remarks are from a letter he wrote to the Earl of Shelburne in 1767, quoted by Duncan Campbell Scott in "Indian Affairs, 1763–1841," the first of his three essays on Indian administration in British North America and Canada, commissioned for *Canada and Its Provinces: A History of the Canadian People and Their Institutions*, eds. Adam Shortt and Arthur Doughty, published in 1913. Chester B. Beaty's *The Landscapes of Southern*

Alberta offered useful background information about Chinook country. The newspaper description of Fort Macleod is from the papers of the Methodist missionary John Maclean in the United Church of Canada Archives in Toronto; the first grumpy account of the town is from a letter written by Mary E. Inderwick to her sister (and published in the *Alberta Historical Review*, ed. Hugh Dempsey, in 1967), and the second is by John D. Higinbotham in his book *When the West Was Young*. The list of buildings in Fort Macleod is from both John Maclean's journal notes and from *Fort Macleod—Our Colourful Past: A History of the Town from 1874 to 1924*, published by the town's diligent History Book committee and a source for many other details; I have also learned from the monographs *Fort Macleod: The Story of the Mounted Police*, ed. H. G. Long, and *A Walking/Driving Tour of Fort Macleod's Historic Downtown and Residential Area*, put together by the Fort Macleod Provincial Historic Area Society. The account of the mail system is from Edward Brado, *Cattle Kingdom: Early Ranching in Alberta*, to which I have often turned in writing this book; and from North-West Mounted Police Inspector Cecil Denny, quoted in a typescript by William Pearce, "The Early History of Western Canada," in the Thomas Fisher Rare Book Library at the University of Toronto. I am indebted for the line about flies walking to Gary Holthaus, in *Wide Skies: Finding a Home in the West*; for the description of the berries to Alex Johnston's *Plants and the Blackfoot*; and for the legend of Chief Mountain and the naming of Cowley to *A History of the Early Days of Pincher Creek*, prepared by members of the Women's Institute of Alberta. The Blackfoot place names are from Hugh Dempsey's *Indian Names for Alberta Communities*. Some details about Harry (Kamoose) Taylor are from an obituary written by Fred Haultain and published in the *Lethbridge News* in March 1901; about Francis Dickens, from Roderick C. Macleod's article in the *Dictionary of Canadian Biography*. The newspaperman was Bob Edwards, writing in his Calgary tabloid the *Eye Opener*; the description of "Lord" Brook is from the Pincher Creek reminiscences. Some details about Taylor's Table, and about Fred Haultain in chapter 2, are from Grant MacEwan's *Frederick Haultain: Frontier Statesman of the Canadian Northwest*, as well as *The Haultain Story*, a monograph compiled by Doris and Claud Stevens for the Fort Macleod Historical Association.

CHAPTER TWO. The discussion of treaties throughout the book is drawn from a range of sources, in particular Michael Asch's eloquent *On Being Here to Stay: Treaties and Aboriginal Rights in Canada* and Hugh Dempsey's *The Great Blackfoot Treaties*. Also, Gerald Friesen's *The Canadian Prairies: A History* offers a refreshingly regional account of these times. Adams Archibald is quoted by Sidney L. Harring in his essay "'There Seemed to Be No Recognized Law': Canadian Law and the Prairie First Nations" in *Laws and Societies in the Canadian Prairie West, 1670–1940*, eds. Knafla and Swainger. George Stanley's memorable phrase is from his chapter "The 1870s" in *The Canadians*, eds. J. M. S. Careless and R. Craig Brown. The anecdote about the pace of railway construction is from Pierre Berton's *The Last Spike: The Great Railway 1881–1885*. There are fascinating insights into both native and non-native conceptions of territory in Mark Warhus's *Another America: Native American Maps and the History of Our Land*. Current Aboriginal land claims, and the mappings that they represent, also offer valuable insights into the misconceptions and misunderstandings as well as the malice and mischief that have been part of the history of occupied countries. Thoreau's sentence is from *Walden*. Red Crow's tribute to James Macleod is quoted in Dempsey's *Red Crow*; and my comments on the idea of a commonwealth echoes a much earlier meditation by Lewis G. Thomas in "The Umbrella and the Mosaic," written during Canada's centennial year and published in *Ranchers' Legacy: Alberta Essays by Lewis G. Thomas*, ed. Patrick A. Dunae. The quotation describing the "plains outpost" is from Edward Brado, who also provided the anecdote about the cowboy wearing velvet slippers to the dance. The story of Jerry Potts is from several published accounts, most notably Hugh Dempsey's *Jerry Potts, Plainsman*, and from my grandfather's stories. The stories about Ned Maunsell throughout the book are drawn from accounts in the various histories of western ranching mentioned in these Endnotes, as well as from two sources: "The West of Edward Maunsell," Parts 1 and 2, edited by Hugh Dempsey and published in *Alberta*

History in 1986–87; and from the Maunsell papers in the Glenbow Museum. John Maclean's tribute to Red Crow is from his book *Canada's Savage Folk: The Native Tribes of Canada*, the irony of its title taking away from the well-informed ethnographic accounts he provides (with some fictional portraits, one of which is titled "Apokena: The Adventures of a Blackfoot Indian in the Land of the White Savages"). Annabel Crop Eared Wolf's tribute is from her monograph *Matsiyáítapapiiyssini: Káínai Peacekeeping and Peacemaking*, and my own commentary on *Káínai* peacemakers and peacekeepers owes much to her work. The broad sweep of Blackfoot history, the details of some of the events, and some of my descriptions of the life and livelihood and cultural traditions of people in this and the following chapters are informed by the two-volume collection *Alberta Formed, Alberta Transformed*, eds. Michael Payne, Donald G. Wetherell, and Catherine Cavanaugh, published to celebrate Alberta's centenary as a province, with essays by (among others): John W. Ives, "13,001 Years Ago: Human Beginnings in Alberta"; Alwynne B. Beaudoin and Gerald A. Otelaar, "The Day the Dry Snow Fell: The Record of a 7,627-year-old Disaster"; Trevor R. Peck and J. Rod Vickers, "Buffalo and Dogs: The Prehistoric Lifeways of Aboriginal People on the Alberta Plains, 1004–1005"; Fritz Pannekoek, "On the Edge of the Great Transformation: 1857–58"; Hugh Dempsey, "1870: A Year of Violence and Change"; Sarah Carter and Walter Hildebrandt, "'A Better Life With Honour': Treaty 6 (1876) and Treaty 7 (1877) with Alberta First Nations"; Bill Waiser, "Too Many Scared People: Alberta and the 1885 North-West Rebellion"; Brian Calliou, "1899 and the Political Economy of Canada's North-West: Treaty 8 as a Compact to Share and Peacefully Co-exist"; and David Hall, "1904–1905: Alberta Proclaimed." Mike Mountain Horse's *My People the Bloods* offers a testimony of tribal stories and personal recollections; Hugh Dempsey's *Indian Tribes of Alberta* is an important sourcebook. The description of the tipi design is from Dempsey's *Red Crow* and John Ewers's work on the "Painted Tipis of the Blackfeet Indians" for the Museum of the Rockies in Bozeman, Montana. Crop Eared Wolf's exploits gathering horses are described in Dempsey's *Crop Eared Wolf & Other Horse Thieves*, written as a curriculum resource for the Ontario Institute for Studies in Education. My use of phrases such as "bringing in" or "bringing home" horses instead of stealing them is influenced by Methodist missionary John McDougall's description of horse raiding, quoted by Sarah Carter in *Lost Harvests: Prairie Indian Reserve Farmers and Government Policy*. My mention of the long tradition of mischief in human societies draws from Lewis Hyde's *Trickster Makes This World: Mischief, Myth, and Art*. Thoreau's comments on *"extra vagance"* are from *Walden*. The story of *Natawista* is recounted at the beginning of Dempsey's *Red Crow*, and the celebration of her triumph at the dance is by R. B. Nevitt in *A Winter at Fort Macleod*.

CHAPTER THREE. The pretentious ranching patron was Alexander Staveley Hill, one of the principal backers of the Oxley ranch near Willow Creek, and he is quoted in Brado's *Cattle Kingdom* from John R. Craig's 1903 account of *Ranching with Lords and Commons; or, Twenty Years on the Range*. For the banking background and some details about Cowdry Brothers Bank, I have drawn from the archives and family papers, and also turned to Henry C. Klassen's *A Business History of Alberta* and his article "Cowdry Brothers: Private Bankers in Southwestern Alberta, 1886–1905" in *Alberta History* (1989). Marshall McLuhan's phrase is from *The Gutenberg Galaxy: The Making of Typographic Man*. The brief discussion of medicine bundles is drawn from Clark Wissler's 1912 article "Ceremonial Bundles of the Blackfoot Indians," referred to by Hugh Dempsey in his essay "Blackfoot" in the Smithsonian's *Handbook of North American Indians*, Vol. 13, *Plains*, which is an indispensable source of information, alongside the stories and songs of Blackfoot elders and tribal historians. For my comments on the relationship between trade and culture, I drew on James Dempsey's essay "Effects on Aboriginal Cultures Due to Contact with Henry Kelsey" in *Three Hundred Prairie Years: Henry Kelsey's "Inland Country of Good Report,"* ed. Henry Epp. L. V. Kelly's book *The Range Men: The Story of the Ranchers and Indians of Alberta* is an invaluable resource, written so close to the time by someone who knew most of the characters and much about the business of ranching.

CHAPTER FOUR. The winter count is taken from Hugh Dempsey's monograph *A Blackfoot Winter Count*. William Pearce's comments are from his "The Early History of Western Canada"; and background on Pearce is from Simon Evans's magisterial *The Bar U and Canadian Ranching History*, to which I am much indebted. The letter from Snookum Jim is in the Pearce typescript; it is also quoted in, among other places, a genial collection of sayings titled *Sounds Like Alberta (1754–1905)*, eds. Colin A. Thomson and F. Lee Prindle. The story of the arrival of the North-West Mounted Police at Fort Whoop-Up has often been told; but all accounts of that time and place are indebted to Paul F. Sharp's *Whoop-Up Country: The Canadian-American West, 1865–1885*.

CHAPTER FIVE. William Hornaday's extraordinary assessment is from his report "On the Extermination of the American Bison," published as part of the annual report of the United States National Museum in 1887. Among other books that I consulted were Andrew C. Isenberg's *The Destruction of the Bison: An Environmental History, 1750–1920*; Harold P. Danz's *Of Bison and Man*; and the essay "Buffalo and Dogs: The Prehistoric Lifeways of Aboriginal People on the Alberta Plains, 1004–1005" by Trevor R. Peck and J. Rod Vickers in *Alberta Formed, Alberta Transformed*. John Macoun's description of a grass fire is from *Manitoba and the Great North-West*. I am grateful to Sean Kane and his elegant writing on "wonder" for my quotation from *Sir Gawain and the Green Knight*. The Spanish observer on the pampas was Vázquez de Espinosa, and both his and the traveler's report in 1777 from the Rio Grande are quoted by Deb Bennett and Robert S. Hoffmann in "Ranching in the New World" from *Seeds of Change*, eds. Herman J. Viola and Carolyn Margolis. John C. Ewers's *The Horse in Blackfoot Indian Culture* is an indispensable resource on this subject. The comment on buffalo horses is from John Maclean's notebooks; and it was John Cotton who said the Blood had the fastest horses, quoted by Hugh Dempsey in "The Wise Old Ones," from *The Amazing Death of Calf Shirt and Other Blackfoot Stories*, in which Dempsey also gives a description of the laughing dance (told to him by his Blood father-in-law, James Gladstone). The statement "we thought we had more time" is quoted from the permanent Glenbow exhibition. Thomas Huxley is quoted in *The Resilient Outport: Ecology, Economy and Society in Rural Newfoundland*, ed. Rosemary E. Ommer. Josiah Wright Mooar's buffalo count is mentioned in Tom McHugh's *The Time of the Buffalo*, and the calculation of Cody's carnage is from Don Russell's *The Lives and Legends of Buffalo Bill*. Echoing Psalm 50, Red Crow said to North-West Mounted Police officer Percy Neale at a meeting in 1888, "God has taken all the game away." My comments on the Sun Dance here and later are drawn from Hugh Dempsey and others, including Walter McClintock in *The Old North Trail: Life, Legends and Religion of the Blackfeet Indians*, and from the essay "Sun Dance" by JoAllyn Archambault in *Handbook of North American Indians*, Vol. 13, *Plains*.

CHAPTER SIX. The speeches by David Laird, Pemmican, Crowfoot, Red Crow, and James Macleod are from Hugh Dempsey's books *Crowfoot: Chief of the Blackfeet* and *The Great Blackfoot Treaties*; and the descriptions by Frank Oliver and Cecil Denny are from John W. Chalmers's *Laird of the West*. The deadly consequences of the government's actions and inactions are recounted in chilling detail in James Daschuk's *Clearing the Plains: Disease, Politics of Starvation and the Loss of Aboriginal Life*. It is a point made not just by First Nations historians but by many others. The story of the move by the Blood to the new reserve is told by Dempsey in *Red Crow*. Big Swan's turn to a lawyer over a fraudulent surrender of Peigan land is mentioned by Claudia Notzke in "The Past in the Present: Spatial and Landuse Change on Two Indian Reserves" in *Essays on the Historical Geography of the Canadian West: Regional Perspectives on the Settlement Process*, eds. L. A. Rosenvall and Simon M. Evans. "Surrenders" sought from the Blackfoot also receive attention in Hana Samek's *The Blackfoot Confederacy 1880–1920: A Comparative Study of Canadian and U.S. Indian Policy*, and in Keith D. Smith's *Liberalism, Surveillance, and Resistance: Indigenous Communities in Western Canada, 1877–1927*.

CHAPTER SEVEN. My account of the roundup draws on the work of Simon Evans and Lewis G. Thomas, as well as reminiscences in Frederick W. Ings's *Before the Fences: Tales from the Midway Ranch*, ed. Jim Davis, and *Leaves from the Medicine Tree*, compiled by the High River Pioneers' and Old Timers' Association; and there are valuable essays in *Cowboys, Ranchers and the Cattle Business: Cross-Border Perspectives on Ranching History*, eds. Simon Evans, Sarah Carter, and Bill Yeo. The Stimson-Nolan exchange is told by Edward Brado; and stories about John Ware are included in almost every account of that time and place, most thoroughly in Grant MacEwan's *John Ware's Cow Country*. Richard Slatta's *Cowboys of the Americas* is a book I have turned to many times, along with a dictionary of Spanish terms from the American West called *Cowboy Talk* by Robert N. Smead. The composition of the song "Riding Old Paint," as well as of the western cowboy community in the late nineteenth century, has been recounted by Hal Cannon, founding director of the Western Folklife Center, in a National Public Radio program titled "Who Were the Cowboys Behind 'Cowboy Songs'?" broadcast on December 4, 2010. Many of the details about the Blackfoot turn to farming are from Dempsey's books as well as contemporary accounts. It is from Sheilagh Jameson's essay "Women in the Southern Alberta Ranch Community, 1881–1914" in *The Canadian West: Social Change and Economic Development*, ed. Henry C. Klassen, that I take the quotation from Lewis G. Thomas about horses.

CHAPTER EIGHT. Frank Oliver's tirade is quoted by Grant MacEwan in his book on Haultain. For some unfamiliar details about the 1885 uprising I have turned to Desmond Morton's *The Last War Drum: The North-West Campaign of 1885*. Gordon E. Tolton gives a sense of the paranoia that was fostered following the uprising in *The Cowboy Cavalry: The Story of the Rocky Mountain Rangers*. The comments by Archbishop Taché and Father André are from newspaper clippings kept by John Maclean. My description of the Blackfoot trip east draws on Hugh Dempsey's *Red Crow*, where he also quotes Red Crow's acceptance speech to the Gros Ventre.

CHAPTER NINE. The description of the trading in town following treaty payment is from the *MacLeod Gazette* in the fall of 1888, quoted in *Fort Macleod—Our Colourful Past*; and some details of benefits to the town are from John Maclean's notebooks. The stories about Dave Cochrane are from L. V. Kelly, Edward Brado, and Robert E. Gard's *Johnny Chinook: Tall Tales and True from the Canadian West*. My portrait of Annie Saunders is drawn from the essay "Assembling Auntie" by Cheryl Foggo in *Alberta Views* (2009). The tradition of horse races is recalled in almost every account of the foothills during this time; some of the details here are from Frederick Ings and from *Leaves from the Medicine Tree*; as well as from Lewis G. Thomas's essay "The Ranching Tradition and the Life of the Ranchers" in *Ranchers' Legacy*, and Shelley A. M. Gavigan's *Hunger, Horses, and Government Men: Criminal Law on the Aboriginal Plains, 1870–1905*. J. W. Morrow's *Early History of the Medicine Hat Country* provides some entertaining anecdotes about horses and horse breeding, and much else. The story about the tie between bronc riders Franklin and Stewart is told in Hugh Dempsey's *The Golden Age of the Canadian Cowboy: An Illustrated History*, along with entertaining comparisons between the Canadian and American frontiers. There is a brief tribute to polo in *A History of the Early Days of Pincher Creek*. The Alberta cowboy's comment about "barb wire" is quoted in Richard Slatta's *Cowboys of the Americas* from Florence B. Hughes's "Listening in at the Old-Timers Hut," published in *Canadian Cattlemen* in 1941. A detailed account of the invention and invasion of barbed wire can be found in Henry D. and Frances T. McCallum's *The Wire That Fenced the West*.

CHAPTER TEN. The rancher who described his winter wear was Fred Godsal, quoted by Simon Evans. Godsal also described I. G. Baker hospitality, and the common foothills practice of extending kindness to strangers is celebrated by Edward Brado. John Maclean's comments, and his question about food and implements left with surface burials, are taken from his journals and notebooks; Maclean's popular book was *Canada's Savage Folk*. I was first alerted to Maclean's warning about the "danger of educating [Indians] away from their real life" by its mention in the article "Reverend John Maclean and the Bloods" by Arni Brownstone in *American Indian Art Magazine* (2008). The calculation of the start-up cost of a ranch is from Alexander Begg's accounting in John Macoun's *Manitoba and the Great North-West*, included in David Breen's section, "The Ranching Frontier in Canada, 1875–1905," in *The Prairie West to 1905: A Canadian Sourcebook*, ed. Lewis G. Thomas.

CHAPTER ELEVEN. Nat Cowdry's son, Vincent, went on to a distinguished medical career; he is credited with establishing the medical field of gerontology. The story about the police officer who felt "very sorry for Cowdry" is in Etta Haultain's memoir *With the Mounties in Boot and Saddle Days*. Teresa Jordan's remark about the trails west is from her essay in *The Stories that Shape Us*, eds. Teresa Jordan and James R. Hepworth. Some of my commentary and quotations about the frontier are from the lively account by Richard White and Patricia Nelson Limerick in *The Frontier in American Culture*, ed. James R. Grossman.

CHAPTER TWELVE. The railway contract to the Montana border is described by Henry Klassen in *Eye on the Future: Business People in Calgary and the Bow Valley, 1870–1900*. Haultain's biographer is Grant MacEwan. The marriage of D. W. Davis and Revenge Walker is recounted by Edward Brado; and the description of her outfit at Fort Whoop-Up is by Donald Graham, quoted in Dempsey's *Red Crow*. Sarah Carter's observations are from her essay "Creating 'Semi-Widows' and 'Supernumerary Wives': Prohibiting Polygamy in Prairie Canada's Aboriginal Communities to 1900" in *Contact Zones: Aboriginal and Settler Women in Canada's Colonial Past*, eds. Katie Pickles and Myra Rutherdale. The anthropologist, quoted by Carter, was Esther Goldfrank in *Changing Configurations in the Social Organization of a Blackfoot Tribe during the Reserve Period*. Carter provides further insight into the condition of women in her essay "Categories and Terrains of Exclusion: Constructing the 'Indian Woman' in the Early Settlement Era in Western Canada" in *Great Plains Quarterly*, 1993. James Dempsey has given a good account of Crop Eared Wolf's buffalo robe, along with many other forms of warrior pictographic representation, in his *Blackfoot War Art: Pictographs of the Reservation Period, 1880–2000*; and this specific robe is discussed by Dempsey as well as by Marius Barbeau. (It is now back with the Crop Eared Wolf family, with a copy made by the Blood artist Running Coyote in RCMP headquarters.) Arni Brownstone's *War Paint: Blackfoot and Sarcee Painted Buffalo Robes in the Royal Ontario Museum* and *War Paintings of the Tsuu T'ina Nation* provide crucial insight into this venerable tradition of "writing without words." Kate McAll of the BBC produced a radio program "Another Country, As a Tale That Is Told," recorded with me on location in southern Alberta and broadcast on BBC Radio 3 several times between November 2002 and September 2003. It included my discussion with Frank Weasel Head about the quirt; and I have been careful to go no further than he and Gerald Conaty took me in my interpretation of that gift. My reflections on gift-giving are indebted to Lewis Hyde's *The Gift: Imagination and the Erotic Life of Property*.

CHAPTER THIRTEEN. Big Swan arrived in time to sign Treaty Seven, but in the treaty text he is mistakenly listed as *Akka-Makkoye*, or Many Swans—a reminder that written documents, no matter how they are sanctioned, offer no guarantee of truthtelling. Edmund Morris's account of the robe can be found in *The Diaries of Edmund Montague Morris: Western Journeys 1907–1910*, transcribed by Mary Fitz-Gibbon. A full run of *The Outlaw* is in the United Church of Canada archives in Toronto, a partial run in the Glenbow, and a few issues here and there in other libraries. The ideologies around settlement of the West are analyzed by Doug Owram in *Promise of Eden: The Canadian Expansionist Movement and the Idea of the West, 1856–1900*. Shelley Gavigan is also a valuable resource on this subject; and Hugh Dempsey's *Charcoal's World* illuminates what he describes as a clash both between the secular and the sacred and between two cultures, "neither completely understanding what was motivating the other." Coleridge's affirmation is from his periodical *The Friend*. My comments on covenants and codes and "chosen people" are much influenced by Donald H. Akenson's *God's Peoples: Covenant and Land in South Africa, Israel and Ulster*. Red Crow's statement is quoted by Hugh Dempsey in *Red Crow*, and by Hana Samek in *The Blackfoot Confederacy 1880–1920: A Comparative Study of Canadian and U.S. Indian Policy*. The most complete account of the residential schools is in the report of the Truth and Reconciliation Commission, *Honouring the Truth, Reconciling for the Future* (2015). John Rastell's poem, titled "The Interlude of the Four Elements," was published in *Early English Poetry, Ballads and Popular Literature of the Middle Ages*, Vol. 22, ed. J. O. Halliwell (London, 1848). The phrase "essential gaudiness" is from the poet Wallace Stevens.

CHAPTER FOURTEEN. John Maclean's account of White Calf's denunciation is from his notebooks. John McDougall's description of the "almost despotic power of the ration house" is quoted in Keith D. Smith, *Liberalism, Surveillance, and Resistance*. The movement of the bands to the gathering place for the Sun Dance is described in more detail in John C. Ewers's *The Horse in Blackfoot Indian Culture*. The belligerent agent who ordered the beef tongues cut in two was memorialized in the winter count as "Indian Agent James Wilson [who] stopped the Sun Lodge." Looking-glasses (mirrors) had come into Blackfoot use some time earlier, and (along with the telescope) into their language (as John Maclean confirmed in his notes when he was learning Blackfoot). My account of Hettie Edwards relies on an essay by Patricia A. Roome, "'From One Whose Home Is Among the Indians': Henrietta Muir Edwards and Aboriginal Peoples" in *Unsettled Pasts: Reconceiving the West Through Women's History*, eds. Sarah Carter, Lesley Erickson, Patricia Roome, and Char Smith.

CHAPTER FIFTEEN. Edward Brado has a good account of the circumstances leading up to the purchase of the Cochrane cattle. Some of the material about Robert Wilson in the following pages is from his own accounts in the Glenbow archives; and some from selected Blood agency files, also there. The description of the 1906/7 Big Die-Up draws from the ranching historians mentioned earlier in these Endnotes, from Max Foran, and from Wallace Stegner's *Wolf Willow*. Leslie Hall Pinder's phrase forms the title of a monograph published as *The Carriers of No: After the Land Claims Trial*. The struggle over surrender of both land and culture is well documented by Hugh Dempsey, and well remembered by the Blood tribe. The first of the reports on "the Indian question" was by the Spanish priest Bartolomé de las Casas in 1515, proposing remedies to prevent the harm being done to the Indians, one element of which was the recognition of self-governing Indian communities; another, tragically, was to replace their forced labor with that of enslaved Africans—a recommendation he later recanted. The "young girl . . . named Margaret" became my godmother; and *her* mother was the young Métis girl who visited Louis Riel in prison. The song "Hello, Central, Give Me Heaven" was written by Charles K. Harris and first recorded by Byron G. Harlan. The description of the Calgary Stampede draws on a wide range of accounts, among them *Legends of Our Times: Native Cowboy Life* by Morgan Baillargeon and Leslie Tepper. Edward Brado tells the story of Ned Maunsell securing Tom Three Persons's release from the police cells in Fort Macleod. Agent Dilworth's vindictive action against the rodeo hero is recorded in Mary-Ellen Kelm's *A Wilder West: Rodeo in Western Canada*.

INDEX